CULTURAL HERMENEUTICS:
ESSAYS AFTER UNAMUNO AND RICOEUR

Cultural Hermeneutics

Essays after Unamuno and Ricoeur

MARIO J. VALDÉS

UNIVERSITY OF TORONTO PRESS
Toronto Buffalo London

Toronto Buffalo London
www.utppublishing.com

ISBN 978-1-4426-4946-0 (cloth)

Library and Archives Canada Cataloguing in Publication

Valdés, Mario J., 1934-, author
Cultural hermeneutics : essays after Unamuno and Ricoeur / Mario J. Valdes.

Includes bibliographical references and index.
ISBN 978-1-4426-4946-0 (bound)

1. Unamuno, Miguel de, 1864–1936 – Criticism and interpretation.
2. Ricoeur, Paul – Criticism and interpretation. 3. Hermeneutics. 4. Arts – Philosophy. I. Title.

B4568.U54V34 2016 194 C2015-904602-5

This book has been published with the help of a grant from the Federation for the Humanities and Social Sciences, through the Awards to Scholarly Publications Program, using funds provided by the Social Sciences and Humanities Research Council of Canada.

University of Toronto Press acknowledges the financial assistance to its publishing program of the Canada Council for the Arts and the Ontario Arts Council, an agency of the Government of Ontario.

Canada Council for the Arts
Conseil des Arts du Canada

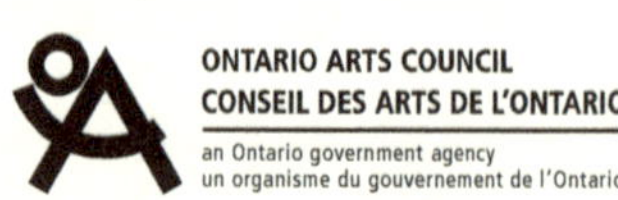

Funded by the Government of Canada
Financé par le gouvernement du Canada
Canada

I dedicate this book to María Elena de Valdés whose intelligent observations are on every page I have ever written from 1962 to the present.

I want to recognize the editorial assistance of Michael Jordi Valdés in completing this book.

And to remember Ronald Schoeffel, Humanities Editor at the University of Toronto Press, who was a wise and generous colleague and friend. He was my editor in all my previous publications with the University of Toronto Press.

Contents

Preface

The aim of this book is to establish the rationale for the comparative study of the work of Miguel de Unamuno (1864–1936) and Paul Ricoeur (1913–2005). It was written in Paris, Salamanca, and Toronto between 2008 and 2011, thanks to the grant I received from the Social Sciences and Humanities Research Council of Canada and to the support I received from María Elena Valdés and Michael Jordi Valdés. This book consists of new, unpublished material from the archives of Unamuno in Salamanca and Ricoeur in Paris as well as completely rewritten pages from my previous publications. None of the unpublished texts from the archives have been cited directly, respecting the copyright restrictions of both archives, but they have been invaluable in confirming the conclusion I reach in this book.

This book closes the circle that began in 1960 when I first read Unamuno. Unamuno was and is the spirit of a free Spain. Ricoeur was the most complete man of principle I have ever known. I wrote my PhD thesis on Unamuno's work (1962); I met Ricoeur in 1970 and had the privilege to live in his home in Chatenay-Malabry in 1972 and in 1988. In this book I have revisited all of my work on Unamuno and Ricoeur, giving them stronger centrality and continuity so that this double inquiry has become one.

A Note on Sources

The titles of the works used in this book are given in the language of original publication. Quotes from texts in languages other than English are taken from published translations, and the bibliographic information is given in the References section at the end of the book.

If there is no published translation, the translation is mine and is so indicated. Sources for quotations are given in the text by title and page number of the English translation. The dates of publication indicated in the text are always the dates of the original publication rather than the translation.

CULTURAL HERMENEUTICS

Introduction

Why Unamuno and Ricoeur?

In the second decade of the twenty-first century, what assessment can be made of Unamuno's work – a "complete works" of ten large volumes – and that of Ricoeur – twenty-five books and fifty-one articles in philosophical journals? Unamuno consistently held that all philosophy originates in a specific rootedness in a community and the everyday world of human action. Consequently, he argued that there is no such thing as a neutral proposal for action, for all plans and projects are based on the needs and ambitions of the individuals who engage in such action. First-time readers of Unamuno's major work *Del sentimiento trágico de la vida* are struck by the vehemence and unrelenting passion with which he addresses issues. Some are put off by this display of verbal power. A few readers, like Sidney Hook, never consider the substance of his thesis and dismiss him as obsessive. Fortunately, this view is the exception, and more careful readers like William Barrett have understood Unamuno. Barrett has written an Afterword to the Kerrigan translation of *Del sentimiento trágico de la vida* that I cite as an example of a more thoughtful reader:

> The reader will respond to Unamuno's passion with his own capacity for passion ... Nobody can come away from it without being quickened once again for that ceaseless contest with death – and particularly death of the spirit – that goes on day by day, and sometimes even hour by hour, in the lives of all of us. (374)

Barrett's comment brings to mind Hegel's statement in *The Philosophy of Mind*: "Nothing great has been and nothing great can be accomplished without passion. It is only a dead, too often, indeed, a hypocritical morality which inveighs against the very form of passion" (211).

In the opening pages of *Del sentimiento trágico de la vida* Unamuno offers this remarkable paragraph, which would be echoed in the writings of philosophers such as Karl Jaspers and Maurice Merleau-Ponty, as well as in the later work of Paul Ricoeur:

> Philosophy responds to our need to form a complete and unitary concept of life and the world and following our conceptualization, the impulse which engenders an inner attitude or even action. But the fact is that the impulse in question, instead of being a consequence of this conception, is the cause of it. Our philosophy, that is, our mode of understanding or not understanding the world and life, springs from our impulse towards life itself. (*Selected Works* [hereafter *SW*], IV, 4–5)

Ricoeur was the consummate philosopher's philosopher. His modus operandi in all of his writing was to present the work of his philosophical referent as carefully as possible and then provide a commentary highlighting both agreements and disagreements, amending his own position in response to what he had learned from that commentary.

His work covered the full spectrum of the human sciences. Perhaps what first drew my attention to the philosophy of Unamuno and Ricoeur was the way in which they engage the questions under discussion. A perceptive commentator on Ricoeur has written the following assessment, with which I fully concur:

> There is, in fact, no surer rule for the reading of Ricoeur than to watch for the way in which he construes his chosen question in terms of an apparent conflict between two contrasting aspects or poles – and then proceeds to mediate between them: drawing the contrasting aspects together while yet preserving a certain productive tension or dialectic. One acute commentator [Mary Schaldenbrand] has interpreted the entirety of Ricoeur's work in terms of this dialectic of kinship through conflict. (Lowe, "Introduction," ix)

This observation could be applied to any of Unamuno's major essays, as I pointed out as early as 1962 in my PhD thesis, later published as *Death in the Literature of Unamuno*. Of course, Unamuno and Ricoeur had a strong affinity in a number of ways, as we will show in the course of this book.

Both philosophers had a system of inquiry, although neither set out a philosophical system such as we find in Hegel or Spinoza. Both viewed reality as a process, and both developed an open dialectic to cope with the problems they addressed.

Over the last forty years of his life, Unamuno never wavered from his social philosophy. From *En torno al casticismo* (1895) to *San Manuel Bueno, mártir* (1933), he wrote that men and women can rise above the noise of the intellectual and political fashions of the day if they recognize that the fundamental subject of philosophy is the human being and the community of individuals who are the agents of history, and realize that history is not linear and unidimensional in spite of what one reads in national histories. Each generation must struggle to achieve the well-being of the community. Nostalgia for a golden age misses the point – there is no going back, and life is struggle and has always been so.

Paul Ricoeur began to develop the concept of open dialectic with his first major studies. Although he often referred to it directly, he always did so in a pragmatic sense and not by way of dogmatic declaration. He explained his approach as follows:

> One way of finding a way between these two extremes may be to take as our guide an attempt to think about the dialectic between love and justice. Here by dialectic I mean, on the one hand, the acknowledgment of the initial disproportionality between our two terms and, on the other hand, the search for practical mediations between them – mediations let us quickly say, that are always fragile and provisory.
>
> The insight promised by such a dialectical approach seems to me to have been overlooked by the method of conceptual analysis that seeks to extract from some selection of texts by ethicists or theologians who talk about love in the most systematic recurrent themes. ("Love and Justice," 23)

An Overview of Two Philosophies

As early as the 1880s, Unamuno formulated three distinct perspectives that are both exclusive of one another and interdependent. The first grew out of his reading of Spinoza and Hegel. The second was elaborated in the first decade of the twentieth century and culminated in his longest and most reflective work, *Del sentimiento trágico de la vida* (1912). This perspective was dominant over his remaining years, although the first never disappeared completely. All of Unamuno's major works of literature are imbued with this perspective of the self's search for meaning in the face of finitude. From his *Niebla* (1917) to *San Manuel Bueno, mártir* (1933), Unamuno refined and perfected this powerful approach, according to which the human being responds to the absence of belief in divine intervention in the affairs of men and women and must cope with the threat of finitude. Unamuno held that God was a willed God created by the desire that there be God. The ethical maxim of life, according to Unamuno, is to live in such a way that one's death will be a tragic loss for others, who will have lost an irreplaceable part of their own life. This second perspective came to be what would later be called an existential philosophy and was to remain with Unamuno until his death in 1936. The third perspective is more sporadic and arises primarily out of Unamuno's poetic anticipation of his own death and the idea that traces of himself will survive in his writing. These traces of the man of flesh and blood are his words, which his readers will give new life.

These three perspectives are distinct insofar as the starting point for each is replaced only in part by the others but nothing is left behind. He moves from a perspective of material existence to the deeply felt anguish of human existence in the second perspective and finally to the intellectual existence of the third perspective. The three are interdependent, for the second can only exist as a complement to the first and the third has its only place as the trace of the individual's work in the second, which is that of the finite self in a material world. For the individuals who have lived, struggled, and died, the only visible trace is the work they have left as a testament to their having lived. This is the trace of those who have lived.

Paul Ricoeur's philosophy started to take shape in post–Second World War France. His first books, *Karl Jaspers et la philosophie de l'existence* and *Gabriel Marcel et Karl Jaspers. Philosophie du mystère et philosophie du paradoxe* (both 1947), revealed his concern with the human being's will to act and create. But it was with *Philosophie de la volonté (I). Le volontaire et l'involontaire* (1950) that he made clear the direction of his unique merging of phenomenology and existentialism. He set out to make the human will the primary subject of his philosophy. Ten years later, in 1960, he continued his philosophy of the will with two significant works: *Philosophie de la volonté. Finitude et culpabilité. I. L'homme faillible* and *Philosophie de la volonté. Finitude et culpabilité. II. La symbolique du mal.* These two books mark an important turning point in Ricoeur's work. In them, he left behind the descriptive phenomenology of his 1950 works and turned to examine the concrete situation of the human being who loves, suffers, and dies, the one whom Unamuno had called the man of flesh and blood.

Ricoeur fully articulated his hermeneutics in the "Introduction" to his major work on Freud: *De l'interprétation. Essai sur Freud* (1965). His philosophy of the human capacity to create new meanings is a major complement to Unamuno's philosophical anthropology, written between 1912 and 1924.

The principal books of Ricoeur's hermeneutics followed his analysis of Freud: *La métaphore vive* (1975), *Interpretation Theory: Discourse and the Surplus of Meaning* (1976), and the three volumes of *Temps et récit* (1983–5). *La métaphore vive* is an important work in the history of hermeneutics. Ricoeur's open dialectic becomes a dialectic inquiry of world-making. *Interpretation Theory* has become the hermeneutic primer in the world beyond France. It has never been published in French but has gone through numerous editions in English, Portuguese, Spanish, Polish, Dutch, Danish, and Japanese. *Temps et récit* is recognized as a masterpiece in the philosophy of language and as the high point in the development of his hermeneutics, which began to take shape in 1966.

In the last years of his life, Ricoeur concentrated on the self–other relationship – the same relationship that was Unamuno's principal concern from 1917 until his death in 1936 in such literary works as *Abel Sánchez, El otro, Niebla,* and *San Manuel Bueno, mártir*. Ricoeur's last works on this topic are *Soi-même comme un autre* (1990), *Le juste I* (1995), *Le juste II* (2000), *L'histoire, la memoire et l'oubli* (2000), and, finally, *Parcours de la reconnaissance* (2005).

Ricoeur died in May 2005, leaving unfinished *Vivant jusqu'á la mort,* edited and published by Olivier Abel in 2007. His last words bring Ricoeur closer to Unamuno on the topic of death and one's legacy: "But there is the trace of others, to which mine do link up in some way. This is part of the hope that mine will survive" (*Living Up to Death*, 87).

A Common Ground

Is it an uncanny coincidence that Unamuno and Ricoeur moved in the same direction in their very different ways of writing? Or is it that the vast network of acknowledged shared thought from philosophy and theology came together for both, moving them towards a hermeneutics of self? In *Temps et récit,* Ricoeur presents a spiral process of the human being's configuration not only of metaphorical meaning but also of the conceptualization of the individual's world. The apex of the spiral is the collective prefiguration of past world-making as available in the present; the act of making sense of the phenomenon of life's experiences is the configuration of meaning. The driving force of world-making is the encounter between the individual and his or her interpretation of lived experience. The spiral continues as refiguration, which is the engagement with others in the necessary conflict between individual interpretations of life.

As Ricoeur explains in *La métaphore vive,* and especially in the three volumes of *Temps et récit*, the process of figuration is at its most acute in the interpretation of literature. When we disregard for a moment the angst that so colours Unamuno's writing, we find a marked correlation between Unamuno's *En torno al casticismo* (which outlined Unamuno's first perspective, of the material world) and Ricoeur's concept of the prefiguration of symbolic expression. Unamuno's material world exists through human perception and expression in language. Similarly, his second perspective of individual action is close to Ricoeur's concept of configuration, through which the human being grasps the meaning of discourse. Finally, Unamuno's third meaning of discourse, which considers the appropriation of the symbolic expressions of others as the realization of a person's humanity, is a concept that is clearly within the range of Ricoeur's refiguration. What brings these two philosophical approaches closer together is the realization that both Unamuno and Ricoeur saw language as the basis of the human being's engagement with the world. For Unamuno, a tree is not a tree until I say so to myself and to others. For Ricoeur, the human being is constantly redescribing the world in which he or she lives.

Ricoeur's most acute commentators sense there is a powerful unity in his work, a unity that goes beyond the specifics of the topic under discussion in each essay and book. But with few exceptions, such as Domenico Jervolino, the common flaw in their approach to Ricoeur has been the attempt to find unity by means of a system. Ricoeur's philosophy cannot be forced into a system akin to those of Hegel and Husserl. Although Ricoeur gained philosophical depth from his study of Hegel, Kant, and Husserl, his philosophy describes and elucidates a *process* and is not a system. Since a process cannot be arrested so that it can be examined and explained, the only way to understand it is to examine its sources and its effects. This is the age-old problem in the study of flow in physics. Reality can be seen as a dialectic process of conflicting powers and continuous tension between them. *This* tension will not dissipate; it is reality. Ricoeur's word for the process of reality is *tension;* Unamuno's is *struggle*. For both philosophers, what is to be examined is human expression in all its diversity and distinct manifestations, both lasting and ephemeral. The world-making of the human being is the expressive process of reality that is always now. But human expression, in distinction to a flow of water, has left traces of previous moments. Men and women of the past have left us their legacy in their work. Both Unamuno and Ricoeur develop a philosophy of interpretation that is an encounter with otherness that transforms moments of the other into moments of the present of the reader. Unamuno was fond of saying that he was one with Kierkegaard in Copenhagen and that this was so because when he read Kierkegaard in Danish, he created him as his other with whom he was engaged in dialogue. The philosophical weight of this sentiment was obvious to Unamuno, who asserts in *Del sentimiento trágico de la vida* that language is the true basis of reality (English trans., 338). In *Soi-même comme un autre* (1990), Ricoeur outlines with great care his position, which can be summarized as "man is language." He carries this position into his hermeneutics and reaches a concept of reader–other identification often stressed by Unamuno. Ricoeur writes: "By narrating a life of which I am not the author as to existence, I make myself its co-author as to meaning" (English trans., 162).

Chapter One

From Unamuno to Ricoeur

1. The Open Dialectic

What separates Ricoeur from other contemporary philosophers who have considered language as the best way to gain an understanding of the human condition, philosophers like Ludwig Wittgenstein and Jacques Derrida, is that Ricoeur, like Heidegger before him, held that to be human is to be in language. Unamuno would only add that the human being is language bound and that so is the world he or she makes.

Ricoeur's theory of interpretation, unlike that of Unamuno, was highly developed. In *La métaphore vive* (1975), and *Temps et récit* (3 vols., 1983–5), Ricoeur outlined the intrinsic polarities in language. In this task, he began with the dialectic of noun (naming), verb (acting), and event (meaning). He then examined sense and reference, self-reflection, the avowal of finitude, and, especially, the inescapable opposition in language between literal and metaphorical meaning. Ricoeur insists that language cannot be reduced to univocity of meaning. The interpreter is always called upon to enter the semantic impertinence of metaphor and create meaning out of the ashes of literal meaning. In other words, the literal meaning does not disappear; rather, it remains behind as the negative force that obliges the interpreter to think with the imagination. The resulting tension produces metaphorical meaning. For Unamuno this tension is real and is the constant force behind reality as we know it. For Ricoeur, metaphor is "being as," which means being and not being at the same time. Unamuno and Ricoeur agree that we think through contradiction. The metaphorical process of gaining meaning out of opposition and differences is, in philosophical terms, the open dialectic of "being as" or the overcoming of non-being by being. The dialectic of both philosophers is not viable in the Hegelian system of total knowledge; rather, it is a tension that produces truths that are always finite and limited. The conflictual nature of human experience is central to Unamuno, as is well known; it is also fundamental to Ricoeur. From *Le conflit des interprétations* (1969) to *Du texte à l'action* (1986), Ricoeur's hermeneutic comes closer to articulating an anthropological hermeneutics based on the human struggle to act and live and, if possible, to survive. What Unamuno expressed metaphorically, Ricoeur articulated in philosophical discourse.

Ricoeur was twenty-three years old when Unamuno died in 1936. He was studying philosophy under Gabriel Marcel (1886–1973). Although he had read chapters of *Del sentimiento trágico de la vida* (1912), his link to Unamuno's thinking is indirect. It comes through Gabriel Marcel's teaching. Marcel was a Christian existentialist, and his thought converged in many areas with Unamuno's, especially in *Del sentimiento trágico de la vida* and *La agonía del cristianismo* (1924). By contrast, the points of convergence between Unamuno and Ricoeur are minor if considered in isolation from their respective philosophies. Perhaps the most important are the following concepts, which are central to *Del sentimiento trágico de la vida* and *L'homme faillible* (1960). Both philosophers reject the objectification of the human being. Unamuno's "man of flesh and blood" and Ricoeur's "affective fragility of the individual" argue strongly for human feelings as the privileged mode through which the pre-objective reality of the person is revealed. Ricoeur argues that Descartes's consciousness is not self-consciousness; Ricoeur holds that consciousness per se is not the unity of a person in itself and for itself: "It is not one person, it is no one. The I of 'I think therefore I am' is merely the form of a world for anyone and everyone" (*L'homme faillible*, 46). It is in the fourth chapter of *L'homme faillible* that Ricoeur joins with Unamuno: "The universal function of feeling is to bind together. It connects what knowledge divides; it binds me to things, to beings, to being" (131).

In the same vein there is the rejection of all ideological or categorical forms of reductionism, be it Marxist or Freudian. The real is not the abstract description we encounter in empiricism, but the culmination of human experience. Being, for both Unamuno and Ricoeur, is the process of living affirmation; it is not the quantification of the material world. The key to understanding both philosophers is the concept of process and struggle. Life is a constant struggle of opposing forces of which life and death are the defining points of reference.

In both Unamuno and Ricoeur, struggle is productive rather than destructive. Between Ricoeur's philosophy of creative tension and Unamuno's affirmation of life over death, there is a deep kinship. This unacknowledged kinship is derived from many sources besides Marcel. We have traced those common sources to Protestant liberal thinkers of the early twentieth century, to Hegel and Nietzsche, to a common will not to compromise but to push a question to the end, and, last but not least, to the open dialectic. If reality for Unamuno is struggle, for Ricoeur it is conflict: "Conflict is a function of man's most primordial constitution; the object is synthesis; the self is conflict ... No conflict between ourselves and some process susceptible of conferring upon us an assumed personality could be interjected if we were not already this disproportion of living and thinking, of which our heart suffers the primordial discord" (*L'homme faillible,* 132). Unamuno often wrote that "all or nothing" was an intellectual response to the passion of living. In the same vein Ricoeur writes that "life does not want all; the word 'all' has no meaning for life, but only for the mind" (*L'homme faillible,* 130).

Ricoeur developed a *modus operandi* for all his major works that Unamuno had also used, albeit in a less philosophical fashion. The essence of Ricoeur's writing is an open debate with other philosophers; the essence of Unamuno's is a mode of conflict that engages the other as my other and in time produces a net gain in ideas that are neither mine nor the others'. Walter Lowe explains Ricoeur's philosophy succinctly:

> There is, in fact, no surer rule for the reading of Ricoeur than to watch for the way in which he construes his chosen question in terms of an apparent conflict between two contrasting aspects or poles – and then proceeds to mediate between them: drawing the contrasting aspects together while yet preserving a certain productive tension or dialectic. One acute commentator [Mary Schaldenbrand] has interpreted the entirety of Ricoeur's work in terms of this dialectic of kinship through conflict. (Lowe, ix)

And so it is with Unamuno. Jorge Luis Borges wrote the following obituary of Unamuno on January 1937: "The leading writer in our language is dead ... He was, before all else, an inventor of splendid argument. He debated the I, immortality, language, the cult of Cervantes, faith, ethics, the regeneration of vocabulary and of syntax ... I know of no better homage than to continue the rich discussion he began and to go on to plumb the secret laws of his soul" (Kerrigan, xxi).

In Unamuno's philosophy the self is always in conflict – that is, it is always caught up in the tensional situation of struggle (*lucha*) – and this is so because at each instant it creates itself in creating its image of what it is to become. The self is therefore in struggle with others, with the past, and with the inauthentic. A number of philosophers elaborated a similar philosophy in the second half of the twentieth century, philosophers such as Maurice Merleau-Ponty, Eric Weil, and, especially Paul Ricoeur. Before we begin examining the common ground between Unamuno and Ricoeur, it is necessary to review Ricoeur's turn to hermeneutics and elaborate on his philosophy of the self as maker of reality.

Ricoeur's epistemology is just as significant as any of the major concepts he developed in anthropology, hermeneutics, or moral philosophy. In Ricoeur's philosophy there is an epistemic requirement to think dialectically. The fundamental philosophical antinomy of such concepts as identity and difference, unity and diversity, the universal and the particular, an antimony that forces us to choose one or the other, is obviated in the open dialectic, in the course of which the tension between polarities moves us to think in terms of process rather than absolutes. Ricoeur's dialectic, like that of Unamuno, is derived from Hegel. Both Unamuno and Ricoeur rejected the Hegelian synthesis; in the tensional force of the open dialectic they recognized the thinking that transforms reality into a reflective articulation of shared experience. Our world differs from the shared world of the past, hence our experiences will not be identical to those of individuals of the past *or* the future.

In 1976 Ricoeur was invited to participate in a lecture series at the University of Kansas. He was one of ten speakers to address the general topic of "Freedom and Morality." He surprised many when he announced that his lecture was titled "What Is Dialectic?", which on the surface was not relevant to the general topic. He began with this basic question: If dialectic is valid, what are its hypothetical assumptions? One would be that certain things do not exist unless there is another opposite thing at the same time – for example, life and death. A second hypothetical possibility for the dialectic would be a logical contradiction where one proposition cancels out the other. A variant of this would be the physical zero resulting from the equilibrium of opposing forces. But if the dialectic makes sense in the broader realm of experience, a third kind of opposition can be supposed, what we can call productive opposition as in the positive and negative poles of an electrical charge. This opposition in one way or another generates a new reality in our experience that is qualitatively different from the opposing forces. What are some of the paradigms for this productive dialectic? There are three that interest Ricoeur: history, literature, and the self.

Turning first to history, Ricoeur asks, "Is there anything at all that designates history as a totality?" His answer: "If one repudiates the notion of absolute knowledge, it is merely necessary to reply in the negative to this question" ("What Is Dialectic?" 175). History is not and cannot be construed as a fixed account of the past, yet it remains as a record of human action. The question now turns on what aspect of human action can best be approached by considering specific oppositions and their development into a play of forces. Human desire for specific objectives is mitigated only by rational deliberation on ways and means. Between these two poles – desire and deliberation – a tension is produced. This tension indicates that the poles of wanting and reflection are set in full opposition between immediate action and strategy. Because the human being is rational, he or she will respond to the tension and move towards resolution. Tension leads to conflict, and conflict demands resolution lest there be negative consequences. The writing of history is consequently a form of resolution of the willed action of the past by providing a reflective explanation of how desire played out in the strategies of the participants.

In the relations between persons at the economic, social, or political level, all forms of the dialectic present the same fundamental structure: an initial opposition reasserts the opposing poles as a positive force; this creates new paradigms, new thinking that neither collapses the poles into each other nor favours the vanquishing of one by the other. Thus it is that neither the self nor the other can exist separately. They find meaning only in their interaction.

The third instance of the dialectic that Ricoeur examines is the creation of new meaning through metaphor. When we read that "time is a beggar," a semantic impertinence immediately stops us. We can dismiss the incongruence by recognizing the words as a metaphor, but for those of us who need to understand what we read, this is not a valid response. Metaphor is not a trope; rather, it is a form of attribution born out of the tension resulting from the incompatibility of the words in the metaphorical statement. In the above example, the words *time* and *beggar* undergo an alteration of meaning that results from the predicative operations that bring them together. *Time* in this poetic sequence signifies more than the measurement of an interval between two moments, while *beggar* signifies more than an importunate vagrant. In this poetic context each word finds an additional signification that permits it to make metaphorical sense. In this regard, metaphor is an enigma. The words, taken literally, are incompatible. This semantic collision leads to a logical absurdity where any semblance of meaning would be annulled by incompatibility. But the reader comes to the rescue and gives life to the metaphor by selecting out of a range of possibilities the verbal significations that permit a new meaning to arise. These significations have only a contextual existence within the statement, whereas lexical significations are codified by language. Among the multiple possibilities that emerge from the statement "Time is a beggar," I prefer the futile plea of the subject to remain in the course of the relentless current of experience.

At the core of Ricoeur's hermeneutics is the concept of an open dialectic, a post-Hegelian dialectic of opposition without resolution but with a continuing tension between the poles. These productive oppositions can be observed, recognized, and identified in human action in response to the binary concept of life and death, or the self and others; they can also be gleaned from creative metaphors that defy literal meaning. This concept of the dialectic can be nothing more than the process of life proceeding by productive oppositions. Human action can be viewed as dialectic at work, but is the opposite true? Is the dialectic human action? This enlargement of the inquiry leads to the conclusion that the dialectic of praxis becomes the dialectic of human experience as a whole.

We turn now to Unamuno, who is the most complex thinker in all of Spanish philosophy. His philosophy makes a radical break with established philosophical discourse by rejecting systematic thinking. He insisted that the only true subject of philosophy is the human being, not as an abstract subject of *cogito* but as "the man of flesh and blood, the man who is born, suffers, and dies" (*SW*, IV, 3). He concludes: "The logical point of departure for all philosophical speculation is not the 'I,' nor its representation (*Vorstellung*), that is, the world as it immediately appears to the senses, but rather it is a mediate or historical representation, humanly elaborated and given us principally in the language through which we know the world ... Thought rests upon pre-judices; and prejudices are embodied in the language ... All philosophy, then, is essentially philology" (IV, 336–7). Or might we not today, after Gadamer and Ricoeur, say philosophical hermeneutics?

Ricoeur's starting point, as stated in the introduction to *Soi-même comme un autre* (1990) with regard to Descartes, was as follows: "The I who does the doubting and who reflects upon itself in the cogito is just as metaphysical and hyperbolic as is doubt itself with respect to all knowledge. It is in truth no one" (6). A few years earlier, in *A l'école de la phénomenologie* (1986), Ricoeur had written this paragraph, which could serve as an introduction to the work of Unamuno: "As soon as we start thinking, we discover we are already living in and by the means of worlds of representations, idealities, norms. As far as that goes we move in two worlds: the pre-given world which is the other's limit and ground, and a world of symbols and rules through which the world has already been interpreted when we begin to think" (225).

Unamuno's major work on the dialectic was *The Tragic Sense of Life,* written in separate essays in 1912 and published in a single volume a year later. The full title is *Del sentimiento trágico de la vida en los hombres y las naciones.* This was not an approach to writing the dialectic; rather, it was a metaphysical concept of the first order, as it was with Ricoeur. I will take time to elaborate this concept in Unamuno's thinking before returning to Ricoeur. Throughout his adult life, Unamuno was plagued with depression and despair. After each major psychological crisis he emerged stronger, prepared to take on all obstacles like a twentieth century Don Quijote. To understand this fluctuation between almost arrogant self-confidence and depression plagued by inner doubts, we must review his life not as a series of set periods but rather as a process of development that eventually became a way of living in terms of the dialectic of opposition in what can only be called a constant tension or will to be.

Unamuno's early faith was shaken by empirical Positivism, especially by Herbert Spencer's philosophy, and this nineteenth-century philosophy weakened his Catholicism; but this did not supplant his need for faith. Even before he read Spencer, Hegel's dialectic had left a lasting imprint on him. Referring to these early years, he later wrote: "Hegel's concept of identity between pure being and pure nothingness were ideas that produced vertigo in my still tender spirit not yet sufficiently balanced to stand at such heights of metaphysical acrobatics" (*Recuerdos de niñez y mocedad,* VIII, 144). And to his friend Federico Uriales he wrote in 1901: "I learned German in Hegel, stupendous Hegel, who is one of the philosophers who has left the deepest impact on me. Even today I think that at its base my thinking is Hegelian" (Zubizarreta, 3). And many years later, in 1925, he would write: "And what does it mean, to doubt, it is more than Cartesian or methodical doubt: it presupposed the duality of combat" (in Reinhardt, 19–20). "To negate life is to die, and to negate death is to be born again. And this precisely is the dialectic agony" (23).

The open dialectic would become the basis for all of Unamuno's writings. Unlike Hegel, Unamuno sees no synthesis but only a continuous struggle between two poles. This manner of thinking and writing explains some of the otherwise unanswerable complexities of Unamuno's work. The year 1884, which marked the end of Unamuno's university studies, also marked the beginning of a gradual development of three philosophical perspectives, each succeeding the other in three outstanding essays: *En torno al casticismo* (1886) *Del sentimiento trágico de la vida* (1912), and *La agonía del cristianismo* (1924). But it is important to note that each philosophical perspective was immersed in literary texts that expanded the philosophy into the imaginative configuration of his readers.

The polemics and conflicts that surround Unamuno criticism stem from the fact that many critics have attempted to simplify and reduce the open dialectic into a fixed, coherent system. Unamuno was not Lutheran, although he read and discussed the work of Lutheran theologians, nor was he an atheist or a nihilist, nor was he a follower of Nietzsche, although he read and commented on his work. He read and admired Kierkegaard, but there are marked differences between the two philosophers. Unamuno was also devoted to the works of the American pragmatist William James, albeit with reservations. Some critics contended that Unamuno's poetry revealed a deep attachment to the Spanish mystics Santa Teresa de Ávila and San Juan de la Cruz, but this line of thought must be contextualized as part of Unamuno's first perspective. Others have sought to identify his thinking with the writings of the Church fathers and early Christianity. Any one passage from his writings taken out of context can make a good case for any of the modes of thinking thus far mentioned. Unamuno was in his own words just a man of flesh and blood who opened his mind to a broad spectrum of Western philosophy and literature. The extraordinary range of interpretations of his work is in part due to the open dialectic and the evolution of his philosophical perspectives. His work must be considered not as one system or another but as a process of reflection moved by the open dialectic described above.

With a few notable exceptions, most critics of Unamuno can be placed in one of two categories. There are those who have focused on his relations with the individuals whom he found to have an affinity to his way of thinking. There is, however, no evidence of anything more than an acknowledged affinity with writers such as Henri Féderic Amiel (1821–81) and his *Journal intime* (1883–4), Etienne Pivart de Sénancour (1770–1846), especially his *Obermann* (1804), William James (1842–1910) with regard to his *The Varieties of Religious Experience* (1902), or Søren

Kierkegaard (1813–55) and his works such as *Fear and Trembling* (1843) and *Concluding Unscientific Postscript* (1846), which Unamuno read in Danish.

Then there is another group of critics who, because Unamuno rejected a linear system of inquiry and used multiple sources, have concluded that Unamuno was an eclectic thinker who concerned himself with the problems of philosophy but was not himself a philosopher.

Julián Marías, José Ferrater Mora, François Meyer, and Pedro Cerezo Galán are the notable exceptions to these two categories. Marías was one of the first philosophers to study Unamuno's major works philosophically. It was through Marías's friendship with Gabriel Marcel that Unamuno's philosophy became known in French philosophical circles. His literary writing was well known, but his philosophical essays were not appreciated until the emergence of existentialism. For Marías, the intellectual core of Unamuno's thought was the problem of immortality. And as a consequence of the lifelong confrontation with that problem, he slowly developed a way of thought at whose core was the individual man's personal awareness of death. This was not a concept of death per se, but rather a driving force that thrust Unamuno into diverse corners in search of an answer to one essential question: How does one live with the threat of death as finality? Since Marías's study in 1943, his perspective has prevailed among serious students of Unamuno. Unamuno's writings have also been examined by José Ferrater Mora, who has penetrated the multifaceted core of Unamunian thought and has insisted on Unamuno's place as a philosopher. The task before us is to bring out this philosophy that has been outlined but not developed by Ferrater Mora, for it is an implicit rather than an explicit philosophy that is dispersed over the fifty-two years of writing. Ferrater Mora sums up his opinion as follows:

> This [concrete eternal] can be understood in two ways. First, as something whose permanence is being continuously produced or created; true permanence is, Unamuno believes, the result of an effort, of an act of will, of a conatus to such an extent that there is no fundamental difference between being and wishing to be. Second, as something whose duration is constantly threatened by annihilation, just as war is the guarantee of peace, death – the imminence of death – is the guarantee of life. To last forever is not to go on existing, to continue to be, it is to conquer unceasingly its own being. This explains why for Unamuno to live is primarily "to agonize, namely, to fight against death." ("On Miguel de Unamuno's Idea of Reality," 520)

Thus, although two Unamunian views of reality are given, José Ferrater Mora does not develop the relation they may have to each other, nor does he connect them to the different perspectives that Unamuno realized. We contend that these two views are parts of a philosophy that Unamuno developed over the years and that manifested itself in three perspectives, and that each of these in turn used the same open dialectic of oppositions on the same problem before him: immortality and death or non-being. The language of dialectic dramatized the basic thought of Unamunian philosophy: that being is essentially an "in struggle" fact of existence. Thus, his philosophy is not a linear logical system, nor is it eschatology of a world mind; rather, it is a dynamic surge that is "being-in-struggle" without end. The perspectives are not counter-resolutions of the same problem, but rather complementary manifestations of the problem as world, the individual man, and the tradition of man's thought.

The first perspective is that of the metaphysical problem of existence in the totality of reality. The position reached in *En torno al casticismo* (1895) is that of a reality that is ever changing flux in a stream of projection that has only an eternal now as time. When Ferrater Mora's analysis is applied to this perspective, it can be stated in these terms: first, the stream of flux that is reality is being continuously produced, and second, the continuous affirmation of this totality is a constant negation of non-being. Since there is no personal consciousness in this perspective, there is only one view, one time, and one interrelationship – the totality of existence. This is seen as an eternal stream of struggle. It is "in struggle" because as existence it is always conquering being, again and again. Here, the Unamunian dialectic pattern is at its broadest scope, for all there is, was, or can be is a single constant affirmation of being and negation of non-being.

In the second perspective Unamuno takes the starting point of the individual man who is there in the world. No longer is metaphysics the traditional quest for the essence of existence; rather, existence is put first in the position of the individual's being cast there in the world. Ferrater Mora's two points on this perspective are as follows: First, existence is the fact that precedes all other facts, but *continued* existence is the result of an act of the individual's will; the force of the will to exist is what projects the individual existent so that there is no difference between being and wishing to be since the human being is free and is always remaking himself. But the self that Unamuno thinks he is, is not the same as the self he wants to be, because the latter is a horizon that is never reached. This leads to Ferrater Mora's second point. The existence of the self is the unceasing reconquest of its being from non-being. In this perspective, this is the individual self's struggle unto death. It is in this perspective that Unamuno's philosophy may be viewed as within the general concerns of the existentialists. It is in this perspective that the human being finds himself as being-in-the-world. The self's existence takes precedence over everything else, and a man can realize his freedom when he learns how to live each day as if it were the last. His self thereby becomes authentic, and he realizes his freedom and his commitments to the world; this is what opens the self to the world as he personalizes it. As the personal self engulfs all of his world, this world is put into a dialectic of oppositions, except that now this pattern is the self's reconquest of its being as long as the "in struggle" remains. This authentic light of the self is the tragic sense of life.

The third perspective does not concern the totality of existence, nor does it concern the personal self in its world; rather, it is the spiritual legacy of man's thoughts. This is the universe of ideas, traditions, and memories that all coexist in the minds of men and women. But primarily, it deals with an individual's thought. Upon death, what happens to all of the ideas and thoughts that a self has generated during a lifetime? Some will be remembered for a time and then will be disseminated, losing the unity of being the thought of that particular individual. This individual who created the thought may thus be lost. But if the thought of the self has been expressed in written words, there is the possibility of continued re-creation by others. There is also implicit in this perspective the idea that the community of authors is a constantly enriching continuum leading to a greater spiritual universe. Of course, much that is written is destined for oblivion, but that which expresses a sense of truth to others will be read and re-created by others. Thus in this perspective Ferrater Mora's views apply in this way: Through the efforts of readers, an author's words are always threatened with oblivion, but they can be re-created. The words that express the intimate feelings of a person and that can conquer a continued existence may be lost. Unamuno developed an extended metaphor of the flow of time as a strong current with a counter-current.

Ferrater Mora's second point on non-being has the following application: The eternal flux (which is reality) can be seen as a dialectic of oppositions between being, that is, the constant affirmation of existence, and non-being, which is its continuous negation. Non-being is a linguistic necessity to denote the undoing, negating activity inherent with existence. Therefore, if a focal point can be put on an individual part within this flux, it would become an abstraction when removed from the context of the whole, for totality is set in an eternal "now" and individuality is necessarily temporal and finite. It is precisely this problem that makes it necessary to use a metaphor such as a stream. Consequently, man can reach an intuition of this philosophical perspective through the intuitive contemplation of the whole of reality where he becomes a mere insignificant speck. Thus, death here merely means that this speck is arrested from the continuity and is caught in the counter-current of constant negation, which is, however, never achieved because the affirmation of being continues. Unamuno gives metaphorical expression to this philosophy in his novel *Niebla* (1914):

> A man is left alone and he closes his eyes to the illusion of the future and sees into the fearful abyss of eternity. Eternity has no future. When we die, death turns us about-face in our tracks, in our orbit so to say, and we begin the long trek back, towards the past, toward what once was. And so on without end, unraveling the skein of our destiny, undoing that infinity which an eternity has made of us, and we voyage toward nothingness without reaching it, for nothingness never was, nothingness never existed. (*SW*, VI, 64)

Now, if one takes the same metaphor of the counter-currents in flux and applies it to the existential reality of the second perspective – the individual personal self – there is the following result: "Beneath the current of our existence, within it, flows a countercurrent: in one current we go from yesterday to tomorrow, in the other from tomorrow to yesterday. We ravel and unravel simultaneously" (64).

The personal self is temporal, as are all living things, yet the human being is the being that exists. Only the human being has a future that is a personal projection. Of all living things, Unamuno argues, only the human being has self-awareness. The self is always moving from his yesterday to his tomorrow until death cuts him off and the physical remains deconstruct, but the spiritual legacy of what the individual said and did can become part of the counter-current. Before the individual dies, he lives in a process that is described as a dialectic struggle. The individual's life is a constant affirmation of his or her being in the world. Death is the ever-present counterforce of life. As long as life continues, the current and counter current pull the self in opposite directions: to be all or to be nothing. Unamuno in *Niebla* formulates the dialectic that is life as follows: "From time to time we get a whiff of the other world, we hear mysterious murmurs of its existence, of a world within our own world. The marrow of history is counter history, a quintessential counter process, a subterranean river flowing from the sea to the source" (VI, 64). From the counter-current of death there comes a distant echo of others who have lived, worked, and died but who have left a trace of who they were. In Unamuno's first perspective the dialectic was being and non-being; in the second, it was life and death; in the third, it is a trace of having lived and oblivion.

These three perspectives of Unamuno in their genesis are not rational and can best be considered intuitive, emphatic, and emotive; however, in their articulation they take on a highly developed non-linear logic that we have described as the open dialectic of oppositions. Whatever the perspective may be, in effect, there is a dynamic "in struggle" continuum where being must conquer itself again from non-being. It is the very state of "in struggle" that affirms existence and negates non-being. But the threat that is there, a form of non-being, is the possibility of nothingness for the personal self and of oblivion for the words and deeds of those who have lived.

Contrary to most philosophers, Unamuno found an implicit openness in the purported closed spiral of Hegel's logic. Unamuno was deeply moved by Hegel's *Phenomenology of Spirit* (see "Cuesta abajo," *Obras completas* [hereafter *OC*], VII, 810). The impact of Hegel on Unamuno's thinking has been underestimated. One of Unamuno's handwritten notes with translation to Spanish was in Hegel's *Wissenschaft der Logik* (*The Philosophy of Logic*); however, it is not from this work but from *The Phenomenology of Mind,* a work that is no longer in the Unamuno library in Salamanca but had been there before his death in 1936. (See Valdés and Valdés, *An Unamuno Source Book,* 280.) The note is a translation from the preface to *The Phenomenology of Mind* and in J. Baille's translation reads as follows:

> But the life of the mind is not one that shuns death, and keeps clear of destruction; it endures death and in death maintains its being. It only wins its truth when it finds itself utterly torn asunder. It is this might power, not by being a positive which turns away from the negative, as when we say of anything it is nothing or it is false, and being then done with it, pass off to something else; on the contrary, mind is this power only by looking the negative in the face, and dwelling with it. (93)

As noted earlier, at the heart of Unamuno's thinking was his version of dialectic. Hans-Georg Gadamer's assessment of Hegel's dialectic serves us well to situate Unamuno's dialectic. I cite a few lines from Gadamer's *Hegel's Dialectic*:

> Dialectic was the magic charm enabling Hegel to uncover a necessity in the erratic drifting of human history, a necessity as convincing and rational as that which for ages past, and in the modern era of natural science as well, had been evident in the lawfulness and order of nature. As his point of departure here Hegel took the Ancients' conception of dialectic as essentially being the heightening of contradictions. (105)

Unamuno's idea of dialectic agrees with Gadamer's interpretation of Hegel. The Unamunian change comes where he rejects the place of synthesis and replaces it with creative tension within the contradiction; this leads thinking not to a conclusion but to a series of insights produced by the tension; however, the contradiction remains as a source of the dialectic process.

Finally, in the third perspective, there is a sense of participation in the community of writers. But this third direction is not an answer to the agonic dread of finality, for it is quite evident that the trace of the person who has died is not the survival of the personal self. This direction is expressed in Unamuno's literature in themes of the trace of parents in their children, and the drive for achievement and recognition; and, most of all, in writing that expresses the thoughts and sentiments of the writer with the hope that a trace of the person who wrote will be re-created by others every time they read the writer's words.

2. Reality as Process

The continuity of the Heraclitean flow is reality, and this dynamic process must somehow be grasped. Unamuno found that there were no philosophical words to express his approach to reality; this prompted him to turn to metaphor. Some forty years later, Heidegger would reach the same conclusion in his essays "The Origin of the Work of Art" (1936) and "The Question Concerning Technology" (1949), both now available in *Basic Writings* (1977). He turned to poetic language to break through the barriers he had encountered in *Being and Time* (1927), using poetic creation to express presence. He offered the analogy of painting and the objects painted, and he commented on Van Gogh's *Peasant's Shoes* of 1887. There is an absence in the painting, yet we are aware of the intense presence of the absent peasant in the artist's presentation. Heidegger writes: "From Van Gogh's painting we cannot even tell where these shoes stand. There's nothing surrounding this pair of peasant's shoes in or to which they might belong – only an undefined space. There are not even clods of soil from the field or the field-path sticking to them, which would at least hint at their use. A pair of peasant shoes and nothing more. And yet ..." ("The Origin," 163).

It is this tension between absence and presence that best characterizes Unamuno's concept of reality as a process. A moment in time has an infinite stream within it; the reality as process Unamuno has grasped is not a kaleidoscope of fragments in a series. A moment is not a moment in itself but becomes a moment when man abstracts it and isolates it from the continuum. Unamuno found that the only way to express this perspective was through metaphor. He developed his sense of process through the metaphor of the sea:

> The waves of history with their roar and foam reverberate in the sunlight and roll over an endless ocean, an ocean that is immensely deeper than the surface that undulates over the silent depths which never see the sun. Everything that is reported in our newspapers, "the present historical moment," is nothing more than a surface of the ocean which is taken up and crystallized into books and historical registers forming a hard crust not greater than the surface view of the everyday life in which we live that covers over the immense burning centre that lies beneath. (*OC*, I, 793; my trans.)

Throughout this metaphysical reflection the movement of the sea gives an intuition of reality as the ever-changing surface view, but these waves on the surface are merely an abstraction of the real. It is the surging ocean that is the continuum of the real. Unamuno continues: "A single wave is not different from another, it is the same water, it is the same undulating that runs through the same ocean. Metaphorically the ocean's movement is the unbroken continuum of time" (793). "In the depths of the ocean beneath surface history is where the true tradition of life, the eternal one, resides and it is in the present not in the past; the past is where only the dead lie in the graveyard of human being's rational isolations" (794). The philosophical configuration of the real in rational terms creates abstractions. Reason must isolate and remove its object of analysis from life in order to examine it. The reality of change demands an approach that can only be called a philosophy of the poetic imagination. Rational paradigms of reality are but the ephemeral constructs that human beings form in a vain attempt to understand life. In line with Heraclitus, Vico, and Bergson, Unamuno considered reality to be in continuous flux. Ideas of change and process are not new, but Unamuno's concept of flux anticipates Bergson's *élan vital* of *L'évolution créatrice*. Unamuno uses the metaphor of the sea to elaborate his understanding of written history as the surface that although in motion gives the illusion of permanence; but there is also a deep history of *intrahistoria* that is the unwritten history of everyday life. Beneath the surface, the ocean is all movement.

How can Unamuno refer to his concept of continuous flux expressed solely in poetic terms as the metaphysical concept of the negation of non-being and the affirmation of being? His answer is that this dialectic pattern does not constitute a system of inquiry but rather an *a priori* framework of thought into which his philosophical inquiry can be formulated. Each perspective has to be elaborated on its own terms, from the metaphysical to the existential to the aesthetic.

Unamuno's philosophy does not adhere to linear logic; the only order he follows is that of an open dialectic. Dialogue and linguistic communication are his guideposts. It is true that intuition gives him insight, but this insight is developed through a pattern of oppositions basic to the open dialectic. Consequently, oppositions, contradictions, and metaphors – which are central to Unamuno's writing – can be misconstrued if they are not understood as linguistic devices to capture the essence of the dialectic tension of reality. When he comments on the opposition of being and non-being, he is not indicating two fixed entities, but rather one force engaging another in the struggle that is reality. For Unamuno, the dialectic tension indicates a driving force of coming into being opposed by the counterforce of non-being. This is a continuum of opposition.

The pattern of thought of the open dialectic accounts for some of the differences between Bergson and Unamuno, who acknowledged the proximity of his philosophy to that of Bergson. He wrote in *Del sentimiento trágico:* "What did Bergson, for example, attempt, especially in his work on creative evolution, but to restore a personal God and an eternal consciousness? The truth is that life will not surrender" (*SW*, IV, 159).

Unamuno thought that Bergson had tried to reach the concept of the human being as the personal god but had failed and ended up creating a self-propelling totality. Unamuno contended that his first perspective of reality, as developed in *En torno al casticismo,* had been given a philosophical framework by Bergson in *L'évolution créatrice* (1907). Thus in 1912, when Unamuno wrote *Del sentimiento trágico,* he reaffirmed his first perspective in Bergson's language: "Intelligence is a dreadful matter. It tends towards death in the way that memory tends towards stability. That which lives, that which is absolutely unstable, absolutely individual, is strictly speaking, unintelligible. Logic tends to reduce everything to identities" (*SW*, IV, 100).

Unamuno, in company with Bergson, developed his first philosophical perspective from a poetic sense of totality to a philosophical argument. Non-being is never completed, because it is the necessary dialectic counterpart of being. In this perspective all of life is part of an unending flux, thus there is no death, only change.

Unamuno's relation to Heidegger was different from the close relation he had with Bergson. It is doubtful that Unamuno and Heidegger knew of each other. Heidegger was twenty-five years younger than Unamuno and was steeped in Continental philosophy, which at that time gave no heed to Spanish philosophers. Unamuno knew German philosophy well and had studied Hegel – who had a long-lasting impact on his thinking – but by the time Heidegger's *Sein und Zeit* was published in 1927, Unamuno was embroiled in political combat with the Spanish government of Primo de Rivera, which exiled him to the Canary Islands. He returned to Spain only after the Second Spanish Republic was founded in 1931. He died in 1936 and was never able to return to his careful reading of German philosophy; so we must conclude that Unamuno and Heidegger never read each other. However, critics and commentators of Unamuno have pointed to many uncanny parallels in their philosophies. One of the most perceptive and accurate commentaries was that of Martin Nozick in *Miguel de Unamuno* (1971).

Under the heading "Some Comparisons," Nozick writes: "Martin Heidegger has as his goal the return to the vital center or ground (68) ... When being becomes *logos* and logos is incorporated into language, language becomes the custodian of being, and truth becomes an 'attribute of statement,' a shifting thing determined by 'properties, magnitude, relations'" (69). Unamuno would have agreed, of course, but only insofar as he would have recognized that philosophers and theologians are not necessarily equipped to delineate God, although this does not exempt them from a preoccupation with the problem. More central to Unamuno's thought is that reason is an usurpation of the whole by the part, an arbitrary breaking up of an indivisible unity into discrete parts. Nozick forges the strongest links between Heidegger and Unamuno is in his sixth chapter, "Philosophy and Poetry": "If, as Heidegger avers, the poet speaks Being, it is not surprising that Unamuno should have found his way irresistibly to verse form as a natural correlative to those essays which are as much confession and rhapsody as they are exposition" (170–1). The parallel between Unamuno and Heidegger can be explained by the coming together of several intellectual currents in both philosophers. Both were influenced by Hegel but ended up rejecting his absolute domain of reason; more significantly, both were drawn to the pre-Socratic philosophers, primarily Heraclitus. According to Heraclitus, the essence of reality is the relentless conflict of opposites; it is this tension of struggle that gives unity to reality. One of the most philosophically informed of Unamuno's commentators is Pedro Cerezo Galán, who in *Las máscaras de lo trágico* recognizes that in Unamuno's philosophy "the tension is insuperable ... In Unamuno's dialectic the fundamental phenomenon is the antagonism of opposites, of the opposites of reality, of the *Polemos* which has been determinate since Heraclitus" (419; my trans.).

George Steiner, in his lucid commentary on Heidegger, explains the pre-Socratic basis of this philosophy in the following passage:

> Here Heidegger's example is that of a Greek temple. The temple is earth-rooted and has, literally sprung from the earth. Now it conceals the earth beneath it while, simultaneously, linking it to the sky. Inside the temple the deity is at once present and absent, made manifest in epiphany yet hidden from view. The temple, as a colonnaded space is both open to the outside and enclosed. In a Greek temple the two primordial agencies of the truth of being – openness (*die Lichtung*), and concealment or guarded infolding – conjoin. The sky is, in this new Heideggerian parlance, the place and realization of openness. The earth is the locale of concealment and sanctified in-habitation (*der Verbergung als Bergung*). Both are indispensible if existence is to find authentic embodiment ... But such simultaneity and conjunction are polemical. Here Heidegger invokes the notion of vital strife (*polemos)* derived from Heraclitus. (135)

Vital strife – essentially, the concept of creative struggle – was central to Unamuno's philosophy. Unamuno's dialectic engagement of the ontological Being to the existential self was described brilliantly – albeit twelve years after Unamuno's death – in Ricoeur's *Le volontaire et l'involontaire*

(1950; English trans.: *Freedom and Nature*), which he completed in 1948, only a few years after his liberation from a German prison camp. When we read Ricoeur with Unamuno in the background, both are elucidated:

> Yet everything becomes; there is nothing which is not derived from something simpler. Thus genesis is the temporal line from simple to complex ... The alleged human being is only a moment in human becoming from birth to death. A meaning is built up and lost. Only what becomes is. Here we can see a new devouring objectivity being constituted, an objectivity of genesis or evolution. I lose myself in my own growth which makes and unmakes me. I have no basic meaning. I am only a history, or, better, there is a history which I call "I" and which immediately has a structure which engulfs the "I" as one of its subordinate sectors. (427–8)

Finally, we must inquire about the place of ethics in Unamuno's philosophy of process. He does not elaborate an ethical line of thought, yet it can be readily seen that an ethics is implicit in his philosophy. As Unamuno's unpublished texts become available, the scope of his ethics will be recognized. Cerezo Galán cites the following unpublished note: "Religion provides the foundation for ethics, but it is a hyper ethics, a metaethics" (460).

Awareness of the finality of death gives rise to an ethics of living so as to merit an eternal memory in others. As early as 1905, in the short essay "Soledad," the ethics of myself as another was in place: "There is no dialogue as truthful as the dialogue you have with yourself, and this is a dialogue you can only have when you are alone. In your solitude and only in your solitude you will be able to know yourself as your other, and as long as you do not know yourself as your other you will not be able to see your others as other selves like you" (*OC*, I, 1252). Ricoeur takes these ideas to their full philosophical expression in *Soi-même comme un autre* (1990) as we shall examine in chapter 3 of this book.

3. The Idea of God

During the same years that Unamuno was giving shape to his perspective of the universe as process, he began to address a different concern. The problem now was his personal finitude. This inquiry expanded over the years into a philosophy of self in the major text of this period: *Del sentimiento trágico* (1912). At the same time, Unamuno took up extended readings of German liberal Protestant theologians; foremost among these was his contemporary, Adolf von Harnack (1851–1930). Unamuno's 1894 edition of Harnack's *Lehrbuch der Dogmengeschichte* is the most extensively annotated work in the Unamuno Library (see also Valdés and Valdés). Unamuno's close reading of Hegel's *Wissenschafter der Logik* (also annotated in the Unamuno Library) had a profound and lifelong effect on him. He formulated the metaphor of God as Hegel's Absolute Spirit. That metaphor would remain even after Unamuno could no longer sustain his belief in God. The years 1897 to 1912 were marked by emotional and psychological crises that he eventually overcame and that led to the strong-willed and self-confident thinker we now know. He considered the self's will-to-be as the force that created the need that there be God. The result was a God who dreams reality but who in turn is being dreamed by those who need there to be a God. This is the philosophical position of personal existence as struggle against the counterforce of non-being. The concept that reality is the dream of some higher being is prevalent in world literature; in Spanish literature, the classic example is Calderón de la Barca, and following Unamuno is Jorge Luis Borges. In Calderón's work *La Vida es sueño,* act III, scene 10, we read:

Let us attend on eternity
Which is truly living fame
Wherein good fortune never wanes
Nor glory ever quite stay.

Unamuno quotes these lines in *Del sentimiento trágico de la vida* (*SW*, IV, 291) and goes on to comment that Calderón most probably had faith in the promise of redemption, but what about those others, like Sénancour and himself, who do not believe? What course of action remains? He answers: "All of us each one of us, can and ought to resolve to give as much of himself as he can and even more than he can, exceeding himself, going beyond himself, making himself irreplaceable, giving himself to all others so that they may give him back himself in them" (292). Borges, who was an avid reader of *Del sentimiento trágico* and Unamuno's poetry, wrote an original and highly significant variation on the theme of dreaming reality and one's survival in others in "The Circular Ruins." In this short story a shaman arrives at the ruins of a deserted religious site and takes up the arduous task of dreaming his son, who will eventually replace him. After many failures, he succeeds and dies in a consuming fire.

In 1910 in *Conversación segunda,* recalling the metaphor of the sea as well as the one of the dreaming God, Unamuno interjects the personal note of dread for the coming of death – his death: "Which were but the Sea's dreams. Yes the sea's dreams. The sea also dreams; it dreams eternity, time; god dreams the world, alas the day he wakes up" (*OC,* III, 381; my trans.). It is because of texts such as this that many critics considered him to be a late Romantic, at best a distant echo of Kierkegaard, but at this point in time *Del sentimiento trágico* was foremost in his writing (he would complete it two years later, in 1912). We must understand this development as a process that began in the last years of the nineteenth century as he worked on his essays "Meditaciones evangélicas," which would evolve into two series of three each. "Nicodemo el fariseo" (1899), a meditation on the Gospel of St John, was one of those essays:

> "Jesus arrived and said unto him, Verily, verily, I say unto thee, Except a man be born again, he cannot see the kingdom of God." Nicodemos responds to a literal meaning of the gospel: "How am I to change now, I am in debt to my past; more than that, I am only the result of my life. It is impossible to undo what has been done, nor can I be anything but what I have come to be." (*OC,* VII, 371; my trans.)

Unamuno identifies with Nicodemus's dilemma and questions the meaning of faith. We must consider this crucial challenge, which Unamuno expressed in another essay, "La fe" (1900):

> Question: What is faith? Answer: To believe what we did not see? No, not believe what we did not see, but rather beget, create what we do not see. Create what we do not see, yes; create it and live it and consume it. And then again to create it and consume it once again, living it anew in order to again create it ... and thus on and on, or round and round, in a ceaseless vortex of life. (*OC,* I, 963; my trans.)

Lack of faith cannot mean personal annihilation. Unamuno cannot accept anything less than immortality. In *Del sentimiento trágico de la vida* (1912) he wrote:

> But as I sank deeper and deeper into rational scepticism on the one hand and into emotional despair on the other, the hunger for God was aroused in me and the suffocation of spirit made me feel His reality precisely in

> my want of Him. And I wished there were a God, and that God existed. And God does not exist, but rather super-exists, and He is sustaining our existence by existing us, making us exist. (*SW*, IV, 186)

Paradoxically, the absence of faith made Unamuno feel a greater need for God; he wanted there to be God, he willed that there be God, and what resulted was the overwhelming reality of the need that there be God, but not a God of an independent existence, but one of a supra-existence, a personal God involved in the destiny of men and women. It is in *Del sentimiento trágico* that he reaches his fullest conceptualization of a willed God: "And we may say that He is continually creating Himself in man and being created by man ... All the human imaginations that imagine Him. For God is, and God reveals Himself, in our collectivity; at the same time. He is the most ample and the most personal of all human conceptions" (*SW*, IV, 187).

Unamuno adds that all human beings live in this their God, created by their will: "Reason, the head, pronounces a dread 'Nothing!' Imagination, the heart, speaks to us and says 'All!' And thus between nothingness and the All, in the fusion in us of the All and the Nothing, we live in God, who is All, and God lives in us, and without Him we are Nothing" (*SW*, IV, 196).

The tragic sense of life means that man faces possible annihilation with death. Furthermore, his elimination means the end of everything he knows and has worked towards in life: "We wish to save not only ourselves but the world itself from nothingness. And God is our medium. Thus we do sense His finality" (*SW*, IV, 201). Every year that passes from 1900 to 1912 marks another step towards the culmination of this search for the meaning of personal existence. In the remarkable short story "La locura del doctor Montarco," Unamuno's narrator expresses the emotion behind the tragic sense of life: "Whatever Reason may tell us – that great liar and she is not only a liar but a great whore – in our innermost soul, which we now call the Unconscious, with a capital U, in the depths of our spirit, we know that in order to avoid becoming, sooner or later, nothing, the best course to follow is to attempt to become all" (*Abel Sánchez and Other Stories*, 190). Another step towards the tragic sense of life is reached in "Mi religión" (1907):

> "All right, but what, in short, is your religion?" I will be asked. And I will reply: "My religion is to seek the truth in life and life in the truth,

> even though I know I will not find it while I live. My religion is to struggle incessantly and tirelessly with the mystery; my religion is to wrestle with God, from the break of dawn until the fall of night, as they say. Jacob wrestled with Him. (*SW*, V, 210–11)

This restatement of the problem of the self's extending world is in terms not of victory but of a continuing struggle. The entire philosophical basis begins to take form in these years. Struggle slowly reaches the position of being the end rather than the means.

Again, in "De la correspondencia de un luchador" (1909), Unamuno speaks of the dialectic pattern that will develop into his philosophy in the second perspective.

> You imagine yourself fighting to win, a fight for the struggle itself, and since I anticipate your reply that to fight, to struggle, is a means and not an end, I respond that I have never known, and as time goes by, less and less, what difference there is between the means and the end. And if life which is nothing, if it is not struggle, it is an end according to you, but I believe that struggle could very well be an end in itself. (*OC*, III, 269; my trans.)

There are Nietzschean overtones to these words, but not much more, for Nietzsche's struggle was for power, for the dominance of the superman. This is quite in contrast with Unamuno's struggle, which is not a struggle for a purpose; rather, life itself is in struggle as long as it lasts and even after death – a struggle against oblivion. In other words, existence of the human being is a continued effort to survive, and this is an end in itself: to be in struggle is to exist or to have existed. Unamuno adds: "I have already said that this conflict must be accepted for what it is, and that we must live by it. It remains to explain how – according to my way of feeling, and even to my way of thinking – this despair can be the basis of a vigorous life, of an effective activity, of a system of ethics, of aesthetics, of a religion, and even of a logic" (*SW*, IV, 138).

Unamuno's gradual development of what I have called the will-to-be came from a broad range of sources, English, French, and even Danish but primarily German. He read and assimilated all of the major German theologians and philosophers of the nineteenth century. One of his most lasting sources was Hegel's *Phenomenology of Spirit*, especially the introduction. It is from Hegel that the idea of identity emerges out of the dialectical movement of opposites. Hegel's God is negativity, or the abyss that is the necessary polarity to being. In Hegel's language, God negates himself so that the world can be. In Unamuno's view, the idea of God is the projection of the human being's desire to continue. He is pure desire to be. The individual and collective expression of his desire to continue in being is God. The problem arises when one person's idea of God is threatened by another's idea of God or no-God. The core idea of God as the sum of human aspirations is that my God is our God which makes us human. An early indication of this direction is in the *Diario íntimo:* "Deep within your conscience of yourself is your conscience of God. The God that is in you" (*OC*, VIII, 876; my trans.). The most explicit expression of a man-made God is given in *Plenitud de plenitudes y todo plenitud*: "The power to create God in our own image and likeness, of personalizing the universe does not mean anything more than we have God in us as the genesis of hope" (223; my trans.).

The concept of the open dialectic in Unamuno has metaphysical, anthropological, and aesthetic expression. I have written about these distinct modes of engagement elsewhere (Valdés, *Death in the Literature of Unamuno*). What concerns me here is to offer a historical context for the aesthetics of disbelief. At the core of this aesthetic lies the passage from simple contradiction to the semantic impertinence of the creative metaphor. In a contradictory statement, proposition A is countered by proposition B in such a way that there is no room for compromise. One negates the other. But what is overlooked in this simple example is the action of negation, for what has been active in this encounter is the expression of negation.

Unamuno acknowledged that his concept of dialectic was a transformation of Hegel's logic and that his narration was an open dialectic with no synthesis. Unamuno's dialectic process is one of opposites and antitheses in continuous struggle. The resulting tension grants insight into the problem at hand. Open dialectic is anti-dogmatic and brings about debate, contradiction, and, eventually, for the enlightened, the recognition of differences between persons of principle in the community of commentators. At the root of the open dialectic is scepticism, a distrust of absolutes, and an openness to the views of others. For Unamuno, debate was the only way to open up inquiry and eventually find other minds.

If instead of fixed propositions or interpretations we have ideas that reflect our own reality, there will necessarily be opposition with the ideas of others, and the conflict that ensues is not resolved by the víctory of one idea over the other, but by the net gain in understanding differences.

Poetry, through its propensity for creative metaphor, participates in open dialectic. When one usage is incompatible to another – such as "a tree grew on my forehead" – there is semantic impertinence; that is, the words do not make sense together, but there is the possibility of metaphorical sense. In the words we used above, if we think of an idea as a tree, there is a metaphorical sense. Metaphorical sense develops when we as readers encounter the challenge and instead of eliminating one image or the other – which would be the logical solution – we accept the tension of opposition; this tension then becomes the basis for the creative metaphor. Thus we have an image from Islam, "God is great," countered immediately by "God is but an idea," which we attempt to reconcile with the notion "a great idea." But no sooner have we done this than the true opposition emerges: God is larger than reality. Unamuno enters the struggle with two verses in his *Cancionero:* "How great you are my god! You are so great that you are an idea" (*OC,* VI, 359; my trans.). The second verse has the deflationary effect of apparently reducing God to no more than an idea that is a clear semantic opposition to greatness. Yet there is a way out, for an idea like that of truth can indeed be an idea and still be great. The full semantic impertinence comes in the enjambment between verses two and three. God is great because reality is too narrow no matter how it expands. Therefore the following poem of disbelief emerges. God is but an idea, an idea that is too great for reality no matter how our knowledge of it expands. The metaphor is that God in physical terms of size and space exceeds all comprehension because God is not real, as an idea there is no limit to what countless generations of millions of persons over centuries can imagine. The aesthetics of disbelief are a tensional creativity full of indeterminacy and conceptual richness.

In this chapter I have traced Unamuno's idea of God as a human creation as it developed in the last years of the nineteenth century, culminating in *Del sentimiento trágico* (1912): "It is the furious longing to assign finality to the Universe, to make it conscious and personal, which has led us to believe in God, to want God to be – in a word, which has led us to create God. Yes to create Him! ... It is He who is continually creating Himself in us. We have created God in order to preserve the Universe from Nothingness" (*SW*, IV, 170).

Central to Unamuno's thinking on God and faith is his reading and annotation of Carl Gustav Adolf von Harnack's *Lehrbuch*, which advocates a return to the basic faith of the early Christians and removes the non-essentials of dogma (see Valdés and Valdés, *An Unamuno Source Book*, 111).

In the final paragraph of his intellectual autobiography, Ricoeur came very close to Unamuno's concept of God as the human source of hope. "I cannot say as a philosopher where the voice of conscience comes from – that ultimate expression of otherness that haunts selfhood! Does it come from a person who is other whom I can still envision from my ancestors, from a dead god or a living God, but one as absent from our life as the past is from all reconstructed history, or even from some empty place?" (in Valdés, *The Philosophy of Paul Ricoeur*, 53).

Unamuno dismissed the idea of a dead God, or Aristotle's unmoved mover. He found scant solace in his Spanish tradition going back to Saint Teresa of Ávila and Calderón de la Barca, but he recognized its force. He rejects as meaningless the idea of a living God absent from our life. The indeterminate "empty place" as the absence that must be filled in presence is close to Unamuno's idea of God as a human need. Precisely *because* a "willed God" does not exist, it must be willed. The concept of a willed God is a non-linear, non-progressive, non-self-conscious human response to the tragic sense of life. If Unamuno's idea of a willed God has no inner logic of development, and if it is driven by the human struggle for self-preservation, we must recognize Unamuno's debt to Hegel and Nietzsche.

To understand the sometimes violent furor over Unamuno's concept of God as the manifestation of the human will-to-be, one must put his work in the context of the first third of the twentieth century in Spain, when the Catholic Church was under attack by liberal forces and the Church's hierarchy responded by sowing hatred for public figures who did not adhere to the orthodox narrative of creation. For most of the Francoist post–Civil War period, Unamuno's works were banned, especially *Del sentimiento trágico*, *La agonía del cristianismo*, and the novel *San Manuel Bueno, mártir*.

We should compare Unamuno's concept of God with the views of the British physicist Stephen Hawking on God. In a recent article, "Stephen Hawking Will Now Take Your Questions" he was asked: "If God doesn't exist, why did the concept of His existence become almost universal?" Hawking's response: "I don't claim that God doesn't exist. God is the name people give to the reason we are here. But I think that reason is the laws of physics rather than someone with whom one can have a personal relationship" (4). Unamuno would agree in principle but would also insist on the passionate rejection of death, calling it the most unfair and unjust fate awaiting us all. He would certainly agree with Dylan Thomas and his rage against death in his poem "And Death Shall Have No Dominion." In the book of critical interviews conducted by François Azouvi and Marc de Launay, *Critique and Conviction,* we find major directions or signposts in Ricoeur's thinking. It is here that he is most candid on the topic of God and an afterlife:

> I find myself meditating – *andenken!* – on a God who remembers me, beyond the categories of time (past, present, future). In order to give due weight to this digression, I venture to add to it a speculative extension in the wake of the process theology stemming from Whitehead, where it is a matter of a God who becomes – and not who is, in the static and immutable sense of Greek philosophy, from which Augustine descended. Supporting this speculation on the schematism of the memory of God, I figure to myself that human existence that is no longer but which has been in some way gathered into the memory of a God who is affected by it. (158)

And if we ask where one fits within this memory of God, Ricoeur responds:

> I demand nothing. I demand no "after." I cast upon others, my survivors, the task of taking up again my desire to be, my effort to exist in the time of the living ... But I do not have the right to interiorize, so to speak, this anticipation that I will have survivors in order to convert it into a representation of my own afterlife, in continuity with my actual life. (158, 159)

4. The Tragic Sense of Finitude

Ricoeur was born in 1913, the year Unamuno published *Del sentimiento trágico de la vida* as a book. Besides the nineteenth-century liberal German theologians, the link between Unamuno and Ricoeur was Gabriel Marcel. Here I will outline Unamuno's radical philosophical development after 1913, the parallel with Gabriel Marcel, and, finally, Ricoeur's contribution to the tragic sense of finitude in *Fallible Man* (1960).

Unamuno's *Del sentimiento trágico* was first published monthly in a journal in 1912 and as a book the following year. This work marks a radical departure from any traditional philosophy since all supernatural determination of reality is abandoned, as well as any consideration of a basic essence of existents. The new philosophy of the self puts existence itself before any other consideration. The existential fact of the individual's being-there in the world becomes the basis of the entire inquiry. In chapter 2 of *Del sentimiento trágico,* "The Point of Departure," Unamuno rejects Descartes:

> The defect in Descartes' *Discourse on Method* does not lie in the methodical prior doubt, in the fact that he begins by resolving to doubt everything, which is no more than a mere artifice; the defect lies in his resolving to begin by leaving himself out, omitting Descartes, the real man, the man of flesh and blood, the man who does not want to die, so that he can become a mere thinker, that is, an abstraction ... The truth is *sum, ergo cogito* – I am, therefore I think, though not everything that is, thinks. (*SW*, IV, 39, 41)

This starting point puts Unamuno into the mode of thinking we have come to call existentialism. If existence precedes rational deliberation, the individual is uncompromisingly free and alone. The self is its own maker through its will to be, as Tillich would say. To exist is to be there, cast into a world that others have made and that now must be appropriated by the self. The essential factor about this existence is contingency, not necessity. It is in this state that man finds himself, and it is this state that he tries to overcome through the belief in a causative superior being. It is when this faith in God wavers that the individual is forced to take a second look at himself and at his world. This is what Unamuno calls "the depths of the abyss": in order to survive he must learn to live in the tragic sense of life.

Thus the real individual woman or man first exists, rationalizes his position, but then the ultimate contingency of death makes some individuals reflect, doubt, and search for life's meaning. These individuals find themselves alone in the abyss and then, through their will, learn to live from this inner strife as they realize they are making their own future. Unamuno states clearly, in this essay, the basis of existential anthropology – the tragic sense of life.

The personal self is in this world and knows the world from his or her own perspective and lived experience:

> What exists for us, in fact, is precisely what we need to know, in one or another way, in order to go on existing. Objective existence is, in our minds, dependent on our own personal existence. (*SW*, IV, 28–9)

The rational analysis of the individual is a secondary sociological development:

> And if the individual survives through his instinct for self-preservation, society owes its being and its continuance to the instinct for perpetuation in the individual. And, from this instinct, or rather from society, springs reason. (*SW*, IV, 29)

So it is the individual who wants to move beyond the appearances of reality. But if he seeks to probe into a sense of his being, he cannot advance through reason alone. As Vico had written in the eighteenth century, he must nurture a poetic sense of life. In Unamuno's appropriation of Vico, the poetic sense of life comes from an awareness of the significance of being in the world and of the finality of death. This state of awareness is what Unamuno called the tragic sense of life, which commits one to the world and to live every day as if it were the last, which results in a profound sense of responsibility and commitment to one's others.

The philosophical personalization of the environment by the Self, which for Unamuno is at first an aspiration (see "El secreto de la vida" [1906]), by 1912 has become the consequence of the tragic sense. *Serlo todo,* to be everything, is the total experience each individual has with the world:

> If you look at the universe as closely and as inwardly as you can, that is, within yourself, if you sense, and not merely contemplate, everything in your consciousness, where all things have left their painful imprint, then you will plumb the depths of tedium, not only the tedium of life, but of something more: the tedium of existence, the bottomless well of the vanity of vanities. And thus you will come to feel compassion for all things: you will feel universal love. (*SW*, IV, 153)

Recall that this God is the personal God of the self's creation and of the self's life-world. This is not a transcendent concept of God, for the above-cited lines cannot in any way be taken as a form of pantheism of Spinoza's universe or the world of Schopenhauer.

This *amor universal* is not the world-being of Hegel, nor is it Krausist idealism; rather, it is the self's identification with his world. The *serlo todo* means precisely this final status of existential awareness of the all, which is the self's world. Each individual is a unique, irreplaceable self. Ricoeur's idea of the God of Christianity is close to Unamuno's philosophy of self, albeit in a very different mode of expression.

The world, therefore, exists in the self and has been re-created there by the self, which singles it out, is aware of it, feels for it. This material enclosure of the self is not the Thomistic concept of the material limitations imposed on the soul; it is, rather, the personal effort of the individual to personalize his world, his total living relationship with everything around him. The tragic sense of life, which opens the personal self to the world for personalization in commitment, is the result of an awareness of death. But this is not the passive state of inner wisdom of Siddartha. Quite the contrary, it is a state of emotional and intellectual struggle, which rages within the authentic person. And this continuous struggle with finitude does not put the self-world relationship into two poles, for that would be an abstraction rather than a personalization. The pattern of struggle that is the tragic sense is a positive force; its function is to make all living relationships personal ones for the self so that others will be perceived as unique individual forces that are also making their way, just like the self that has personalized them. Unamuno wrote the following exposition:

> We may formulate it thus: Act so that in your own judgment and in the judgment of others you may deserve eternity, act so that you may be irreplaceable, act so that you do not deserve death. [*SW*, IV, 285]

> In all truth every man is unique and irreplaceable: another I is inconceivable; each one of us is ... worth the whole Universe.
>
> The feeling of solidarity originates in myself; since I am a society, I feel the need of making myself master of human society; since I am a product of this society, I must socialize myself, and from myself I proceed to God – who is I projected to the All – and from God to each of my fellows. (*SW*, IV, 302)

Thirteen years later Unamuno wrote *La agonía del cristianismo* (1925) while in exile in France – a period of emotional crisis equal in depth to the one of 1897. Again the problem is the finality of the self that becomes an unceasing struggle unto death. "Agony means struggle. The life of a person in agony is one of continuous struggle, a struggle even against life itself and against death. This is the meaning of Santa Teresa's ejaculatory prayer, 'I am dying because I cannot die'" (*The Agony of Christianity*, 6–7).

The struggle against life itself and against death repeats the idea that the self's utter freedom must be lived with the will to face the contingency of life and must, therefore, remake itself at every moment as the will-to-be. The tragic sense of life is born in the opposition between the intellect that insists that all living beings must die and the will that cannot accept the finality of death for the self. From the moment of the self's awareness of life unto death there is a continuous struggle to continue.

Gabriel Marcel is the intellectual connection between Unamuno and Ricoeur. In temperament and writing style, Marcel is much closer to Unamuno than to Ricoeur. His essays are deliberately non-systematic free commentaries on social and moral issues. He is strongly opposed to abstractions that reduce the human being to statistical data. Marcel, like Unamuno before him, insists on focusing on the human being of flesh and blood, who lives, suffers, and dies. In contrast to Sartre, his contemporary, for whom the fundamental human experience is loneliness, the anxiety of having been thrown into an incomprehensible world, Marcel's philosophy emphasizes the human being's relation to others. Unamuno's novel of 1933, *San Manuel Bueno, mártir,* offers a fictional image of this philosophical position. Marcel had a warm friendship with the Spanish philosopher Julián Marías. When Marcel read Marías's book *Miguel de Unamuno,* he expressed astonishment that as early as 1887 Unamuno had approached the basic ideas of the self and others that he and philosophers in France were just recognizing. Marcel was also a dramatist whose works addressed the moral issues of his philosophy. Marías explains the difference between the plays of Marcel and the novels of Unamuno:

> The fundamental difference [with respect to their literary works] is that Unamuno was primarily a novelist and not a playwright. His plays can be "reduced" to his novels, that is, he studies human life in a narrative form, and not through dialogue, whereas Marcel never wrote novels and his dramatic representation of human life is based in the scenic and verbal confrontation of intimacies rather than in the reflection of imagination. ("Love in Marcel and Ortega," 556)

A few lines from Marcel's *Pour une sagesse tragique* (1968), translated as *Tragic Wisdom* (1973), will help us build the bridge between Unamuno and Ricoeur:

> I depart most resolutely from Heidegger's thought as it is commonly interpreted. Indeed, I am brought back to the criticism I felt I had to make of *Sein zum Tode:* that this notion radically minimizes the importance of the death of the other, the death of a loved person ... Our task is to understand what I have called the original light ... given this tragic world we live in where each of us participates in being-towards-death, not only towards his own death ... but much more profoundly and intimately towards the death of the being whom he loves and who for him counts infinitely more than himself, to the point of his being, not by nature but by vocation, decentered or poly centered. (211–12)

Finally I want to cite what Ricoeur finds to be the foundation of Marcel's thinking:

> Although one may wonder whether the fragmentation of individuals, collectivization and bureaucratization are really the most inexcusable signs of the division of the world against itself, the essential matter for the present discussion is that the most primordial experience on which philosophy reflects already attests to the existence of a break affecting the integrity and wholeness of human experience ... This exigence, or urgent need, can be called the need for transcendence only if philosophy continues to recognize the adversary to which it is joined, which we have called the temptation of despair. ("Gabriel Marcel and Phenomenology," 488)

Ricoeur's *Fallible Man* (1960) is the textual evidence of Marcel's link with Unamuno.

> The universal function of feeling is to bind together. It connects what knowledge divides: it binds me to things, to beings, to being. Whereas the whole movement of objectification tends to set a world over against me, feeling unites the intentionality, which throws me out of myself, to the affection through which I feel myself existing ... It seems then, that conflict is a function of man's primordial constitution; the object is the synthesis; the self is conflict. (131, 132)

To summarize, in the twentieth century there is a line of development in philosophy culminating in philosophical anthropology. Unamuno and Ricoeur stand out among the philosophers in France, Germany, Spain, and North America who have expanded this mode of inquiry into all aspects of human engagement.

The basic difference between Unamuno's *Del sentimiento trágico* and Ricoeur's *Fallible Man* is that whereas Unamuno sought to come to grips with the human being's finitude and remove the destructive implications of alienation and despair, Ricoeur's work is, simply put, a philosophical reflection on human being. Unamuno's power derives from a passion for life akin to that of Kierkegaard, while Ricoeur's hermeneutics is developed from Heidegger and Gadamer. In spite of these differences there is a confluence of the two, which is to realize self-discovery through the configuration of texts.

5. A Hermeneutics of Self

In May 1971 Ricoeur embarked on the new hermeneutics when he delivered the lecture "From Existentialism to the Philosophy of Language" (published as the appendix to the English edition of *La métaphore vive*). He gave the following explanation: "The kind of hermeneutics which I now favor starts from the recognition of the objective meaning of the text as distinct from the subjective intention of the author. This objective meaning is not something hidden behind the text. *Rather it is a requirement addressed to the reader*. The interpretation accordingly is a kind of obedience to this injunction starting from the text" (319; emphasis mine). This new hermeneutics was directed to what the encounter between text and reader disclosed. He was still at the beginning of this radical shift within hermeneutics, and a number of major challenges lay ahead for him, including exchanges with his post-structuralist contemporaries, Foucault and Derrida.

In *Les mots et les choses* (1966), Foucault, at the peak of his influence, dismissed all referentiality in poetic discourse. His dramatic flair carried the day: language is a self-sustaining system in which words have no necessary relation to things; humanity is therefore locked into a madhouse with massive diachronic shifts between alternative epistemes. The illusion of coherence was a tribute to Foucault's rhetoric rather than to his philosophy. Ricoeur stood fast, quietly asking for proof that

> the passage from one episteme to another comes close to the dialectic of innovation and sedimentation by which we have more than once characterized

traditionality – discontinuity corresponding to the moment of innovation, continuity to that of sedimentation. Apart from this dialectic, the concept of transformation, wholly thought of in terms of breaks, risks leading us back to the Eleatic conception of time, which according to Zeno, comes down to making time something composed of indivisible *minima*. And we must say that the *Archeology of Knowledge* (1969) runs the risk with its methodological stance. (*Temps et récit*, III, 219)

Derrida is the other major thinker who questioned the creative power of discourse. Throughout his multiple twists and turns, it is clear that he also denies referentiality to poetic discourse. Ricoeur addresses Derrida's "White Mythology" (1972) in chapter 8 of *La métaphore vive:* "The perplexing tactic has proven to be only one episode in a much vaster strategy of deconstruction that always consists in destroying metaphorical discourse by reduction to aporias" (287). Ricoeur identifies two prongs in Derrida's argument: (1) the proposition that, like coins, metaphors wear out and, in the effacement that follows, drift towards idealization; (2) a rejection of opposition of operations, as for example, syntax and semantics, or figurative usage and literal usage. Ricoeur's response is just as innovative: the wearing out of the coin and the consequent effacement of its images is not the end of the story, for the metal can be recycled. Ricoeur cites Michel Le Guern (*Sémantic*, 87) in support of his argument: "Lexicalization brings out the total disappearance of the image only under special conditions." Ricoeur then adds: "In other cases the image is attenuated but still perceptible; that is why almost all lexicalized metaphors can recover their original brilliance. The reanimations of a dead metaphor, however, is a positive operation of de-lexicalizing that amounts to a new production of metaphor and therefore of metaphorical meaning" (*La metáphore vive*, 291). And this is so because lexicality, like metal, can be recycled. The underlying basis for split referentiality is the cyclical process of lived language from the prefigurative matrix to the action of configuration and on to the reflection of refiguration, which renews and adds to the lexicality of the prefigurative domain of live languages.

From *De l'interprétation* (1965) to *Du texte á l'action* (1986), Ricoeur's hermeneutics evolved from the interpretation of texts to the interpretation of meaningful action. In the text–reader dialectic, the reader liberates the text from the world to which its author first responded; the text opens up through the reader's participation in unknown worlds. This last turn moves his hermeneutics into the domain of a hermeneutics of culture, one that is not limited to written texts but rather is aimed at all creative work of persons and communities.

Throughout *La métaphore vive,* Ricoeur states that language is a way of living arising from living discourse among speakers who have something meaningful to say to one another. Ricoeur's thinking on language developed from his reading of Émile Benveniste's *Problèmes de linguistique générale* (1966). Ricoeur states that the reduction of language to signifiers is an abstraction of the discursive reality. Language use is an event of communication in which human beings transcend their subjectivity in creating the intersubjective phenomenon of meaningful communication. New meaning can emerge in dialogue between participants in the language event.

The respective philosophical views on language held by Unamuno and Ricoeur are noteworthy. Consider the position often expressed by Ricoeur in conjunction with the metaphorical writing of Unamuno. Ricoeur held that human perception of reality is determined by language. The world we inhabit is the language we live in. He recognized that as a system, language is a self-referential process of communication between persons in which signs get their meaning entirely through their relationship of similarity and difference with other signs in the system. In ordinary usage, this is the basis for persons to understand one another. Historically, Ricoeur thought of language as the prefigurative storehouse of experience, and as a storehouse it grows, evolves, and discards signs no longer useful for expressing human experience. His philosophy of language can be summarized as follows: The human being lives in language. Language makes manifest the world we inhabit, but because the use of language is individual, we inhabit a personal sense of the world that is only similar to the world of others. We are susceptible to a shared view of reality because of what Wittgenstein calls language-games.

Now let us briefly quote Unamuno on language: "Language is what gives us reality, and it does so not as a mere vehicle of reality, but as the true flesh of reality, of which all the rest, dumb show or inarticulate representation, is merely the skeleton" (*SW*, IV, 338).

Ricoeur's major work of the 1980s was *Soi-même comme un autre* (1990). For anyone seeking to trace the development of Ricoeur's philosophy from a hermeneutics of discourse to a hermeneutics of text and, finally, to a hermeneutics of self, the key readings are ch. 7 of *La métaphore vive,* "Metaphor and Reference," especially s. 5, "Towards the Concept of 'Metaphorical Truth.'" Next, the hermeneutics of text has its fullest expression in *Time and Narrative*, vol. 1, pt 1, ch. 3, "Time and Narrative: Threefold Mimesis," which is a bridge to the next stage of development. It is also necessary to consider vol. 3, pt 2, ch. 10, "Towards a Hermeneutics of Historical Consciousness." The last stage in this philosophical development is in *Soi-même comme un autre*, ch. 1, "The Question of Selfhood," and especially, pt 2, "Towards a Hermeneutics of the Self," and ch. 5, "Personal Identity and Narrative Identity."

It is clear that the premise on which the inquiry in *Soi-même comme un autre* is based is the distinction between two aspects of personal identity: sameness and selfhood. The defining concept behind sameness is that a person remains being one person in spite of the variety of life's stages he passes through. The sense of selfhood is the relationship each person has with himself. Now then, in the action of living we can refer to a person's character, which Ricoeur defines as "the set of lasting dispositions by which a person is recognized" (121). Therefore we realize that in this philosophy of identity, sameness and selfhood overlap in what he has designated as character, but on introspection the two disassociate entirely from each other, thus forming a polar opposition.

In *Soi-même comme un autre*, Ricoeur establishes a fundamental dialectic between idem and ipse. Idem is the continuity of the self across time and in the world. Ipse represents the present thinking and acting of the self. This is what we refer to as conscience. Ricoeur elaborated the dialectic of self through four questions. With respect to idem, (1) who is speaking, (2) and who is acting? And with regard to Ipse, (3) who is telling his story, and (4) who is responsible for his words and actions?

In a much less formal style and with some wit, Unamuno expressed similar concepts about the dialectic tensions of the self in his *Tres novelas ejemplares y un prólogo* (1920). He comments on the Oliver Wendell Holmes essay "The Professor at the Breakfast Table" and distinguishes four separate aspects of individual identity. First, there is the person I think I am, which corresponds to Ricoeur's ipse; second, there is the person others think I am, which is designated by Ricoeur as idem; third, there is the person I was in the past, as I remember, which is also included in Ricoeur's idem; and fourth, there is the person I would like to be, which is part of Ricoeur's ipse. The thinking of the two philosophers, although expressed in different styles and quite different contexts, comes together in a dialectic of body and conscience. The body and the actions of the body have been in continuous development over years, and this is what is known by others. The conscience is the reflexive thinking of the individual and ultimately the mental unity of the one responsible for words and actions. Unamuno's fictional depiction of this philosophy of personal identity is in his novel *Abel Sánchez* (1917), written three years before *Tres novelas ejemplares y un prólogo.*

In *Soi-même comme un autre,* Ricoeur identifies three main features of the hermeneutics of the self: (1) the reflective process must move in its interpretative purpose through a series of analytical examinations into the purported problems of interpretation. This important first feature reasserts Ricoeur's fundamental premise of rational inquiry. (2) The hermeneutics of self engages the dialectic of selfhood and sameness. This feature clearly distances the hermeneutics of self from the philosophies of the *cogito:* "To say self is not to say I. The I is posited – or is deposed. The self is implied reflexively in the operations, the analysis of which precedes the return toward this self" (18). (3) The final dialectic is that of selfhood and otherness. The significance here is that the otherness Ricoeur delineates is not the otherness of comparison but rather the otherness that is constitutive of selfhood as such. Thus Ricoeur held "that the selfhood of oneself implies otherness to such an intimate degree that one cannot be thought of without the other." (3). To these three features Ricoeur puts four questions that will be the working stations of the hermeneutics: "Who is speaking? Who is acting? Who is telling his or her story? Who is the moral subject of imputation?" (169).

In an extraordinary interview conducted by François Azouvi and Marc de Launay and published in 1995, Ricoeur gave one of his most candid statements on the questions of belief in God and personal mortality that so engaged Unamuno. Setting aside the marked differences in temperament and style between Unamuno and Ricoeur, the common ground set out on these matters is so solid that one wonders why commentators have not remarked on it. Ricoeur said:

> My mistrust of the proofs of the existence of God had led me always to treat philosophy as an anthropology – this is still the word I adopted in *Soi-même comme un autre,* in which I border on the religious only in the final pages of the chapter on the voice of conscience, when I say that moral conscience speaks to me from farther away than myself; I cannot say then if it is the voice of my ancestors, the testament of a dead god, or that of a living god. In this case I am agnostic on the plane of philosophy. (*La critique et la conviction,* 150)

Let us compare these remarks with the earlier view expressed by Unamuno on the question of faith and ethics: "I should like to establish the fact that uncertainty, doubt, the perpetual wrestling with the mystery of our final destiny, the consequent mental despair, and the lack of any solid or stable dogmatic foundation, may all serve as basis for an ethic" (*SW*, IV, 283–4).

To summarize Unamuno's and Ricoeur's hermeneutics, the interpretation of texts becomes a step towards a greater semantics of Being. For both philosophers, hermeneutics refers both to the explication of texts and to an inquiry into the nature of human self-understanding.

Throughout his sixty years of work, Ricoeur kept his philosophical discourse separate from his writings on religion; the latter were primarily biblical exegesis. But in the final fifteen years of his writings, we encounter crossovers, always limited to a few lines but growing more and more intense as he contemplated his own death. It was primarily through his philosophy of selfhood that he confronted the question of human mortality and the desire that there be God. He introduces the concept of "l'homme capable" (loosely, "the human who is capable of living unto death"). Unamuno also thought of the capable self as one who lives this life as fully as possible, striving to make his or her willed action valuable to his others and thus to himself. For both philosophers, the potential for self-realization for myself and my others is in all human beings but only some live up to it.

A concept gradually emerges as Ricoeur's reluctance to cross over from philosophy to religion subsides here and there, enough for us to get a clear picture. The concept of God is seen as a human response to the absence of certainty. It is a form of reaching out in hope towards goodness. Here Ricoeur joins Unamuno, for whom God is a relentless human need whose effect is a struggle to be, a striving for the good in the sense of Plato's philosophy. Its hallmark is the voice of concern that cannot be silenced. In this regard, we need only recall the commentary we have made with regard to Unamuno's *Del sentimiento trágico* (1912), recognizing points of contact with Spinoza, Kant, and Hegel.

Both Unamuno and Ricoeur comment on the idea that each and every living organism seeks to continue to live (as explained by Spinoza); and both recognize a kinship with Kant and his premise that the human being has a determination to reach out beyond the self towards an ideal concept, whether it be God or Plato's good. Unamuno's concept of God calls up the human desire for an ideal beyond the self in which humanity could share. In the writings of both Unamuno and Ricoeur, the idea of God is ultimately realized in the philosophy of the self–other relationship.

In his final book, *Parcours de la reconnaissance* (2004), Ricoeur concluded a line of thought that had begun with *Soi-même comme un autre* (1990) and had emerged as the main argument in *La mémoire, l'histoire, l'oubli* (2000), which many of his commentators, including David Pellauer (*Ricoeur*, 109–11) and David E. Klemm (44–5), have called Ricoeur's philosophical anthropology. It is clear to me that in these three books, Ricoeur carefully delineates a hermeneutics of self and comes closest to Unamuno's ethics. As I have argued here, and as William Barrett has recognized (*SW*, IV, 373–4), Unamuno's work ought to be read as philosophy written by means of metaphor. I contend that taken as a whole, Unamuno's work constitutes a hermeneutics of self.

Ricoeur's philosophical anthropology aims to expand and explain his concept of "capable man." The capable human being has a clear sense of self and does not merely abide by what others think one should be. Such a person is keenly aware of being-in-the-world and acts *with* and *for* others, whom he recognizes as his essential others. The capable human being is, above all, a unique and irreplaceable individual. This is a person who lives, loves, suffers, and survives. He or she participates in the social world of work and communal interest. In this philosophy, every capable human being acts and takes responsibility for his or her actions. The capable human being understands that life is a process and that the world as it appears at any given moment has only limited validity. This person recognizes that existence is a process and that permanence is an illusion. The continuity of life is in the individual and collective memory. One's ideas can survive only in the minds of those who read them. Above all, both Unamuno and Ricoeur held that the capable human being accepts the responsibility to participate and share in the pursuit of the good for himself or herself and their others.

Chapter Two

Unamuno's Hermeneutics

1. Unamuno on Interpretation

I have chosen a minor essay by Unamuno to illustrate his hermeneutic perspective for two reasons: that perspective was the theoretical basis for all his writing, major and minor, and permeated everything he wrote; and in examining a minor work we will not be distracted by commentary on the text. Unamuno's philosophy needs no defence from any quarter, and I do not offer one here. My task is to show a necessary development of his hermeneutics within the wider philosophical problematic and to take these insights to their limits, which are implied but not developed in the text I will be using.

Unamuno published the short article "Cosas de libros" in *La Nación* (Buenos Aires) on 17 October 1918 (*OC*, IV, 437–40; all cited translations mine), one among some two hundred short articles he published that year. The first of the nineteen short paragraphs of the article reads as follows: "To know something is, in some way or another to have expressed it" (437).

This introductory paragraph places the author in the tradition of Humboldt's philosophy of language. The very structure of awareness, we are told, is linguistic. To be aware of anything is to verbalize. Experience thus becomes accessible as meaningful through the organizing patterns of language; thus, we must conclude, thinking and language are ineluctably entwined.

Unamuno then dramatizes the commonplace situation of the tourist who takes a number of photographs in order to remember and reconstruct the places he has been. The point is that the photograph as visual communication is basically different from linguistic communication, oral or written. Unamuno posits that the photo is a memory device that can be used to strengthen the memory of the experience depicted. But at the same time, expression is the primary ordering of reality in the mind of the speaker. Both Gabriel Miró and Antonio Machado were deeply impressed by this concept of Unamuno.

The fourth paragraph reads as follows: "If I have a somewhat clear notion of my own ideas it is because I have put them down in writing and therefore I can read them. To express something is to understand it; nobody can be sure of knowing anything until he has expressed it" (438).

We are now deep in the heart of Unamuno's theory of knowledge. In brief: I know the world through my experience; I am aware of experience because I organize and form it; I can organize the world because I express myself. Thus language becomes the great mediator between man and the external matter that surrounds him, and it is only through the organizing function of language that external matter is knowable.

The fifth paragraph is a key one:

> Language, expression, is the father of human reflexive knowledge, Dr Ward, along with others, maintains that everybody has his own world and that there is no way of knowing whether or not our worlds coincide and agree. What stands as actual for a particular man may not be so for another. Every spirit is an exclusive owner and possessor of his own truths and his own errors. For each man there is a world; for each self there is a not-self. There is no common element for the various different ways of experiencing. What there is, is a common language and that is enough. (438)

Unamuno is here commenting on the philosophy of mind of the Cambridge philosopher James Ward (1843–1925), who was influenced by the Theistic philosophy of Lotze. Unamuno had an unusual knack for finding kindred spirits in the most diverse quarters. The choice of Ward as support for his argument is excellent. Unamuno does not provide the bibliographical information for his source; however, Ward's many articles on philosophical problems were later collected and published in two books: *Psychological Principles* (prepared by the author himself) and *Essays in Philosophy* (compiled by his colleagues after his death). The former volume contains some ideas that are very sympathetic to Unamuno. For example, in chapter 12, "Intellection," Ward writes on the acquisition of language:

> But thinking – as permanent activity at least – it may be fairly said, owes its origin to the acquisition of speech. It must here be noted that the higher

> development of the individual is only possible through intercourse with other individuals, that is to say, through society. Without language we should be mutually exclusive and impenetrable, comparable almost to so many physical atoms; with language each several mind may transcend its own limits and share the minds of others. (286)

In a subtle manner, Unamuno's commentary on Ward and his insistence on language's central role closely anticipate the Wittgenstein of *Philosophical Investigations*.

Unamuno adds commentary by Henry Jones on Ward's position in order to make his main point, which is that the only link between minds is language. Losing no time, Unamuno involves his reader in the argument: "Somos hijos todos del lenguaje, de la expresión" (We are all creatures of language, of expression). Then in the next paragraph, he expresses a philosophical position that I have already cited as being closely in harmony with Ward's principles of psychology. By coincidence, Ward's final position on this matter, quoted above, was published at the same time as Unamuno's article, although there is no proof that Unamuno read it. Undoubtedly, Unamuno would have been fascinated by Ward's theory as finally stated in 1918. Although other parts of *Psychological Principles* had been published earlier, the chapter in question was published for the first time in that book in December 1918.

The seventh paragraph presents Unamuno's version of the nominalistic thesis, which he shared with Ward and a few others of his generation in Europe and America:

> What is shared in common by two or more men, what they can communicate, is nothing but language, expression. Language is the foundation of society and sociability. What does it matter if you and I see a poplar, a sheep, a cart in a different way if we call them poplar, sheep, and cart? It is usually said that most arguments are about words. Obviously! Definitions are the only things we disagree upon. (438)

Unamuno has now begun to present the radical duality that he consistently ascribed to language. Language is to be understood as a mediating force that makes human existence possible. But this mediation has two levels: the first we can term the organizing power, through which the individual encounters reality and which is therefore the central basis of self-identification; the second is the transcendent power, through which the individual communicates with his fellow man. The tension between the two is the logical result of contact and encounter between persons. It follows that man inherits the medium and is taught how to use it, but that the inevitable result of such use is the growth of self-consciousness, that is, the first level of language as a capacity to know. Thus, as the individual exercises his capacity for knowing, he inevitably clashes with others who are doing the same. This is not a problem of the physical encounter of each person as a living organism; the problem is entirely with the individual appropriation of the encounter, which is different in each case. The common ground between the two persons who confront the tree is not in the tree itself; rather, it is the way in which they account for the tree, which is to say the linguistically dominated appropriation of the thing. When it becomes desirable for the tree viewers to share their views, they will fail to communicate if they attempt to base their agreement on the object; however, they will succeed if they base their search on their expression of the object.

Unamuno repeatedly insists that the common matrix of perception as being is expression. The living present, by which I mean self-identity, the possibility of repetition, the exploitation of secondary attributes, the very essence of the physical being confronted with the object – all are contained in the concept of awareness, a concept that cannot be broken down into a subject and an object and that comes to be because the individual appropriates reality through expression.

The eighth paragraph contains the now familiar allusion to the Book of Genesis. Unamuno symbolizes man's appropriation of reality through the organizing power of language in terms of the myth of creation. Adam's naming of things and animals is seen as emblematic of man's verbal creation of his universe.

Unamuno must make one last expansion to his thesis on language so that it can encompass "paralanguage":

> We do not become aware of most things we see until we have seen drawings of those things. The marvelous prehistoric cave paintings of reindeer, bison, and goats prove the existence of a human society, that is to say, human knowledge. When one of the cave dwellers drew a bison, he knew and all the others knew that bisons existed. Until then, even if they had eaten the meat of bison they did not know bison existed. (438–9)

It should now be apparent that the dual levels of language discussed in response to the eighth paragraph are essential concepts for even an elementary understanding of Unamuno's philosophy of language. The essence of awareness in man is the semiotic presupposition of the sign *as* sign at the level of organization and appropriation by the self. The semiotic presupposition must be understood in relation to the second level of language, which is meaning, that is, the attempt to express, to use the signs. Unamuno's thesis is that the semiotic level is achieved through the semantic level of expression. To Unamuno's credit, he treats the two levels of language from the perspective of a theoretical inquiry. Thus he is alluding to the birth of language in prehistoric man as a dialectic of sign and expression that eventually gave man the symbolic media of art and speech and made possible the abstract appropriation of matter.

In the tenth paragraph, Unamuno begins a series of illustrative notes that touch upon the acquisition of language in children, educational theory, natural science, and history. In this rapid survey he does little more than suggest the consistent applicability of the theory he has been developing. Since I am not seeking to examine these insights in this chapter but rather to underscore the theoretical inquiry itself, I need not comment in detail: "What professors now call learning from things, many say is nothing more than the learning of names. And so it is. For the name is the thing itself. A child with no language, graphic or spoken, of figures or of sounds, does not know the world in which he lives, nor does he know of his own existence" (439).

Unamuno is not a proponent of some aspect of classical nominalism that would deny the material reality of the world. He insists on a radical nominalism; he holds that the world is knowable only because it has been organized by us, through the use of acquired language:

> Someone might ask what would happen to a child, who from an early age was abandoned but given food and clothes. The experiment cannot be done, but if it were done, we would see that he would soon die of hunger. And not because of anything else but for lack of some kind of language. Things, since they do not speak nor write would not teach him anything. The so-called Book of Nature is nothing but a sentence and if Nature is a book it is because man has put letters to it. Without language, nature is a blank book. Nobody would learn anything from his own experience if the dictionary of everybody else's experience, language, were not at hand. Nobody would be able to distinguish symptoms in Nature if it were not for the names we have given them. (439)

The wolf-children of France and India provide Unamuno with valuable support for his theory of language. The children who have survived in a wild state have done so through the instinctive succour of other animals.

The next paragraph focuses on the severe limitations that sense impressions impose and on the abstract-symbolic nature of experience:

> A few months ago I went to the Italian front and brought back books, memoirs, diaries, pamphlets, sketches, drawings, maps, photographs, and thanks to all of this I know something about the front that I saw and of what a front in the present war might be like. Those at the front only become aware of the front when they have seen it through a linguistic translation. One realizes that one's vision of the war, one's understanding of it, is only slightly expanded when one has been to the scene of war and listened perhaps to the blast of the cannon. (439)

The last four paragraphs (16–19) serve as a conclusion to the theoretical inquiry and need a closer examination.

> Theoretical and practical people? Nonsense! When a man who has made something is not capable of explaining what he has made by means of one language or another, one cannot have confidence that he will be able to do the same thing over again. What can happen is that someone after having done something can learn how to do it again by articulating the process to himself. And if he does not express it to himself, if he does not reduce the multiplicity of experience to language, he will not be able to do it again with any degree of accuracy. The claim that one is able to do something, but not to express it, clearly is false. Expression is not only articulated language, and simply doing something is not always expression, but all reflective action presupposes expression. (440)

The first of Unamuno's general propositions on interpretation is here stated: the ground of awareness in man is the use of language. In other words, in order to be aware of something, we must express being. Unamuno makes a subtle point when he insists that although activity can be a form of expression, it can also be a habitual response and therefore non-expressive. We are therefore faced with the problem of defining what Unamuno means by *expression*. The term and the concept that underlie it are not confined to this essay and are in fact fundamental to Unamuno's philosophy. In brief, the self *is* when it is engaged in a dialectic struggle against negation; the activity I have characterized by the term "struggle" is a constant reaffirmation of self. This reaffirmation is a conscious effort by the self to continue being. Therefore, all activity by the self that asserts and reaffirms the self is expression. The conclusion we reach with this line of reasoning is that the division between theory and practice is arbitrary, for in fact theory is not available except through the practice of thinking. Of course, theory as the expression of the practice of the theoretician is always faulty because the expression has not accounted fully for the necessary differences between the self and others.

The second of Unamuno's propositions on interpretation is in the seventeenth paragraph:

> This is the stuff of books? Yes! And so are all human concerns. And even men themselves are men because of books, when they are such. The fetish of primitive man, the crude drawing on his hut, the adornment he wore, are also books, that is to say, they are all part of a collective memory; where there are no books, there is not even the onset of rationality. (440)

Once we have equated human awareness with expression, we are prepared for the second proposition: because the link between men is their common language, the collective memory of a group is based on their inherited mode of expression – linguistic as well as non-linguistic. Things, therefore, are never things by themselves; they are always interpreted and appropriated by human consciousness. The qualities ascribed to things result partly from the knower's needs and partly from the inherited values of the world view latent in the language through which we conceive those things. Thus, for example, we might think of wooden stairs as firewood if we were in desperate need of warmth; and the custom of piercing the ears of an infant girl could be considered perfectly acceptable in some cultures. An even more radical, culturally determined interpretation would be the response to non-pasteurized ripe cheese.

Unamuno, the writer, had experiences as part of a social collective, but he, like everyone, was constrained by the idiosyncrasies of the immediate time and place in which he found himself. Thus we can say there is a physical barrier of time and place that prevents the individual from knowing more than his immediate empirical response to stimuli. However, since man is both freed by language and bound by it, he can simultaneously break his physical barriers and grasp through abstraction the greater view of his collectivity. But we must remember that his perspective is not objectively constituted, for his view is collectively and privately biased. This is not a temporary condition but rather an inherent characteristic of awareness. The third proposition is therefore that the highest goal of the interpreter is not objective detachment; on the contrary, it is radical self-awareness of one's subjective perspective.

The final paragraph conveys the broadest dimension of Unamuno's hermeneutics: "While all around me, people do not want to know what is happening, what is happening to them, what happens in the world. There seems to be no other problem than subsistence, material subsistence; the total effect of the war is nothing but the rise of the cost of living. It will be terrible to wake up!" (440).

Unamuno's final proposition for a theory of interpretation is stated as general social criticism – which was, of course, the essay's ostensible aim. In terms of a theory of interpretation, Unamuno is telling us that our world view is the elementary background against which we interpret the activities in which we engage directly and indirectly. Our world view can be largely an inherited web of clichés with little or no reflection, or it can be a perspective of whose dimensions and limitations we are aware. Thus the fourth proposition of interpretation is that of radical awareness of the position of the interpreter and the world view from which he has organized and knows reality.

The reflective reader may have noted the marked resemblance that Unamuno's philosophy bears to that of Hegel. The Hegelian *Weltgeist* is continually in flux, but unlike Unamuno's reality, the World Spirit progresses continually towards liberty. Hegel's philosophy is eminently historical: the World Spirit unfolds its potentialities through the stages and struggles of Stoicism, Romanticism, moral world view, religion as a vision, and on towards complete self-knowledge and freedom. The essential difference is that for Hegel, the Absolute Spirit was the historical destiny of a process, whereas for Unamuno, self-knowledge and freedom were the attainable goals of a lifetime and were in fact translated into a way of life. Undoubtedly, Unamuno has added an existential anthropology to the metaphysical system received from Hegel. Unamuno's theory of interpretation aims at the individual achievement of liberty to the extent that the self escapes the prison of unreflexive routine and the mere repetition of the past. The achievement of interpretation is measurable in terms of the communication attained by the self with its pre-rational self. This relationship is a continuous dialectic that must constantly reinterpret reality as the present encounter in the world. The four propositions of Unamuno's theory of interpretation are as follows: awareness of self and world is possible because of language; the collective memory of man is gained through the language-dominated world view; the aim of interpretation is not objective detached observation, but rather the self-awareness of one's subjective perspective; and the social aim of interpretation is to gain the freedom that awareness of one's intersubjective world view can bring to the interpreter. This is as far as Unamuno's thought can take us in the elaboration of a theory of interpretation. I have suggested that Unamuno provides a starting point, but I must also insist on the originality and significance of his writing. He is in the company of Giambattista Vico and Wilhelm von Humboldt, radical thinkers whose legacy is an inexhaustible source of discovery. For those who care to take their challenge and go further in the inquiry into reference and meaning, we have only to look forward to Ricoeur's major contributions in *La métaphore vive* (1975) and *Temps et récit* (1983–5).

2. Unamuno on Knowing the Other

Ludwig Wittgenstein in *Philosophical Investigations* addressed the philosophical foundations of what has been termed the contextual theory of semantics. He wrote: "Here the term 'language-game' is meant to bring into prominence the fact that the *speaking* of language is part of an activity, or of a form of life" (11e). The activity called "language-game" by Wittgenstein is a rule-governed occurrence that I will henceforth designate as speaking in semantic context.

There have been a number of different interpretations of Wittgenstein's expression "a form of life." I find J.F.M. Hunter's discussion of the term particularly interesting and informed. In this essay I will expand these observations with some basic insights taken from sociolinguistics. Hunter's commentary links forms of life to the behaviours dictated by specific activities. He sees playing the language-game as performing with a general competence in using the expressions required by the activity (96–7). But remember that this activity that employs and, as we will see presently, creates language, the basic paradigm of contemporary sociolinguistics, is appropriate here. The process of socialization is, in my view, quite central to Wittgenstein's argument. The competence that Hunter considers implicit in playing the "language-games" of life is basically the ability to use language effectively in the numerous socially prescribed situations of living. I used the word *effectively* rather than *correctly* because correctness often implies that language is in accordance with the rules of established usage. Whereas here, the skill of producing correct grammatical utterances is subordinated to the demands of the particular situation of daily life in which the utterance is made. The fundamental forms of life, such as childhood and adulthood, must be expanded to encompass parent, friend, son, and daughter, and even beyond, to take in employer, employee, professional, teacher, student, and so on; finally, all of the above are subject to a range of socializing distinctions of work, class, education, religion, regional upbringing, and (in some cases) gender. A broad range of these distinctions come into play in the multiple sociolinguistic situations of daily life. These are the specific forms of life in which the language-game of speaking produces reasonably clear utterances. The degree of competence is determined by the ability of the speakers to move from one form of life to another.

As is well known, in many language communities there are social dialects as well as regional dialects; so it is that, like George Bernard Shaw's Professor Higgins, one can identify not only the speaker's place of origin but also his or her social class and education. Put briefly, the forms of life are the rules for playing the language-game in a specific semantic context. Thus, a large part of playing the language-game is being aware of the social role being played by the speakers in the situation at hand – for example, the speaker's status in relation to the others in the immediate context and, specifically, in relation to the person being addressed; the socially prescribed attitude towards the interlocutor; and the aims of the utterance (an employee speaking to an employer, lovers speaking to each other, a child asking for something from a parent, etc.). Spoken language interacts with non-verbal behaviour that serves to clarify and reinforce the various roles and relationships as prescribed by the situation. Every student of acting must learn to enact this enunciative interplay in a great variety of language-games. The principal factors involved in the competent playing of language-games are rapid estimation of the other's authority, power, social status, and attitude towards the issue at hand, as well as an assessment of the significance of differences in sex, age, occupation, socio-economic status, and education. The term "register," as used in sociolinguistics, will serve well in this essay as a category of language usage that establishes the rules for the language game.

There is another side to Wittgenstein's theory of semantic context and that is the psycholinguistic factor. In entry 43 he wrote that "the meaning of a word is its use in the language" (20e). The situational context gives meaning, or the lack of it, to all utterances. Further along in *Philosophical Investigations* he questions the activity of game playing with the context:

> For I *can* give the concept "number" rigid limits in this way, that is, use the word "number" for a rigidly limited concept, but I can also use it so that the extension of the concept is *not* closed by a frontier. And this is how we do use the word "game." For how is the concept of a game bounded? What still counts as a game and what no longer does? Can you give the boundary? No. You can *draw one.* (32e–33e)

In other words, the idea that every word must have one correct meaning is a logical absurdity. Furthermore, discourse itself that tends to organize words and set their function cannot be fixed in abstract terms, but only in the specific semantic context of usage. My premise, therefore, is that meaning is created by enunciation in specific contexts. In the case of literary texts, the major task facing the reader is to ascertain what the appropriate context is for the utterances that are being concretized through the act of reading. Basically, this is what literary critics of the New Critical School called the "purported reality." My task in this essay is twofold: (1) to examine the free-standing dialogue as a subgenre of the essay in the writing of Miguel de Unamuno and, specifically, the context-creating devices used by Unamuno in dialogue; and (2) to point out that Unamuno's reflections on language and the creation of meaning anticipate Wittgenstein's *Philosophical Investigations* by some thirty-five to forty-five years. The common heritage is Wilhelm von Humboldt.

Let us examine the language-game as played by Unamuno as he transfers philosophy from an academic register to that of the general public (in the case at hand, newspaper readers). Newspapers in Spain and Spanish America often carried his articles on diverse topics. One that regularly published his views on language was *La Nación* (Buenos Aires), a leading paper of the day that aimed at a general readership in the Argentine capital. In his *Nación* column of 11 June 1910, Unamuno wrote about mental constructs, rationalism, variable conceptions of reality, and philosophical realism. Bernard Dupriez has developed useful categories for dialogue that we can put to work here: scenic or conflictive, tonal, and expository (132, 182). In Unamuno's hands the scenic dialogue presents a conflict of registers. The two speakers are the author (or authorial persona) and his opponent, who is usually good-natured but ill-informed and whom the author clearly wants to expose as shallow. Needless to say, the author is not likely to draw much sympathy from readers. He is far too much the arrogant intellectual, someone who provokes irritation and even anger – and perhaps some reflection.

In the second discursive mode – in Dupriez's scheme, the tonal – the author does not have a textual interlocutor. Instead he addresses the reader directly, anticipating questions and answering them. This question-and-answer dialectic is as effective as the questions being asked. A very different kind of persona emerges here. This person does not have the answers; rather, he is concerned about the questions and the possible answers that would be forthcoming in a public debate.

The third discursive mode, the expository, features extensive quotations from other authors and Unamuno's commentary in the form of a truncated dialogue. Of course, in all three discursive models there is a tendency towards a form of dialogue wherein the speakers may be two aspects of the self.

In this essay I am considering texts rather than the concrete life situations of people holding conversations. For several reasons, this obvious distinction is important for my argument. First, dialogue is the most natural mode of verbal exchange. In the dialogic experience, the referential frame is the concrete physical situation of speakers conversing with each other in a given place at a certain time. Second, the written dialogue consists formally of the replacement of third person pronouns by pronouns of the first and second person. Thus, there is a double characterization of the two speakers. Third, written dialogue that is free of the constraints of time, space, and presence of the speakers nevertheless has an indelible referential link to spoken dialogue; there is an implicit truth-claim that this is a presentation of a verbal exchange. This truth-claim is far more striking in drama but is also present in narrative and even, albeit in a much weaker form, in poetry. We can now turn to a brief review of Unamuno's three discursive modes in the dialogue form – the conflictive, the tonal (i.e., the dialogue of self-representation), and the expository – and the effects of each.

The dialogues I will be using in this essay are in volume III of the *Obras Completas;* all translations are mine. "Conversación primera" of 11 June 1910 opens with a full discussion in progress. The authorial voice is presenting the case against the Romantic notion of poetic originality. He is quoting from English-language authors, whom he cites and translates. Embedded in the dialogic exchange are short, third person passages assessing the situation. At a key point, the authorial persona tells his interlocutor: "Originality is not minting new coins but knowing how to use them. And who has told you that someone can understand and use an idea better than the person who first discovered it?" (*OC*, III, 372). At this point he quotes the much admired Ernest Renan: "'To the philologist a text has only one meaning, but to the person who has put his life experience into the making of the text, for the person who is alive and continues to experience life, the scrupulous interpretation of the philologist cannot suffice'" (372–3). Setting aside the conflictive elements in the dialogue, diverse sources are being marshalled here to develop a cogent argument for what we today would readily recognize as post-structuralist hermeneutics. Unamuno's principal context-creating device here is the dialogic framework of question and answer, within which texts are placed so as to maximize impact. The reader's growing involvement in this dialogue reflects a strategy for avoiding authorial imposition – everything remains open, in flux, and subject to changes of dialogic relationship that Unamuno hopes to establish.

"Conversación segunda," also published on 11 June 1910, is primarily a conflictive dialogue. Here, there are no third person asides. There is no orderly presentation of ideas as in the expository dialogue; the rapid crossfire of this dialogue generates a harsh, middle-class, commonsense rejection of poetry's utility. The argument draws upon Plato's rejection of poets as deceivers and emphasizes sensible people's low tolerance for self-deception. The poet's rejoinder after the materialist has left is, naturally, in the form of a poem. For the materialist, poetry is mere embellishment; for the poet, it is the imaginative task of remaking the world. Thus, these very old arguments that have never been resolved are renewed once again. Unamuno's dialogue brings out the dialectic situation that they *can* never be resolved because they represent the essential conflict of two life forms and two registers of language-game playing.

"A mis lectores" was published in *La Nación* a few years before the other articles, on 6 July 1909. This truncated dialogue assumes questions from readers and, in answering them, dramatizes the authorial persona that Unamuno had by then been cultivating for a number of years (and that he would continue using until his death in 1936). This is the persona of a provocative thinker who catalyses reflection in the reader.

Unamuno begins paragraph after paragraph with the phrase "Yes, I know" as he responds to questions and criticisms. He writes: "I know that I will not convince you, because you must be a balanced, tranquil discrete person, perhaps not too compassionate. May God preserve you!" Later he adds: "Yes, I know that I am not liked by many of my readers, and one of the reasons that make me most unpleasant is my aggressiveness" (*OC*, III, 394).

The context being created is clear. The paradigm of question and answer creates a situation of intense interrogation. The more provocative the question or criticism, the more intense the persona's rejoinder. In the following passage there is even an assumed attack: "No, don't you believe it, this is not a presumption of superiority. If you suspect this, it is because you do not know me. No, it's not that at all. I do not condemn your beliefs, I do not consider the advice you give as bad advice. What I do tell you is that it does not help me" (*Obras Completas*; vol. III, 395).

The most remarkable of these early dialogue articles by Unamuno is "Conversación tercera," published in *La Nación* on 3 August 1910. This is an expository dialogue and is much closer to the Platonic model than any subsequent ones. I use it here to meet the second of my objectives, which is to show how aware Unamuno was of the philosophical position he had taken. There are at least four distinct qualities to this dialogue in terms of philosophy of language: (1) cacophony, where language loses meaning, (2) the hermeneutic problem of misunderstanding, (3) the problem of crossing from one register (rules of the language-game) to another, (4) the concept of dialogue as the basis for shared meaning. He begins:

- This is a boiling kettle; there is no way we can understand each other. Each one says his piece, they all speak at the same time and no one understands himself or the rest.
- Perhaps that is for the better.
- What?
- Yes, out of chaos came the world. And every people when they awake enter into a chaotic period. All of this agitation is an indication of something; it would be far worse if no one were agitated.
- But one can hardly understand anyone ...

> – That is true. And perhaps in a hundred years if some patient historian studies our agitation he may come to the conclusion that many of us who today think of ourselves as opposed to each other were in fact in agreement. There are ways of expressing the same need with words that are not only different but opposed. (*OC*, III, 385)

In this way, Unamuno introduces the dialectic basis of dialogue. The two sides of a debate can thus be seen as necessarily complementing each other so as to make up the whole. The text continues:

> – But the worst of it is that there are persons who not only do not understand, they do not want to understand …
> And that's as it should be, my friend. One cannot and ought not to speak in language that is too close to one's life when speaking to a general audience … When addressing a general group one has to speak in a collective language. (*OC*, III, 385)

The idea of register is linked to the requirement to seek a collective language that transcends the essential subjective starting point. Unamuno's authorial persona continues the response: "Each one translates what he hears into his own language" (*OC*, III, 386).

We thus now face the problem of subjective relativism – the impossibility of communication or the sharing of ideas and interpretations:

> The public at a political meeting goes to hear what they already know will be said to them … But when you get up and say things that the public did not expect or even presume to exist, things that perhaps they have never thought of before or at least had never thought them the way you think them, then you are lost among the frogs and the fish [frogs, those who hear what they want to hear in spite of what is said, and fish, those who do not hear]. Then they will say that you speak in paradoxes, that you are incoherent, or that you contradict yourself. And the contradiction is usually in their head and not in yours. (*OC*, III, 387)

Unamuno depicts subjectivity as a kind of turmoil amidst appetite, intentions, obligations, and needs. "And the first principle is to live. And since we live in struggle, from our struggle, because of it and for it" (*OC*, III, 389). The subjective turmoil is unique to each person; it follows that this basis of all experience must be translated into a discourse we share with others.

But if we always speak to the collective in a collective language, is it possible for us to share personal insights such as aesthetic experiences? The radical sceptic would respond *no*. We can *impose* our generalized view of personal experience, but we cannot *share* it. Unamuno would concur with this, as would Wittgenstein. The exception is, according to Unamuno, if the writer or speaker can have a shared experience. Such an experience would be different in each person; even so, it is possible for the encounter we know as dialogue to produce a meaning that is shared by two. It would not be the dominance of one over the other or the synthesis of the two points of view, but rather an insight brought about through the dialogic activity itself.

The philosophical question Unamuno addresses is how communication between two separate minds is possible. The simple answer – that communication is possible because there is a common language – does not suffice, because it assumes that the language itself is a clear channel of communication once the users have gained a certain competence. Unamuno, anticipating Wittgenstein, holds that the linguistic code can produce meaning only in a semantic context. This directly links effective communication to the relative competence of the speakers at playing the language-game – that is, engaging others within the context.

This conclusion leads into the following hermeneutic problem: How can one person share an interpretation of a polysemic text without imposing closure on it? Unamuno's answer, anticipating Ricoeur, is that it is through the "play" of dialogue that individual interpretations can engage each other in the creative dialectic implicit in the dialogism between speakers of the same register and with the same linguistic competence to play the game. Put simply, it is in dialogue that we can share different interpretations and remake our interpretations. This is the dialectic that Ricoeur addressed with his concept of the conflict of interpretation. Conflict in this context is not just a positive feature – it is a necessary one, if we are to emerge from the prison of our own view.

In Unamuno's thinking, the conflict of interpretations is reality. The real does not appear through the self's private viewpoint, but only through the struggle with the viewpoints of others. In a more philosophical form, Ricoeur writes in *Temps et récit* that refiguration is the necessary engagement with the interpretations of one's others and that it is only through the dialectical engagement with differences that a richer, more profound interpretation reaches the archive of prefiguration.

3. Unamuno's Myself as Other

Spain is a nation of opposites that expand beyond ordinary contradictions; these polarities are evident in Spain's geography, its linguistic diversity, cultural make-up, history, and politics, and, of course, in its art. This is the country of Luis Buñuel, Pablo Casals, Pablo Picasso, Joan Miró, Salvador Dalí, and Federico García Lorca – all artists of the twentieth century whose work reflects the intimate and public tensions of a society forever engaged in a shifting dialectic of polarities. Of all the great artists and thinkers of Spain's twentieth century, no one looms so large and so central to an understanding of present-day Spain as Miguel de Unamuno. To understand Unamuno's work is to understand Spain; to understand Spain is to understand Unamuno.

In this section I examine the self–other concept that Unamuno developed over the last forty years of his life. I will comment on three seminal texts: "The Madness of Doctor Montarco" (1904); *Abel Sánchez* (1917); and *San Manuel Bueno, mártir* (1930). These three dates mark equidistant points in Unamuno's writing career. In 1904, he was forty years old and beginning his career as a writer, still very much the iconoclast rebel demanding that Spain regenerate itself after the debacle of the Spanish-American War of 1898. By 1917 Unamuno was at his intellectual summit. He had recently published his major philosophical essay, *Del sentimiento trágico de la vida* (1912), and his modernist masterpiece, *Niebla* (1914). He and José Ortega y Gasset were Spain's intellectual leading lights, but while Ortega y Gasset sought to make Spain an intellectual partner in Europe, Unamuno threw himself into the task of challenging the way Spaniards viewed themselves as a nation. Unamuno set out to provoke Spaniards of all walks of life to think for themselves and to reject dogma.

The year 1930 witnessed the last great effort by the old warrior: he had recently returned, in triumph, from exile in France amidst great expectations generated by the founding of the Second Spanish Republic (1931–6). *San Manuel Bueno, mártir,* was written at a time of turmoil and the cataclysmic political extremism that in a few short years years would result in the tragic sea of blood of the Spanish Civil War (1936–9). Unamuno died on 31 December 1936, defiant, independent, and rebellious to the end. He had lived seventy-two years, half in the nineteenth century and half in the twentieth, and he had written the way he lived – with intensity and passion, as the unrivalled defender of the rights of the individual and of the community of individuals against the arbitrary rule of the state. In many ways his political views were half a century ahead of his time: he rejected all political systems that sought to suppress individual rights, whether in the name of God, nation, or political party. For Unamuno, all dogmatism was the same, for it effectively denied the right of individuals to form a community of individuals.

Perhaps the best way to start this section is to contextualize the three narratives historically and intellectually. "The Madness of Doctor Montarco" was published in the popular monthly magazine *La España moderna* and has only been reprinted in Spanish in the complete works of Unamuno. In this story, Unamuno weaves together specific historical and biographical matters. Most obviously, he alludes to the public reception of his radically modernist parody of sociology in *Amor y pedagogía* (1902), a work that was widely viewed as inappropriate for a university professor. We can also discern a number of Unamuno's seminal ideas about life and society. He often raised hackles when he wrote that the instinct that most drives humans to act is not self-preservation, as the social Darwinists would have it, but rather the desire for more, the appetite to be God, that is, to continue to be the person one is but also to encompass and assimilate what one wants from the other. In "The Madness of Doctor Montarco," the protagonist remarks that reason is not an end in itself but rather is a weapon in the struggle for life as the individual's personal domain. The narrator observes – as Unamuno often does in his essays – that reason is a conservative force dedicated to preserving the established order that protects life as it is known at the time, and that reason will tolerate challenges only to the extent that they do not threaten this order. He repeatedly asserts that reason must be used in the service of authority – or, as Goya once put it, when reason sleeps, it dreams monsters. Unamuno's strong characters, such as Pachico of *Paz en la guerra* (1897) and Gertudis of *La tía Tula* (1921), are well aware of the struggle for dominance and use their powers of rational analysis to achieve that dominance. Unamuno's moral philosophy rested on the mutual respect of individuals, each with his or her desire to be, whose differences would be adjudicated by respect for the other's rights.

Doctor Montarco's reading habits are also Unamuno's. The latter read *Don Quijote* as a philosophical text and was well informed on British and German science. Quite clearly, Montarco shared with Unamuno a complete rejection of the generic categories of essay, prose fiction, drama, and poetry. Unamuno's focus, as a reader of others *and* as a writer, was on the author's situation within the text. For him, a text was constructed of fundamental polarities that were more or less hidden, more or less revealed by the specific linguistic elements applied to it. Style, for him, was more than self-expression; it was also a translucent presentation of the inherent conflict in the author's point of view. The more the written words obscured the author's inner conflict, the less it was style and the more it resembled gesturing. And so it is in "The Madness of Doctor Montarco." On the surface, the good doctor's conflict seems trivial: he wants to have a private life as a writer of creative prose as well as a professional life as a doctor devoted to general practice in provincial Spain. The reader should recognize immediately that this situation is a clear parallel to that of Unamuno himself, who by 1904 was professor of Greek and Latin at the University of Salamanca and was also the author of *Amor y pedagogía,* a famously outlandish parody of Spanish intellectual life. But even a superficial examination of the story of Doctor Montarco reveals a much deeper conflict: an existential polemic between the person *others* think we are – and, therefore, one we try to act out, like a dramatic role – and the person *we* think we are or would like to be.

The problem is that these personae are not fixed but rather are embarked on a conflictive process of development. The public persona is constantly threatening to take over the identity of the private persona, and meanwhile, the private persona despises the hypocrisy of the public persona and tends to blame others for forcing the self to play this part. In this story, the narrator observes the public persona and through his friendship is able to glimpse the private persona. As the story begins we are informed that this is a new beginning for the doctor, who has been forced to leave his hometown and start anew in a different place of practice. The balance between the public and private personae appears to be working; however, the narrator foreshadows the conflictive situation that lies ahead when he informs us that Doctor Montarco has confessed to him that some gestures are natural enough at first but become artificial once they have been repeatedly praised. There are *other* gestures that we acquire through imitation and hard work that end up becoming completely natural to us. The slippage between the two is constant as long as the public and private faces are more or less equal.

The war begins when one side is thrown off balance as a result of external pressure. Two days after publishing a story, one that is halfway between fantasy and humour, Montarco is deeply upset. It seems that the townspeople are looking askance at him, for he is all seriousness in his practice of medicine yet is also capable of writing farce. The poor doctor loses his practice and is sent to an insane asylum under the care of a former fellow medical student, Dr Atienza. It is here that the story takes its last and most unusual turn. Montarco's real transgression was not that he broke some code of medical propriety but that he attempted to make people think for themselves, to reconsider and redescribe the world they had accepted so uncritically.

Unamuno's *Abel Sánchez* can be called psychoanalytic fiction, for it delves into the psychosis of pathological envy by means of a narrative that alternates between third and first person. Unamuno was not just interested in the schizoid condition of individuals; he also considered these symptoms at the level of communities. In the novel, the narrator, Abel Sánchez, is the object of the pathological envy of his lifelong friend and companion, Joaquín Monegro, who, ironically and symbolically, is the protagonist in the story that has his friend's name as its title. Abel is congenial and well liked by everyone; Joaquín is wilful, aggressive, and highly competitive, not unlike the young Unamuno. From the outside – that is, from the perspective of the third person narrator – the reader's sympathy is with Abel. Joaquín is too intense, too overbearing, and the reader, like the characters in the novel, tires of the constant harangue from this problematic character. Yet we also have selected first person entries from Joaquín's diary that offer insight into a wounded and painfully obsessed victim of a psychosis of severe insecurity.

In Joaquín's first entry in his diary, he begins to portray himself as the reverse image of his friend even though they are not opposites but merely different. It is Joaquín who constructs the oppositional character traits of the two: Abel is the congenial one, and Joaquín the antipathetic one, without either knowing why. Joaquín has been left alone. Ever since childhood, his friends have left him to himself. Joaquín's obsessive envy of Abel has taken root. When Abel informs him that he will marry Helena, the young woman the two friends have courted, Joaquín writes in his diary that he feels as if his soul has frozen, the icy cold pressed upon his emotions as "if flames of ice were suffocating me." Joaquín now nurtures a hatred for Helena and an even stronger hatred for Abel.

The British psychiatrist R.D. Laing offered a description of seething envy that could have been a description of Joaquín Monegro. The patient contrasts his own inner emptiness, worthlessness, coldness, desolation, and dessication with the abundance of their opposites in the object of his envy. A desperate yearning develops for what the other has, along with hatred for all that belongs to the envied. Unamuno and Laing (96) share various sources – most notably, Freud's *Beyond the Pleasure Principle,* Kraepelin's lectures on clinical psychiatry, and Minkowsi's writings on psychiatry. What interests us here is Unamuno's creation of a fictional character who could serve as a clinical case study of pathological envy.

There is another aspect of *Abel Sánchez* that critics have repeatedly pointed out and that is the oblique but pointed contextualization of the novel within Spain. On his deathbed, Joaquín Monegro sobs:

> Why have I been so envious, so bad? What did I do to become that way? What mother's milk did I suck? Was there a philter, a potion of hate mixed with it? A potion in the blood? Why must I have been born into a country of hatreds? Into a land where the precept seems to be: "Hate thy neighbor as thyself." For I have lived hating myself; and here we all live hating ourselves. (173)

Unamuno was part of European modernity, which dominated arts and thinking after the Great War, which had shattered most of the social standards inherited from the nineteenth century (God, national state, the class structure, etc.). The emphasis had shifted to the individual and to the exalted freedom to express oneself – a freedom that now surpassed even the extreme individualism of Byronic Romanticism. Nations had gone to war without fully comprehending that they risked destroying humanity. In *Abel Sánchez* the personal hatred and evil of Joaquín, born of self-hate, is equated with a national psychosis of mutual hatred in the Spanish nation. Unamuno had no idea how prophetic his novel was to be. A mere twenty-two years later, Spain would plunge itself into one of the bloodiest and most tragic civil wars in history, one that cost the nation more than a million lives, that exiled millions more, and that devastated all aspects of national life. Civil war, then, can be seen as the social extension of the symbolic polarity of envy and hatred that plays out the tragedy of Cain and Abel once again. In the end, both sides lose, and it remains for the next generation to seek relationships that do not involve mutual destruction.

The last of the three narratives I discuss in this section, *San Manuel Bueno, mártir,* is unquestionably Unamuno's masterpiece. This short novel serves as the philosophical summary of an intensely lived life. Unamuno completed the novel shortly after returning to Salamanca in 1930, after spending six years in exile for his opposition to the military dictatorship of Primo de Rivera. It was first published in a journal of popular venue in 1931 and then in book form in 1933, three years before Unamuno's death and the civil war's outbreak. The story is a simple one that many other writers have taken up – a man of the church loses his faith in the resurrection but continues to carry out his duties as a priest and to preach the promise of eternal life. So it is not the story's originality that interests us, but rather what Unamuno has written into it about life and death, about the community of individuals, and about writing and literature itself.

The novel's protagonist is Manuel Bueno, whose life is narrated by his lifelong disciple Angela Carballino. Except for the last three pages, where Unamuno himself intervenes, the story is told in the first person by Angela. The Unamunian angst and intense struggle involve not only the intimate battle with suicide but also the public denial of the struggle. Manuel's life is a constant battle to not surrender to the seduction of suicide; it is also an all-out battle to ensure that no one knows this truth and that no one discovers the source, which is the inquiring mind.

Manuel Bueno, the parish priest of the small lakeside village of Valverde de Lucerna in northeastern Spain, has spent his whole life torn between his desire to reveal himself as a non-believer and his desire to conceal his state of mind from others. He finally makes his confession to Angela and her brother Lázaro, and in so doing he makes them accomplices in concealing the truth from the parishioners. We, the readers, share this problem with Manuel since we are the recipients of Manuel's confession through the confession-like testimony of Angela. The essential point is that as a liar, Manuel is irredeemably alone and therefore a prime candidate for suicide. He flees solitude and tries to be active all the time, to the point of exhaustion, so as to avoid being alone. Manuel's confession to Angela and Lázaro is necessary; Angela's confession to us is also necessary. Manuel's confession staves off suicide; Angela's written confession, which in the eyes of the church will damn her beloved Manuel Bueno, will save his story from oblivion.

Unamuno's characterization of Manuel is a subtle gloss on aspects of his own life. It is because of Manuel's great vulnerability to suicide that he has become so adept at concealment. He has mastered the art of leading the community in collective prayer, reiterating their faith in eternal life yet remaining silent himself. What everyone sees – the perfect parish priest – is for the benefit of his parish. He has become a superb actor playing the part of the man he ought to be but is not. If he, for a moment, stopped pretending to be what he is not, and stepped out the persona he has come to be in the eyes of the community, he would emerge as a Christ figure, not as the son of God, but rather as the Christ who died on the cross for the love of others. His parishioners need him to make the sacrifice, but not because of his belief, for he has none; he is a martyr because of his unbelief.

Manuel Bueno's story allows Unamuno to present human truth as an existential truth that is lived out. Manuel's existential truth is neither what he thinks he is or what others think he is, but rather what he has done, what he has lived. Manuel Bueno lived a life of love for others but not for himself. He lived in loneliness and despair until he took in Angela and her brother as his confidants. Unamuno's Manuel owes much to the sense he developed of the tragic Dane, Søren Kierkegaard.

The novel allows the reader to expand the symbolism of snow falling on the lake and melting to encompass Manuel's view of life – that it is a natural cycle in which the individual is completely lost. This symbolism is offset by the symbolism of snow falling on the mountain and giving the illusion of continuity and permanence. But Unamuno never allows us to lose sight of Manuel's profound risk. If Manuel experiences himself as a free agent who can choose to live or die, he is open to the possibility of considering his others as objects to be saved from his despair. If his others are true subjects with lives of their own, they should also be the agents to decide whether they believe or not. In terms of this existential anxiety, the experience of the other as a person would remove his defence against suicide. This explains why Manuel's relationship with Angela begins as that of friend and confessor but, ultimately, is a relationship of son and spiritual mother. Manuel is saved from suicide by his living a lie, but he is saved from the condemnation of living a lie through his mother-confessor, who is his real other, and it is *this* narrative voice, that of Angela, who saves his memory through her narration.

These three texts by Unamuno move the conflictive space from the social to the interpersonal to the internal (i.e., conflict with the self). This progressive development was not accidental. Unamuno's probing of the human condition was a search for a philosophy of existence grounded in language as the dwelling of the human being. What kind of a man was Unamuno? Why did he nurture a contradictory, aggressive, oppositional stance on the issues he discussed and in the characters he created? These questions will never be answered fully, but I can outline the philosophical context that informs the life and writings of Unamuno.

At all levels of action, contradiction suggests conflict whether it is personal or merely a game, but there are certain kinds of contradictions that can only be conflictual – for example, an argument over something claimed by two rivals. When we expand this commonplace experience to a general discussion of life, we realize that most people would prefer not to get involved in conflictive contradiction and that those who do would say it was not the conflict they wanted – rather, their aim was to make the other party recognize the validity of their claim. Unamuno viewed life in general as a continuous struggle against others and – most important – against the other within. It follows that even a person who faces no overt opposition in life can be opposition with himself.

Unamuno's moral philosophy aimed to reduce appearances to the essential characteristics of what it means to exist as a member of a community without losing one's individuality. As painful as the struggle of Doctor Montarco's conflictive life was for him and his family, it is relatively easy for the reader to set it aside as a rather extreme and eccentric example of small-town narrow-mindedness. The plight of Joaquín Monegro is much more difficult to comprehend. It moves into the realm of psychosis, but here too the reader may sense that he or she knows people like Joaquín. However, they represent the nightmare of human existence that is more internalized than public and, therefore, are not fully visible to the other. Indeed, we readers know of Joaquín's pathological envy largely because of his diary. San Manuel's agony is almost completely internal; but unlike Joaquín with his diary, he has not written about that agony; rather, he has confessed it to Angela Carballino, who then narrates it. The three stories together stand as significant literary manifestations of a moral philosophy that drew from Kierkegaard and Hegel, and from Cervantes and Calderón, and in its expression it is indebted to Vico and William James. In the end, Unamuno wrote with an uncommon passion that refused all dogma in a nation of institutionalized dogmatism.

At the core of Unamuno's philosophy of the self is the conviction that one cannot have self-esteem unless one esteems others as oneself. Doctor Montarco was unable to negotiate the conflict between his private and public personae, not because of a personal flaw but because the esteem others held him in was much less than the esteem they had of themselves as guardians of propriety. The public persona suffers the condemnation of his community, and the private person is unable to bridge the gap. Joaquín Monegro is the classic case of someone who finds it impossible to have any self-esteem, because he is incapable of regarding his lifelong friend Abel in any way but with all-consuming envy. Finally in *San Manuel Bueno, mártir,* Manuel loved others but in the end never loved himself. This has been a search for equality between the self and others in the midst of inequality.

The following passage from Ricoeur's *Soi-même comme un autre* summarizes Unamuno's ethics:

> It is this search for equality in the midst of inequality, whether the latter results from particular cultural and political conditions, as in friendship between unequals, or whether it is constitutive of the initial positions of the self and the other in the dynamics of solicitude, as this defines the place of solicitude along the trajectory of ethics. To self-esteem, understood as a reflexive moment of the wish for the good life, solicitude adds essentially the dimension of "lack," the fact that we need friends; as a reaction to the effect of solicitude on self-esteem, the self perceives itself as another among others. (192)

In one of the most extraordinary texts Ricoeur has given us, he evokes, in the strongest possible language, what I have been calling Unamuno's philosophical perspective on survival in others. I cite from the posthumous *Vivant jusqu'à la morte* (2007). The English translation is by David Pellauer (*Living Up to Death*, 2009): "But there's the trace of others, to which mine do link up in some way. This is part of the hope that mine will survive" (87).

4. A Fiction That Is Not a Fiction

> Nothing is more important for teaching us to understand
> the concepts we have than constructing fictitious ones.
>
> Wittgenstein

Unamuno's novels are philosophical paradigms of the cultural complexities of his time and place – early-twentieth-century Spain. This was a nation of radical differences that threatened to tear it apart and eventually did. Throughout his works Unamuno developed a metaphysics that identified reality in a post-Hegelian dialectic of continuous change, an ethics of existential concern for the tragedy of man's existence, and in his later years an aesthetics patterned on a personalistic transmission of the author into the reader's quest for self-knowledge. All of this has been said before, but I would add here that this philosophy had a dialectical method and a fundamental dualism and, most significantly, that both the dialectical method and the implicit dualism have been metaphorically expressed in his literature.

Unamuno wrote the following commentary on Hegel's dialectic that can serve us as a summation of his philosophical position: "The opposite poles of the dialectic exist together and the only possibility of bringing them together is within the same process of existence" (unpublished handwritten note by Unamuno in his copy of Hegel's *Wissenschaft der Logik*).

Unamuno's complete works are strongly unified by his relentless search for a literary expression that could satisfy his need to reach out to the reader and engage him directly. But it would only confuse the issue to call this almost personal need a dominant theme. The Unamunian vision reflects the complex development of a philosopher-poet, and to fit his writing into a category would be to oversimplify and distort it. A brief review of Unamuno's shifting aesthetic solutions to the problem of expressing a growing philosophical concern will provide us with the necessary background for discussing the metaphysical novel in the last twenty-five years of his life.

From the beginning, Unamuno was responding intellectually and intuitively to man's primeval dread of chaos. The maintenance of order in the face of chaos is in its manifold manifestations the Theogonic myth of creation. Unamuno's aesthetics and diversity of genres are unified as multiple re-enactments of this myth. Unamuno's first mythical position elaborated reality as a process, and its literary expression largely entailed extended similes that encountered reality in the eternal cycle of nature; to good effect, that expression used the sea, forests, trees, mountains. This initial simile would later become the metaphor "lluvia en el lago" (rain on the lake) as he responded to the question "¿Qué es tu vida?" (What is your life?)

The continuance of the universe as an eternal process is the fundamental premise upon which Unamuno's work rests; it is never superseded, although it does acquire corollaries, and it is emphatically presented in his final writings, which we will scrutinize in this section. In 1885, when Unamuno began to write *Paz en la guerra,* he was ill equipped to write a novelistic rendition of the Theogonic myth on this primary universal level. This first novel develops out of a purported historical reality; his aesthetic principle in this novel is the mimetic representation of external reality. The predictable result is that the novel's mythical aspects – nature similes of the cycle of regeneration – appear to be gratuitous grafts onto the traditional plot development of the historical novel.

The second philosophical phase, which began even as Unamuno was completing *Paz en la guerra,* is the now very familiar open cry against the personal loss of order amidst the ensuing chaos. Unamuno's response to the Theogonic myth had thus entered into an existential concern for individual's predicament. It was at this time that Unamuno's brilliantly original mind began to unravel the myth with a creative outpouring that would not cease until his death in 1936. After a rather futile attempt at reconciling the mythical quest for the survival of a personal sense of order with dialectic aesthetic in *Amor y pedagogía* (1902), he abandoned more traditional aesthetic formulations; by 1907, with the publication of *Poesías,* he was focused on a radical manipulation of reader–author distance. The years 1912 to 1914 mark the first of several intense periods of enormous creativity. In less than two years, Unamuno completed his strongest existential statement, *Del sentimiento trágico de la vida,* the poetic counterpart to the essay "Rosario de sonetos líricos," the book of short stories *El espejo de la muerte,* which anticipated many of the literary innovations of the following twenty years, and the novel *Niebla,* the culmination of some twenty-five years of literary attempts to address the Theogonic myth. In this novel Unamuno re-enacts the myth as Augusto Pérez, the protagonist, struggles to assert and mould his personal sense of order out of the chaos that had been hidden under a heavy mist of abstract contingency. But what is extraordinary here is that Pérez's struggle for survival is not presented as a traditional representation of external reality, with the narrative voice giving us privileged insight into the character's quest. Rather, the character presents himself through interior monologue even while the narrative voice ridicules him and flaunts its superiority over him. The novelistic reality of *Niebla* depends on the active collaboration of the self-conscious reader.

Between 1915 and 1924, Unamuno participated actively in Spain's political life. He gradually became a public critic on the events of the day. In an age of controversy, in the press and in the lecture hall, he excelled because he was intelligent, informal, belligerent, and not above entertaining with his caustic commentary. During the First World War he campaigned hard for neutral Spain to take up the Allied cause. As a political pamphleteer he wrote hundreds of articles, for the most part uncollected today, dedicated to this end. After the war he took up the bitterly contested question of the Spanish constitution with consuming energy and in his now public role of prosecutor. Unamuno's public stance of political propagandist led him to clash openly and directly with the monarchy. After Primo de Rivera took over the government in 1923, Unamuno's opposition and criticism grew in proportion to the government's attempts to silence him. The climax was not long in coming: on 21 February 1924, he was exiled to Fuerteventura in the Canary Islands; six months later, he escaped from there to Paris. During these years in which he was consumed as a public figure, the private man continued to pursue his *logos*, which had eluded him thus far.

Unamuno's writings now began to cultivate symbolism. From the biblical polarity of *Abel Sánchez* (1917), he moved on to the personal polarity of the double in *Tulio Montalbán y Julio Macedo* (1920). *La tía Tula* (1921) and the overladen novel of Virgin motherhood, *Teresa* (1924), end this period and represent the symbolic escape from the polarities of the myth and a return to the womb of mother nature.

Unamuno's philosophical system, which had by then expanded from an initial metaphysical position of dualistic process into an existentialist ethics, now began its final turn as he assembled the basis of his aesthetics. The idea of the survival of the author's personality through the creative power of his words began to appear frequently after 1907. If examined closely it can be seen as a refined re-elaboration of the Theogonic myth wherein the author, by writing, creates and passes on to others his unique vision or sense of order in the Universe. This concept of aesthetic survival had still to acquire a critical assessment of the mode and substance of the transmission before it could take its place in the Unamunian philosophy. The needed self-examination came suddenly with Unamuno's political exile. A dualistic pattern imposed itself once again; the words of an author are understood by Unamuno to be the expression of an implicit and sometimes explicit polarity between the mask of the public image and the confession of the intimate man. Consequently, his exile, with the ensuing public image, forced Unamuno into a radical examination of his projected self.

Unamuno's writings of exile unfold as bifurcated books of unrelated parallel mythical quests. On the one hand, they present his continuing concern with the Theogonic myth of creation and re-creation amidst the threatened return to chaos; on the other, there is now an additional myth, an Adamic myth of exile and the loss of paradise. The quest is the search for paradise regained or Spain redeemed from the demoniac figures of Alfonso XIII and Primo de Rivera. Even the most casual reader of *De Fuerteventura a París* (1926), *Romancero del destierro* (1927), and *Cómo se hace una novela* (1927), will note that the two separate themes are incompatible. These were dark days for Unamuno, filled with doubt, frustration, and – not infrequently – financial want. But it was precisely in these writings of inner polarity that Unamuno achieved an essential awareness of his work and was able to formulate his aesthetics. Clearly, the Adamic quest for redemption had placed him in the position of a self-proclaimed Messiah, and this public posture opposed and negated the quest for the confession that would re-create the intimate man. The polarity of personality needed to be expressed, but not at the expense of the reader's imaginative participation, for if this were lost, the entire project would fail.

By the final months of his exile, Unamuno had become fully cognizant of the capacity of symbols to create a philosophical literature. The complex tripartite philosophy emanating from the Theogonic myth could only be expressed symbolically. Three works that he wrote in 1929 to 1930 reflect the symbolic aesthetics that he sought: *El hermano Juan* (1929), *La novela de don Sandalio, jugador de ajedrez* (1930) and *San Manuel Bueno, mártir* (1930).

In *El hermano Juan,* Unamuno returns to the Don Juan theme he had touched upon in *Dos madres* (1920) and links it to the love–death motif of *Teresa.* In this play, the protagonist symbolizes sterile love of pleasure without creation. The symbol then grows into the representation of the actor, the mask, the public image that in the earlier works of exile had both hidden and threatened the intimate man. Now, Don Juan is only the public man; he has no intimate counterpart. If we can say that Augusto Pérez of *Niebla* was the self-conscious character, Don Juan is the self-conscious symbol condemned to a never-ending series of return performances as the Sysiphus of the personality.

La novela de don Sandalio, jugador de ajedrez continues to elaborate the public self as opposed to the intimate self. This short novel begins as a conventional epistolary novel: the unnamed letter writer sends frequent reports of his state of mind and spirit to his friend Felipe, whose return correspondence is briefly mentioned in a few of the last letters. In the twenty-three letters of the text, the writer presents himself as a man plagued with anthrophobia. He seeks to escape the tedium and stupidity of man by immersing himself in nature. He finds a large oak whose trunk is partly hollowed, and here he finds a sanctuary; he, like *Teresa's* Rafael, is seeking refuge in nature's womb. But like Pachico of *Paz en la guerra* he must return to the company of men, and in this renewed contact he meets don Sandalio, who becomes his chess partner, but with whom he scarcely speaks. Nevertheless, he begins to imagine the personality of his silent partner. The letter writer consistently refuses to allow others to inform him about don Sandalio. He reiterates in his letters that he has no interest in having his image of don Sandalio dispelled by historical fact. The letters end on a literary note, with the writer calling for the active creative reader to take the place of the common, passive reader, who reads and follows but contributes nothing. As noted earlier, nature symbols and the literary theory of participation are often encountered in Unamuno's writing. However, the epilogue of this short novel quite abruptly takes it beyond the aesthetics of collaboration and establishes it as a metaphysical novel in the aesthetics of symbolic manifestation. Again, Unamuno draws upon a myth of polarity to symbolize the personality.

Unamuno's authorial intrusion begins with the suggestion that the letter writer and his subject, don Sandalio, are the same person. The writer is the intimate part of the personality with his symbolic wish to escape from polarity by returning to the womb, and don Sandalio is his public image – that is, the man others think him to be. But no sooner has our intruder made this interpretation than he suggests that perhaps the recipient of the letters, the purported reader, Felipe, is one and the same as the letter writer and don Sandalio. If so, Felipe is a truly unknown aspect of the personality, and the letter writer is the autobiographical image of himself, with don Sandalio as his public image. The quasi-game is based on the well-known "Prólogo" to *Tres novelas ejemplares y un prólogo*. But Unamuno continues, rapidly adding yet another dimension by acknowledging that all three characters are aspects of the author's personality. And, of course, this re-created personality of the author now exists in the mind of the reader, *his* reader, who reads actively – that is, imaginatively and not passively – and consequently establishes the ultimate polarity of personality – you and I.

San Manuel Bueno, mártir was Unamuno's final novel. He outlined it late in 1929; a first draft was published in 1931; a final version was published together with *La novela de don Sandalio* in 1933. This novel was the culmination of an aesthetic search for the metaphysical novel; it was also a philosophical achievement, for it constituted the *logos* of his philosophical system. The Theogonic myth of creation provides the novel with its primary pattern for dialectic struggle, within which the Adamic myth plays its part. The aesthetic premise for this novel is that of the symbolic manifestations of thought; it does not depend on representations of external reality, or on a didactic revelation of truth. Aesthetically, this novel is a mythic and symbolic manifestation of a philosophical problem.

The pattern of opposites has been a well-known literary tradition since at least the Book of Genesis. A systematic analysis of Unamuno's novel that draws out the various polarities in language, plot, characterization, and the spatial and temporal aspects of structure and theme makes it clear that the author has tapped into an ancient and perhaps essential literary tradition. But as important as this endeavour may be, it overlooks the greatness of Unamuno's literary achievement. Some critics will disagree with my premise that there is a metaphysical as well as a mimetic aesthetics in the novel; even so, I will take courage from my convictions and outline this novel's metaphysical system.

The narrator's presentation of don Manuel as "that matriarchal man" in the first paragraph sets the stage for the development of the novel's metaphysical structure. Don Manuel's capacity to create and sustain the spiritual life of his villagers reminds one of Robert Graves's commentary on the kings of ancient Greece, who maintain their control by claiming the creative primacy of their matriarchal predecessors through ritual. Don Manuel's office as priest gave him the means to control his parishioners; it also demanded that he use ritual to represent the re-creative powers of the promise of immortality.

The introductory presentation of don Manuel anticipates the use of contraries throughout the novel; furthermore, the narrator's relationship to the protagonist structures the novel on a dialectical pattern. The novel begins with don Manuel as the narrator's spiritual father, but by the end of chapter 3, which is before his inner turmoil is fully revealed to us, the narrator begins to feel a kind of maternal affection for her spiritual father. This feeling grows in intensity until it becomes the principal motive for the writing of the memoirs that jeopardize don Manuel's beatification. Angela *must* write, for she is spiritually re-creating don Manuel through the written word or her gospel-like confession. Time in this novel is a juxtaposition of past and present within which the narrator develops the double polarity of time and character. She starts out as the spiritual daughter, but as the novel progresses she moves towards the present, in which she has the reverse role of spiritual mother – that is, the evangelist re-creating the saint. The narrator's ambivalent sense of purpose is always with us, for she reminds us that she does not know to what end her writing will be put. But there are Lazaro's last words to his sister:

> – "I don't so much mind dying," he said to me in his last days, "as the fact that with me another piece of Don Manuel dies too. The remainder of him must live on with you. Until one day, even we dead will die forever." (*OC*, II, 1151)

Lazaro senses that don Manuel is in danger of being forgotten. So, shortly after the master's death, he begins to compile a record of his words, which will later serve as the purported basis for the narrator's writing. The final page of Angela's confession gives her entire project an extra-rational spirit of inner compulsion that cannot in any way be explained as rational behaviour, nor even as common sense. She is a narrator who is unable to determine whether her story is true or false, empirical experience or a dream, reality or illusion. But she is certain she has had an experience of saintliness. Angela Carballino is in the select company of inspired narrators.

Space in this novel is almost entirely symbolic; setting has been reduced to the minimal inference of background for the acts of the master. So let us examine the symbolic polarity of mountain and lake that gives the novel its thematic unity and that also provides the basis for the metaphysical interpretation. The narrator's description of the protagonist progresses through similes of nature; he is compared to both the mountain and the lake. These similes are essentially contradictory, but the extent of their opposition is not apparent until they are metaphorically expanded:

> It was not a chorus, but a single voice, a simple united voice, all the voices based on one. Together they formed a kind of mountain, whose peak lost at times in the clouds, was Don Manuel. As we reached the section "I believe in the resurrection of the flesh and life everlasting," the voice of Don Manuel was submerged, drowned in the voice of the populace as in the lake. (*OC*, II, 1132)

The symbolic polarity of mountain and lake primarily signifies the protagonist's personal struggle to find a reason for living. The mountain as a symbol of faith – more specifically, of the belief in personal immortality – is established with the description of his mission to defend his people's happiness through religion. And the lake symbolizes don

Manuel's conviction that only nothingness lies beyond death. Consequently, don Manuel interprets his own mission as keeping his people from looking too deeply into the lake, for the legend of the submerged city can only indicate that the past is simply an anonymous sedimentary accumulation of the remains of persons who have lived. The threat is the termination of personal consciousness.

Don Manuel's position with regard to the symbols involves both separation and unification. It is he who shields the villagers' faith from the scepticism of inquiry. But his state of mind personifies ongoing opposition. Thus the dialectic of contraries operates on two planes – there is the external reality of life in the village, and there is the internal reality of the protagonist's own consciousness. On both planes, the contraries are dialectical polarities, with each pole acquiring its meaning in opposition to the other. The metaphysical symbols are brought together not only in the narrator's description of don Manuel but also in his own words as Lazaro recalls them:

> I shall not forget the day when snow was falling and he asked me: "Have you ever seen a greater mystery, Lazaro, than the snow falling, and dying, in the lake, while a hood is laid upon the mountain?" (*OC*, II, 1145)

Change and the illusion of eternity are the essential elements in the metaphor. Reality (snow falling on water) is an ever-changing process that can nevertheless appear as an illusion of eternity (the hood of snow on the mountain). The mystery is the illusion itself in the observer. Certainly the natural process of falling snow is part of a continuous cycle of change; only the rate of transformation varies. Nevertheless, the eternal snows of the mountain appear to defy change.

The first level on which the symbolic polarity operates – life in the village – develops into the protagonist's ethical code. His approach to protecting faith is to evade all questions about it and to focus on conduct and social well-being. It soon becomes apparent that he is just as staunchly opposed to theologians who preach sacrifice in this life for the sake of eternal salvation, as he is to social reformers who would ask a generation to sacrifice all for the sake of future generations. In both cases (for don Manuel and for Unamuno, absolute positions are polarizations), they are sacrificing life's only value for an illusion. Only Lazaro is astute enough to see the inconsistency of don Manuel's ethics in relation to his purported position of disbelief in immortality. Consequently, the social dimension of the symbols demonstrates the practical ethics of the protagonist – ethics that are consistent with his metaphysical position and only inconsistent with his role as a member of the clergy.

The second level – the inner consciousness – presents the symbolic dialectic in all its dramatic power. By the time we make the climactic discovery of the protagonist's state of mind, we have been prepared for it by the narrator's characterization of don Manuel as an overt transfiguration of Christ. The parallel drawn between the character's activity and his biblical model is, however, radically transformed – the two are linked as non-believers struggling against despair: "My God, my God, why hast thou forsaken me?" (Matthew 27:46).

The novel is plotted in a loose chronology clearly determined by biblical models and sources. The focal point throughout is not narrative action but rather the words and deeds of the master as remembered and recorded by the disciple. On this level of inner conflict, the symbolic polarities are richly expanded through the explicit identification of the protagonist with the archetype of the conflict of contraries from the Bible. The narrator's Christ-like presentation of don Manuel must be seen in the light of the narrator's relationship to him as daughter *and* mother. As his spiritual daughter, she is part of the mountain of faith that maintains the illusion of immortality, but as his virginal spiritual mother, she responds to the need to re-create him and thus save him from disappearing into the lake of oblivion. The archetype is at its fullest development in don Manuel's open self-characterization as a latter-day Moses:

> Like Moses, I have seen the face of God – our supreme dream – face to face, and as you already know, and as the Scripture says, he who sees God's face, he who sees the eyes of the dream, the eyes with which He looks at us, will die inexorably and forever. (*OC*, II, 1148)

The final touch of biblical archetype used to support the inner conflict is Unamuno's authorial intrusion at the end of the novel:

> – ... we are told how my heavenly patron, St. Michael Archangel – Michael means "Who such as God?" – and archangel means archmessenger – disputed with the Devil – Devil means accuser, prosecutor – over the body of Moses, and would not allow him to carry it off in judgement to damnation. Instead, he told the Devil: "May the Lord rebuke thee." And may he who wishes to understand, understand! (*OC*, II, 1153)

With Unamuno's entrance into the text, the entire pattern of symbolic polarity is recast as a larger conflict. The devil as prosecutor is demanding that don Manuel be damned for having preached eternal life (the mountain) while believing only in death as annihilation (the lake), but Michael the messenger (the author) opposes the rational prosecutor on the grounds that the will to believe is the only faith possible in the reality of man. Consequently, the two central myths are reconciled: the Adamic myth of redemption and the return to paradise is subordinated to but active within the principal Theogonic myth of creation and re-creation. Moses/Manuel does not reach the Promised Land but is redeemed by the author through his writing. Unamuno as author has taken the system of polarities out of the fictional confines of the novel, and by addressing the reader has engaged him directly in the fuller polarity of reality as Unamuno understands it. The novelistic engagement of the reader is thus raised up to the philosophical problem of the reader's existence. This is Unamuno's final contribution to the metaphysics of the novel.

In 1933, when this novel appeared, Spain was on the verge of the tragedy of civil war. The Republican leftist political parties and the conservative Falange were locked in an ideological absolutism that ruled out any possibility of dialogue. At the centre of this impasse was the Roman Catholic Church. Since the mid-nineteenth century, the church hierarchy's political power had been declining, along with its privilege, and it wanted to reverse this tide. The church feared not only a loss of influence but also a substantial loss of property (which the Republic was planning to legislate). But at the same time, many among the lower clergy identified with the working classes. These priests did not preach the gospel of patient suffering in this life for the rewards of the next, as promised in the resurrection. On the contrary, they stressed the value of life and called for social justice. Unamuno took up this contradiction between Roman Catholic theology and church politics. If sacrifice and mortification lead to salvation, how can the gift of life be the highest value, and how can suicide and abortion lead to damnation? This paradox is still with us in present-day Spain.

A hermeneutic inquiry into the culture of 1930s Spain would bring out the violence of political, religious, and social discourse and contrast it with the solitary voice of Unamuno, who called for tolerance of ideological differences and who urged his fellow citizens to debate one another without resorting to violence. The protagonist of *San Manuel Bueno, mártir* does not support the diminuation of this life for the sake of the promise of salvation. In fact, it can be argued that this village priest of the Roman Catholic Church does not believe in the afterlife. Manuel Bueno holds firmly that the highest value we have is the fulfilment of life now. In the context of pre-Civil War Spain, this narrative discourse was as radical as Nietzsche's declaration that "God is dead." We can fully appreciate Spanish literary culture only if we include the religious, political, and social discourse of the period, and our understanding of the novel is far richer in this context, wherein the metaphorical meaning attains full significance.

5. A Philosophy of Self

A Reading of Unamuno's Niebla (1914)

What manner of narrator tells the tale of Augusto Pérez's rather futile life? Augusto is a young man of around thirty who lives in his family home with two older servants, a couple who have been in the family's employ for some time. Augusto lost his father when he was born and was raised by a protective and overbearing mother. He has inherited a fortune and has never worked at anything. He studied at university under the watchful eye of his mother. She has now been dead some two years. Augusto has only one friend, Víctor Goti. He has never been alone with a young woman, much less had occasion to establish any kind of relationship with women. When the novel begins, he is a psychological introvert, neither charming nor brilliant. Indeed, he seems empty of all personality. This thumbnail sketch of Augusto Pérez is, of course, based on what the narrative voice tells us about him and on the limited moments when he is able to speak for himself. Let us consider the novel's first paragraph:

> Augusto stood at the door of his house and held out his right hand, palm downward; looking up at the sky, he struck the posture of a statue. He was not taking possession of the external world, but merely observing whether or not it was raining. As he felt the fresh intermittent wet on the back of his hand, he frowned, not because the drizzle bothered him, but because he would have to open up his umbrella. It made such a fine line folded in its case! A folded umbrella is as elegant as an opened one is ugly. (109)

The omniscient narrator's discursive pattern of punning with Augusto's name – which alludes to the Roman emperor Augustus, whose statue with an outstretched hand claimed the Mediterranean for Rome – is laced with sarcasm. Also, the syntactic pattern of contrastive extremes ridicules the character's actions.

The last two lines are in a free, indirect style; they supposedly express the character's thoughts, but in fact they are the narrator's. The closed umbrella as a phallic symbol is elegant; the open umbrella as a female symbol is ugly. But while these phrases still echo in us, we are unexpectedly given the direct words of Augusto Pérez, and his views are actually at odds with the characterization of him that we have been given. Here let it merely be pointed out that the narrator has openly distorted Augusto. The narrator is omniscient but also unreliable.

Let us consider Augusto's interior monologue:

> It's unfortunate the way we must make use of things, thought Augusto. Usage breaks down all beauty, destroys it. The noblest role of any object is that of being contemplated. How beautiful an orange still uneaten! (109)

Augusto's views on objects such as umbrellas and oranges are, we now recognize, little more than variations of the art-for-art's-sake aesthetic that he has appropriated for his own peculiar situation of introverted alienation. Remember here that at the turn of the century, "art for art's sake" was a prominent aesthetic concept, one that called for the creation of things that had no utility except as objects of contemplation. Thus a closed umbrella made of marble was an object of beauty, and so was a painting depicting oranges, whereas a functional umbrella or an edible orange was ugly.

Augusto's interior monologue provides us with our only unbiased access to his thinking; he continues walking and thinking:

> Just look at this, for example, a ridiculous man rolling chocolate into bars there in the window, in public view. He's an exhibitionist, and an idler. What difference can it make to other people whether he's working or not? Work, work, work! All hypocrisy! As for real work, what about this cripple dragging himself along …? And yet, how do I know anything about that? And at this point Augusto addressed himself aloud to the cripple: "Forgive me, brother!" And immediately after he asked himself: Brother? Brother in what way? A brother in paralysis? (110)

This interior monologue, which is developed as a sort of mono-dialogue, offers us our first extensive look at Augusto and his psychological state. The stream of consciousness with its free association is circular and ultimately returns to Augusto himself. He is obviously concerned with performance, with having something to do, and once again, he gives us some indication of his sexual repression. In his eyes, the pounding of the chocolate maker's pestle for all to see in the shop window is tantamount to masturbation by an exhibitionist. We now have two emerging images of Augusto: the negative, heavily biased view of the unreliable narrator, and the confused mutterings of a rather troubled character.

Chapter 3 offers the first evidence that Augusto has some semblance of personal relations with others. The *other* here is Víctor Goti, whom we will consider later as the novel's prologuist. Augusto and Víctor have for years played a game of chess every week. The dialogue is elementary and never progresses to a level of full exchange, but there is the first indication that Augusto can operate on a minimum level of social intercourse. Chapter 5 gives us some idea of the extremely repressed life Augusto has lived with his widowed mother. He studied law, not to practise but to have an education befitting his social status. Since adolescence, he has been prone to intense mental introversion. When he was a boy of sixteen, his mother would sit him on her lap and hold him there while she contemplated the full ashtrays she had preserved out of reverence to her cigar-smoking husband. Even after he graduated from law school, his mother would tuck him into bed and kiss him goodnight and then wake him in the morning. After she died, Augusto, much like the Peter Sellers's cinematic character in *Being There,* began to spend his entire days in a continuous daydream. If there had been television at the beginning of the twentieth century, he would have been a TV addict like the Sellers character. At the end of chapter 5, he finds an abandoned puppy, which he names Orpheus. The narrator claims that Augusto himself does not know why he chose that name, but after we consider the dog's epilogue, we can speculate on why Unamuno chose the name of the famous mythical poet who descended to the world of the dead. In the narrative text proper, Orpheus is the silent listener to most of Augusto's mono-dialogues. By chapter 10, a sense of alterity has begun to manifest itself in Augusto as his introversion diminishes.

On one of his daily walks, not knowing which way to go, he decides to follow a dog. But after a short distance, he is following a young woman, not a dog. Her body radiates youth, health, joy. His soliloquy has broken off. He is carried along by her. This woman is Eugenia, whom he begins to court without having any idea of who she is. Augusto's mother had dominated him by becoming his essential other. Part of this process was the ritualizing of trivial acts and, through force of repetition, endowing them with symbolic power. One of the most telling of these acts was the practice of sitting the young Augusto on her lap. When Augusto attempted a simulacrum of this ritual by making the laundry girl, Rosario, sit on his lap while he kissed and caressed her, he failed; his erection subsided as he looked into her eyes and saw himself reflected in perfect repetition. He was repeating himself and not the act. Augusto was thereby losing his personal identity and experiencing the psychological dissolution of the self. He pulled back from the brink of destruction, still sexually impotent, castrated by the continuing presence of his Oedipal mother, but with still another opportunity to find himself in his other.

He goes out determined to succeed; he proposes to marry Eugenia. Although she has accepted his financial assistance as well as the proposal, she leaves on the eve of the wedding. The final dissolution begins. Víctor advises him to "devour himself," which is what he has been doing by staring at his reflection in a mirror.

The novel culminates in chapter 31, in which Augusto, after deciding to commit suicide, goes to consult with the well-known philosopher Miguel de Unamuno. The third person narrator who has been telling the main story and who has so abused Augusto now switches to first person narration and alters his tone to one of condescension rather than ridicule. The persona of the implied author Miguel de Unamuno has had an active counterpart in the story itself in the person of Víctor Goti, who is writing the novel that the Unamuno persona is narrating. This fateful encounter between Augusto and Unamuno operates simultaneously at three levels: (1) in the narration itself, the ensuing dialogue is the culmination of a series of interviews in the character's quest for his identity, which he has begun to intuit is linked to his others; (2) but it also functions at the textual level of the long-deferred meeting of the abusive narrator and his hapless victim, who is finally able to reverse the master/slave relationship; (3) finally, it operates at a metafictional level as the creation overwhelms the creator because the creation was never the author's writing alone, but rather the writing as reading whereby it has been realized and completed. A few passages from this chapter will suffice to point out the simultaneous development of the novel. Unamuno's persona explains:

> He started by talking to me about my literary pursuits, especially the quasi-philosophical ones, and displayed a fair knowledge of them,

which, I must admit, pleased me. In short order, he began to tell me his life story, replete with all its miseries. I interrupted him to say he could spare himself the bother, since I was as well versed in the vicissitudes he had endured as he was himself. I proved this to him by bringing up particulars of a very private nature, which he had considered to be most secret. His eyes revealed genuine terror, as if he were looking at a monster. (277)

This passage, which introduces the implied author–character dialogue, has all the levels of textual development. First and foremost, Unamuno has endowed Augusto with the status of a person by placing him on the same level of reality as his own persona, by allowing him previous knowledge of Unamuno's own work and implying knowledge of the present text, since in 1914 Unamuno had not yet written a philosophical novel unless we consider this text. Second, by shocking Augusto with his display of the omniscient narrator's intimate knowledge of the character, he not only brings to a culmination the long-awaited confrontation, but also recognizes that his superior knowledge is limited to what has been written and does not include what Augusto is thinking now as they speak. Unamuno's narrator can only report what he sees. Unamuno, pressing his advantage, delivers what he thinks will be the final blow:

No, you don't exist any more than any other creature of fiction exists. You are not, my poor Augusto, anything more than a figment of my imagination and of my reader's imagination, when they eventually read the story of your fictitious adventures and mishaps that I have invented for you. You are a mere protagonist in a novel, or nivola, whatever you'd like to call it. Now you're privy to your secret …

Then he glanced again at my portrait over the books, and his color returned and his breathing became more regular. He gradually pulled himself together, mastered himself, and with his elbows on my round brazier table, to which he had drawn closer, directly opposite me, his head in the palms of his hands, he suddenly looked at me with a smile in his eyes and said to me slowly:

"Look here, Don Miguel … are you sure you're not mistaken and everything that's happening to me is the exact reverse of what you think and have told me?

'What do you mean by the exact reverse?' I asked him, alarmed at seeing him taking control of his own life.

"Could it not possibly be, my dear Don Miguel," he added, "that it is you and not I who are a creature out of fiction, the person who actually does not exist, who is neither living nor dead? Could it not possibly be that you are a mere pretext for bringing my story to the world? (279)

Unamuno's narrator makes two errors in revealing Augusto's secret to him. He acknowledges that Augusto's reality depends not only on the writer but also and in equal measure on the readers, therefore unwittingly recognizing that control over Augusto is not within his power. Second, by using the past tense with regard to the writing of Augusto's story, he excludes the present moment of dialogical exchange. The turn-around that follows is extraordinary in its open philosophical referentiality.

Augusto, now a liberated autonomous character because he can speak for himself to his readers and not just to himself or to another character, recognizes that the realization of all representation, whether it be in painting as in Unamuno's portrait or through writing, is the concretizing experience of others, those who can view the painting, or read the novel, and respond to it. By turning on Unamuno's narrator, he is inverting the attack into a counterattack. As a persona and as a narrator, Unamuno is merely a pretext for presenting Augusto, but as a writer, Unamuno is the necessary basis for the reader's re-enactment of the story, and as an author, Unamuno will live on only to the extent that his characters, like Augusto, are read.

The prologue of *Niebla* is written by Augusto Pérez's close friend and confidant, Víctor Goti. This initiates the text on a metafictional level and anticipates the existential conflict of chapter 31:

Don Miguel de Unamuno insists on my contributing a prologue to this book of his, in which he recounts the lamentable life and mysterious death of my good friend Augusto Pérez. Since the wishes of señor Unamuno are my commands, in the full sense of the word, I can do no less than write it. For, though I have not succumbed to the Hamlet-like skepticism reached by my poor friend Pérez, who went so far as to doubt of his own existence, I am firmly persuaded that I lack what psychologists call free will. I am somewhat consoled by the thought that Don Miguel possesses no more free will than I do. (97)

Víctor Goti as an equal, that is, as one coexisting on the same ontological level as Augusto Pérez, quite remarkably also claims to coexist with Unamuno. This common level of existence for all three lies only in the domain of the reading experience of the varied and sundry readers of the novel. Beyond the ludic punning, there is no declaration by Goti that should strike a more responsive chord in Unamuno's readers than the claim that Unamuno has as little free will as he possesses. Keeping in mind that Unamuno was an aggressive advocate of the will to be oneself for one and one's others, this statement begs for a response, which indeed Unamuno provides in the post-prologue, but at least on one level, Víctor is correct: he is not the master of his own existence, and neither is Unamuno's narrator; both are completely at the mercy of the whims of their readers, whom they can only hope to influence marginally.

Víctor Goti's comic reductions of Unamuno's ideas on sexuality and alterity do point the way to Augusto's therapy; he emerges from his extreme incestuous introversion when he awakens to sexual attraction for women. The next step would have been to move beyond the woman object to the true other, Eugenia, but he did not get that far.

The epilogue, in the style of Cervantes's *Novelas ejemplares,* has been given to Orpheus, Augusto's dog. This is no ordinary dog, for it knows the work of Plato besides understanding the dog's life his master has lived: "Yes, I understood him all right. He went on talking in any case. He was really talking to himself. He also talked to the dog in himself. I kept alive his so-called cynicism" (299). Orpheus has facilitated Augusto's progress from incoherent interior monologue to mono-dialogue and, finally, to dialogue; he has been part of Augusto's partial return from the prison of the opening pages.

Augusto's accidental or instinctive following of Eugenia gave him a purpose, and this courtship led to his discovery of his sexuality. His sexual appetite for women became evident, but the overcoming of the hiatus did not lead to his self-realization until he was able to engage the other fully and openly. The sense of alterity in the dialogue of chapter 31 is the culmination of his blind search for self. One's self is in being one's other whether this is expressed in action or words. Order is shattered by life's contingencies, and these gaps are overcome by imposing the order of the will, that is, purpose. But the sense of purpose must be the willed expression of any individual, not the automatic response of accepting the purposes one has been given.

The problem for Augusto was to transcend his isolation in a private language and to move back through discourse into the origin of language that is dialogue. Unamuno has consistently held out that the primary function of language is not to inform but to evoke. What Augusto must attain through his use of language is the response of the other. It is only in dialogue that the speaker can know his reality. In the text, this is made manifest in chapter 31, but in the metanarrative there is another level of exchange that is the text–reader relationship, also a dialogical form, where Augusto's ultimate reality lies, as he plainly understands.

Augusto put all his strength and his whole heart into passion for a woman he hardly knew because as a subject of desire she had become all for him. This *all* is the force behind the desire for living for and with another. It is not sexual desire that drives Augusto but metaphysical anxiety. In his mind, Augusto wills Eugenia as the all, and thinks only of her in this light and will only be at peace in that all. For Augusto it is all or nothing. But Unamuno does not merely exemplify the self's need for others, he also displays the interdiscursive nature of reality. The web of discursivity that encompasses Augusto Pérez's fictional life is a metaphor for the reality of cultural life as we live it.

The Philosophical Subtext

Unamuno's philosophy of self is based on the radical premise that the self is a life story that consists of a composite of the stories one tells about oneself and the multiple descriptions of one's person and life told by others, some of which are partially accepted by one but all of which have consequences. These self-descriptions include moral or ethical self characterizations. In other words, they constitute one's relative self-assessment with regard to social values, standards of behaviour, and obligations to persons or institutions. The self is seen as inevitably immersed in a world of values, prejudgments, and, ultimately, moral choices. Self-assessment by its very nature is bound up with the standards for action of one's community.

We can now take a clear position with regard to Unamuno's concept of self. Every individual has a sense of self, that is, of being in the world among others. It is this sense of self that constructs one's self-identity – that is, how one situates oneself in the community's ethical space. People always desire that their actions be judged by others in the context in which they are taken. Thus it is that the sense of who one is, is defined in part by some sense of the truly important issues, values, and standards to be upheld with regard to the common good; and correlative to this is the all-important judgment of how one measures up.

Unamuno's concept of self goes far beyond self-assessment or public image: it addresses the full impact of being and living in the ethical space it is one's lot to inhabit. He takes on the philosophical aporia of ascertaining what is stable and what is constantly changing in the self's identity; indeed, *Niebla* is constructed around that challenge. He sees all persons as having a sense of being self-situated in ethical space. In his novel he stresses the terms that establish this ethical space, which are always changing, sometimes radically.

At the beginning of the twentieth century, Unamuno and his generation of Spanish intellectuals, as a group, called on the Spanish people to accept responsibility, to think for themselves, to be self-reliant in making moral judgments. But Unamuno was making this call in an era when Spain was immersed in a dogmatism that all but precluded free inquiry, freedom of expression, and dialogue. This profound discrepancy between the ideal and the perceived reality serves as the subtext of *Niebla*.

The problem that Unamuno addressed was the failure of the monological thinking subject, which he countered with a dialogical self. This was no mean task, for in 1914 the modern epistemological tradition still overwhelmingly followed the path of representation. In a still unchallenged dualism, these were representations about the world outside the knowing subject and the subject's actions – representations that at least partly revealed the objectives desired or feared by the knowing subject. The self is locked in a prison of consciousness, from which it looks out on an outside world that includes other human agents. The contact between the self and the world is through the representations formed within the knowing subject. Thus the inner space of the knowing subject has a mind capable of processing and interpreting representations. All knowing of self, world, and others is in the centre of consciousness – that is, in the mind of the knowing self. Unamuno thoroughly exposed the blindness of ontological dualism in *Del sentimiento trágico de la vida*. What this monological-centred consciousness turns into a rational abstraction is the configuration called reality, and what it fails altogether to consider is the body and the other. The opening paragraph of *Del sentimiento trágico* sets the stage for Unamuno's radical assault on Cartesian philosophy: *homo sum; nihil humani a me alienun puto* (I am a man; nothing human do I deem alien to me), wrote the Latin playwright Terence in *Heauton Timoroumenos* (25, in Unamuno, *Del sentimiento trágico de la vida*).

Unamuno radically departs from the philosophical tradition, including the philosophy of his contemporary Ortega y Gasset, in his rejection of reason as the locus of understanding. For Unamuno, much of our willed action in the world is governed by the largely unformulated context of the body at work, love, and play. He referred to this background of human action as *intrahistoria*. We sometimes plan ahead what we will do, but more often, we act as beings in the world. The point here is that those representations of acting that we formulate can only be configured against the background of the *intrahistoria* of participation in the action of living. *Intrahistoria*, that is, provides the context in which actions make sense to us. Concrete projections and planned actions become mere islands in a sea of *intrahistoria*. It is in this vein that we can recognize Unamuno's affinity with Heidegger's *Sein und Zeit* (1927), Merleau-Ponty's *La phenomenology de la perception* (1945), Wittgenstein's *Philosophical Investigations* (1953), and, especially, Ricoeur's *Temps et récit* (1983–5).

Unamuno's *Del sentimiento trágico* (1912) places the human body in a new perspective. The body, the man of flesh and blood, is not the mere executor of the mind's projections, nor is it the storehouse of information we require to shape our view of the world. Human understanding is bodily determined – that is, our actions are embodied. This bodily self, the way we act and move, generates our understanding of self and world. To use a commonplace example: I know how to go from my home to the university and what to expect along the way, but if asked to draw a map, I have to recover dozens of indicators and draw what amounts to an abstraction of my everyday action. I know how to find books in the library through everyday manipulations of familiar instruments, without guidelines, which I could construct only with considerable effort. But this is only the surface of the intricate concept of the self's body. The sense I have of myself, my relationships to others, my expectations of their actions in response to my actions, are all grounded in the body's ongoing actions, expression, and participation in the world. This participation in the world that Unamuno delineated with such power at the beginning of the twentieth century is akin to what Pierre Bourdieu sought to express with the term *habitus* in *Le sens pratique* (1980).

Unamuno's dialogical self reflects above all an awareness that life is living *with* and *because of* others. As he pointedly argues at the beginning of *Del sentimiento trágico*, the human subject eludes us completely in the epistemological tradition that runs from Aristotle's *Politics* to

Rousseau's *Social Contract*. That same tradition in the eighteenth century spread beyond philosophy to the science of Linnaean taxonomy and, in the nineteenth century, to notions of mankind, which were pure abstraction. Unamuno wrote in *Del sentimiento trágico:* "Such a man is a man from nowhere, from neither here nor there, neither of this age nor of another, who has neither sex nor country, who is, in short, a mere idea. That is to say, a no-man" (*SW*, IV, 3).

Unamuno constantly refers to the human self as "yo," that is, in the first person singular, but as any careful reader will recognize, this self is a pluralized self. For it is not a question of me alone; it is a question of you and I, it is a question of the other, each and every other. As Cerezo Galán, among others, has insisted, the Unamunian concept of self is dialogical. The knowing self understands and constitutes himself or herself as an inseparable part of the other.

Unamuno's sense of the real is the articulation of experience in language, which establishes the multiple levels of encounter with oneself, with one's others, and, ultimately, with one's own words. Put another way, our identity is the product of all our social interactions. Thus our self-narrative, which gives us our sense of place and purpose, is an ongoing dialogue with our others. But one's self-narrative, which begins in one's thoughts and reflections, does not become a narrative until it is told to another. Unamuno's self is partly constituted through the attitudes of his others towards him, but there is, also and undeniably, the self's action towards what he or she would most like to be. The self arises out of engagement with others, in conversation with all of his or her others. To put it directly, in Unamuno's ontology dialogue is at the centre of one's understanding of life.

In the narrative context, this view is one of a number of Augusto's thoughts that are distorted to make him appear foolish. In the dialectic between the plot (as narrated by the narrative voice) and the character (presented both by the narrator and by himself), the action itself is subject to interpretation. The question is not what the character does but why he does it. As the dialectic of the narrative progresses, a struggle for survival ensues. We anticipate that the narrative as told by the narrative voice will eventually overwhelm the protagonist in such a way that he must succumb to the inevitable unfolding of events. Much to our surprise, in *Niebla* this dialectic moves from the character in his world, to an internal dialectic within the character himself, and, ultimately, to the most powerful dialectic of all – the one between reader and text. Augusto Pérez is a most singular character with a number of unique traits that we learn through the telling of his life story.

In *Niebla* the dialectic of one life story's concordance and the interruption or discordance brought about by the insertion of unrelated stories moves the issue of self-identity to a philosophical level: the reader must cogitate on the similarities and the differences between these gender-related stories. We subsequently approach selfhood as a diversity of imaginative variations on the same theme – the relation of the self to the self's other. *Niebla* does not entertain us with a singular story of ineptitude, female machismo (*hembrismo*), and the narrator's arrogance. The narrative is a complex story about the human need for others, and it is full of contradictions. Paul Ricoeur has said it best: "In this sense, literature proves to consist in a vast laboratory for thought experiments in which the resources of variation encompassed by narrative identity are put to the test of narration" (*Oneself as Another*, 148).

Niebla is a narrative of philosophical inquiry into relations between men and women, mother and son; it is about the need for compassion and kindness, and most of all, it is about the eternal need to speak to another. It is one of the most widely discussed philosophical novels ever written in Spain. It is built around the philosophical aporia of human existence. The basis of human existence for Unamuno is to speak to another, to speak to oneself, to speak to one's problems and joys as in prayer, but to *speak*. In 1905 he wrote, "and as long as you do not know yourself like another, you will not be able to see your others as selves" ("Soledad," in *OC*, I, 1252), and in 1928, while in exile, he wrote in his poetic diary: "I do not exist except in your being" ("Cancionero," *OC*, VI, 1076).

The plight of Augusto Pérez might appear at first to be a most unrewarding vehicle for expressing Unamuno's ontological philosophy. It begins to make sense only when we recognize that Augusto gains insight into his existence through his dialogue with Unamuno. Augusto has come a long way from the alienated loner who could not even carry on a conversation with the concierge of Eugenia's building.

The configuration of selfhood is thus not only the self in his self-reflection and desires. His others grant him the existential circumstances in which to express himself – to himself, to his others, to his dog, and, finally, to his would-be creator, the author of the story. Such is the basis of existence. It is in the encounter with Unamuno that he achieves full status as an autonomous character independent of the whims of his narrative voice/implied author.

On Narrative Identity

In 1991, Ricoeur published the essay "Narrative Identity," in which his kinship with Unamuno's philosophical literature becomes fully apparent. I quote from one of the closing paragraphs:

> In the course of the application of literature to life, what we carry over and transpose into the exegesis of ourselves is this dialectic of the self and the same. There we can find the purgative virtue of the thought experiments deployed by literature, not only at the level of theoretical reflexion, but at that of existence. You know what importance I attach to the relation between text and reader. (in Wood, 198)

The self does not know himself or herself directly, but only indirectly through the detours of cultural signs of all sorts. These are articulated as symbolic mediations, which articulate the action of living, and among them, we begin with the narratives of everyday life. Narrative mediation highlights this remarkable characteristic of self-knowledge – that is, self-interpretation. One of the forms this takes is the reader's appropriation of the fictional character's identity. What narrative interpretation brings is precisely the figural nature of the character by which the self, narratively interpreted, turns out to be a figured self that imagines itself in this or that way. Ricoeur writes the following analysis of selfhood:

> A kind of otherness that is not (or not merely) the result of comparison is suggested by our title, otherness of a kind that can be constitutive of selfhood as such. *Oneself as Another* suggests from the outset that the selfhood of oneself implies otherness to such an intimate degree that one cannot be thought of without the other, that instead one passes into the other, as we might say in Hegelian terms. To "as" I should like to attach a strong meaning, not only that of a comparison (oneself similar to another) but indeed that of an implication (oneself inasmuch as being other). (*Soi-même comme un autre,* 3)

Unamuno, more than any other Spanish writer of the twentieth century, demonstrated that the narrative imagination is a primary entry point for philosophical reflection. From *Paz en la guerra* (1897) to *San Manuel Bueno, mártir* (1933), he showed how specific imaginary features enacted solely in fictional narrative have the power to enrich diverse imaginary mediations, especially with regard to the aporias of existence, truth, and reality. There is no doubt that Unamuno's greatest achievement relates to the narrative identity of self. The story of Augusto Pérez as told by Unamuno and by Augusto himself is the discovery of a narrative identity. The narrative self constitutes an ongoing process of development of self-constancy punctuated by self-correction, which is primarily the deployment of the storyteller's poetic imagination, which brings together past, present, and future. The self's identity does not dispel the polarity between myself and my other's view of myself; rather, it moves identity from a static status to a dynamic one that is constantly in flux in the reader as it flows from the poetic composition of the text.

Chapter Three

Ricoeur's Hermeneutics of the Creative Imagination

1. Polysemia of Poetic Discourse

During the same years of the 1960s that Ricoeur responded to structuralism in France, he was also developing the hermeneutic theory that is at the core of this book. In contrast to other philosophers who had also turned their philosophical inquiry to language, Ricoeur did not focus on standard usage; instead, he chose to focus on figurative language – that is, language full of polysemia and symbolic richness. Figurative language offered Ricoeur a unique opportunity to consider semantic innovation.

Textual analysis and intersubjective interpretation can be seen as having inverted patterns of operation in which each must leave out an essential part of the other because of its very point of departure. Thus the dialectic between the two poles suggests the possibility of a more complete method of inquiry. The problem we seek to investigate is in this way defined as the relationship between experience and language. The two dialectic poles from which we will approach the problem are analysis and interpretation.

Analysis begins with a description of the textual language and structure; consequently, it moves from language towards experience but stops short of it. The presence of a knowing person – here, the reader – is a necessary assumption that cannot be made through analysis of language. For its part, interpretation approaches the language experience problem through the expression of subjectivity. Thus the movement here is from an expression of experience itself towards the explanation of the subjective response to the literary language. However, the literary language cannot be reached unless the investigator is prepared to move beyond the limitations of his subjective response. The literary language itself is the necessary assumption for interpretation.

The dialectic relationship exists as necessary movement towards an assumed pole. In this way we can conceive of analysis as the description of language that is actualized only in experience, and similarly, we can think of interpretation as the expression of subjectivity that is based on language. Both are always present in the process of understanding a text, each is implied in the other, and each is the necessary pole of the other. It follows that a method of inquiry that seeks to fulfil the reader's experience must be dialectic in theory and in practice. Let us consider the preconditions for elaborating this method.

First, we must find and identify the limitations of both analysis and interpretation. Analysis of the literary text bypasses experience and plunges the inquiry into the language of literary discourse. The reading experience is always implied but never treated directly. The undeniable limitation is the reduction of experience to a unitary supposition of actualization. The more complete the analysis of literary language becomes, the more pressing the need to know how the reality of experience takes place and how it realizes the literary expression. Interpretation seeks out the intersubjective common ground of the reading experience. Within the circle of experience, the relative distances from the text are established as that which is basic reference to the exterior world and that which is a secondary construction of self-reference. Within the circle of experience, interpretative theory cannot grasp the organization of the text itself.

Second, we must establish the logical procedure for a dialectic method. The inquiry progresses through a series of inversions. The emergence of knowledge through a dialectic methodology is possible only if we accept cognitive unity as a concordance of the two opposed approaches to inquiry. The forces of analysis and interpretation are exclusive of each other outside of the dialectic. Within the dialectic, however, we experience the inversion from one to the other and use both. The answer to the general question of where the two meet can be anticipated in this second precondition of the dialectic; the two sides of any inversion meet in the phenomenon itself, and here, the phenomenon is the reading experience.

Third, we must outline the successive inversions of the dialectic. The inquiry begins away from the immediate experience in order to penetrate into the fixed external basis of meaning – the text. But it is necessary to recognize the antithesis of this inversion even while we are pursuing it. Therefore, a radical questioning of the questioner himself must follow immediately.

This process of controlled inversions of questioning will be repeated in successive stages of an enlarging inquiry. Within each stage, the direction of the questions is to be fully understood only in light of the inversion that follows. Since these directions – analysis and interpretation – are the two sides of the inversion, each is implicit in the other. I have designed the inquiry in five stages, each with its own inversion. They are (1) fictional language, which approaches the text first from the direction of analysis and then from that of interpretation, (2) fictional structure, which is also examined first from analysis and then from interpretation, (3) fictional context, which is the last of the three stages to move first from analysis and then from the perspective of interpretation, (4) reader distance, which reverses the order of the first three stages: here we begin with interpretation and follow with analysis, and (5) intersubjective value, which is the last stage of the dialectic and, like the fourth stage, begins with interpretation and concludes with analysis.

My central argument on the dialectic can now be stated in more detail. I propose that the inversely related procedures of analysis and interpretation must be joined into one dialectic if we are to attain a full understanding of the literary reading experience. Literature is distinguishable from other forms of expression in its vastly expanded referential aspects, which make the reading experience one of immensely broad and diverse enrichment. I therefore propose a dialectic that incorporates analysis and interpretation in inverse movement to each other. The goal is to open up the reading experience first to the reader himself or herself and then to the community of readers who have shared the same text in an analogous experience.

My theoretical basis on the dialectic can be found in the writings of Miguel de Unamuno and Edmund Husserl (published and unpublished), but principally in the philosophy of Paul Ricoeur, who offers the following insight into the problem of expression and experience:

> In Husserl's first works ... consciousness is defined not by perception, that is to say, by its very presence to things, but rather by its distance and its absence. This distance and this absence are the power of signifying, of meaning ... Thus consciousness is doubly intentional in the first

> instance by virtue of being a signification and in the second instance by virtue of being an intuitive fulfilling. In short, in the first works, consciousness is at once speech (*la parole*) and perception. (Ricoeur, *Husserl*, 204)

According to this theory, the literary work is always and simultaneously language and experience. The method I outline here is an attempt to examine this phenomenon without reducing its multiplicity to any formula; rather, I will respect the intentionality of the text within the subjectivity of the reader.

In my reading of Ricoeur's hermeneutical theory, I have identified five basic presuppositions underlying the interpretation of a literary text:

1. The sentence is the fundamental unit of discourse wherein metaphor and symbol are constituted as event and meaning is discerned.
2. The actualization of written language in a text differs radically from that of spoken language in that the event (writing) is fixed and reference to the author's intentions and world are suspended. Textual reference on the other hand operates as a possible mode of *being in the world*. Consequently, the reading audience of the text is generalized, anonymous, and unprivileged.
3. Meaning in a literary text can be described as movement from *sense* to *reference*. There is an implicit epistemology here and a central question is the analysis of movement as dialectic tension.
4. The text is constituted as an ordered, singular, and generic whole; consequently, the interpretation of metaphorical referentiality must be mediated by the text as a whole. The ultimate limits of referentiality are set by the text itself.
5. The primary task of interpretation is to reveal the intentionality of poetic language. The intentionality of poetic language is to predicate a metaphoric meaning that can be understood in terms of a dialectical tension between mimesis and poiesis, which can be characterized as the common utilization of a collective meaning (communication) and the unique moment of the imagination (metaphoric creation).

Let us consider the applicability of Ricoeur's hermeneutics to poetry before developing its possibilities for narrative study. A phenomenological theory of literature approaches the literary text as the facilitating basis for performances by the reader – performances that are variations on a theme. A fundamental corollary of this principle is that the intentionality of the text itself is variational. This idea takes into account an implicit inventiveness in the text that must be put into play if it is to be actualized. The essential activity of the writer and of the reader is therefore the creative engagement of language as expression. These general observations on the inventiveness of realizing variations of the text are not contrary to the Aristotelian dictum that poetry (texts considered as literature) is ultimately more true than history, for it is only by exploring the possibilities of the mind's free play that we can examine discovery and creativity.

Ricoeur's theory of dialectic tension is best depicted as the intersection between two spheres of discourse. This intersection of the separate spheres can be understood if we recognize that their difference is based on separate modalities of each discourse. Consequently, the intersection is the encounter that is possible because of the oppository relationship implicit in the semantic aims of each discourse.

Metaphor is taken by Ricoeur as a paradigm of the creative encounter of the spheres of discourse. The active metaphor yields a gain in meaning, and this gain is inseparable from the multiple levels of tension present in the metaphor. These levels are identified as (a) tension in the terms of the statement or ultimately of the text that can be focused through the question: *What does the text say?*; (b) the tension in the formal structures of the text, which we can characterize with the question: *How does the text speak?*; (c) tension in the referentiality of the text, which can be understood with the question: *What does the text speak about?*; and (d) the final tension between the text's autonomy and the requirements of the reader's appropriation; the question here is: *How have I read the text?*

The gain in meaning is not a synthesis, for it remains caught in an open dialectic without an absolute. This gain is at the moment of appropriation when there is an intersection of two separate movements. One movement aims at determining more rigorously the conceptual traits of reality; the other movement aims at making referents appear. This is the encounter of the capacity of logical abstraction with the capacity to imagine, concretize, and apprehend the given.

The essential characteristic of the poetic text is thus a creative gain, which Ricoeur examines through four levels of tension operative in the reading of the text. In ordinary language an analogous situation arises when a speaker attempts to express a new experience; he must do so in words that he must appropriate for the occasion. Thus the speaker seeks a formulation capable of carrying his intention from the network of meaningful expressions he finds already established. The first two levels of dialectic tension in the text are accessible through critical description and analysis; the third and fourth levels are primarily levels of interpretation.

Let us assume careful description and analytical rigour. The question remains: How are these data to be tied to the interpretative inquiry of referentiality and appropriation? Metaphorical language in a poem stands out as a statement expressed in specific formal patterns. Ricoeur holds that the utterance is about something and that inquiring about what this something *is* is the task of interpretation. The metaphorical utterance functions in two referential fields at once. This duality explains how two levels of meaning are linked up in the same symbol. Put somewhat differently, two energies or force fields converge: because of the gravitational pull exerted by a second referential field (experience), the first and familiar one (language) is forced to leave its place of origin and move towards an encounter. The dynamism of metaphorical meaning is seen as an unstable convergence of the referential field of experience as it moves towards expression, and the referential field of language is forced out of the familiar, where it begins to move towards experience.

I conclude this presentation of Ricoeur's theory of literature applied to poetry by turning to a specific poem. I will comment on Pablo Neruda's "Oda a unas flores amarillas":

Ode to Some Yellow Flowers

Against the blue, movement of blue,
the sea, and against the sky
some yellow flowers
October comes
And even if it is
so important the sea unfolding
its myth, its mission, its yeast,
on the sand
bursts
the gold
of a single
yellow plant

and your gaze
is chained
to the soil
your eyes turn from the immense pounding sea.
Dust we are, dust we will be.
Not air, not fire, not water
but earth
earth,
Only earth
we will be
and perhaps some yellow flowers.

(*Libro tercero de las odas*, 670–1; translation mine)

What does the text say?

The text has five stanzas. The first four alternate between lyrical descriptive images and brief lyrical statements. The fifth is an extended metaphorical statement.

The first stanza establishes two images of movement: the sea moving its blue against a background of blue, and yellow flowers seen against the sky. The second is a simple and direct statement of temporality: "October comes." The third returns to the images of sea and flowers, which were presented separately in the first stanza but are now linked. This linkage consists of "bursts" in the fifth line. At this point is presented a new image, the presence of the "other" to whom the poem is addressed. The link between the sea and the yellow flowers is in the *perceiver,* who turns from the sea and looks at the flowers on the beach. The fourth stanza is again a brief statement that links the "you" of the third stanza with the lyric voice in the plural "we are, we will be." Temporality is expanded from the present to the future.

The sixth and final stanza expands on the rejection of the sea in favour of the land by reviewing the four elements of pre-Socratic philosophy – air, fire, and water, all of which are rejected in favour of land. The stanza ends with the metaphor of the yellow flowers, which had been one of the initial images.

How does the text speak?

The text is made up of simple parallel structures that set up key images in explicit lyrical contrastive contexts. The first, third, and fifth stanzas have this structure; the single-line second and fourth stanzas serve as breaks or separations for the parallel of contrasts.

The syntactical basis for this structure is the simple syntactical patterns of parallelism:

First stanza – 'Against ...
... and against;

Third stanza – 'and even if it is
... and is chained

Fifth stanza – 'not, not, not ... but ...
And perhaps.'

The first syntactical structures establish a parallel slot for "sea" and "yellow flowers," and it is in this situation that we receive the first contrastive images, blue moving its blue, set against yellow with the sky as background.

The second stanza separates and breaks with the parallel structure of the first stanza. We have here a statement of time with an implicit lyric voice for whom time exists.

The third stanza once again takes up the parallel structure of the first. The sea with its movement is further developed and then contrasted with the solitary "yellow flower" on the sand. The contrast is not merely fixed in the text; it is also acknowledged as the "you" enters the text, fleeing from the massive ever-present movement of the sea.

The fourth stanza is once again an interlude between the parallelism of the third and fifth stanzas. The significant feature here is the first person plural, which effectively unites the lyric voice and the "you."

The fifth stanza utilizes one of the most common parallel structures in Spanish: "not this but rather that," or "ni, ni, ni ... sino." This stanza ends with the extension of the imagery into a fully developed metaphor – "and perhaps."

What does the text speak about?

The poem offers a complex metaphor of human life by means of an elementary syntactical structure. It begins describing two basic images in opposition – the sea in movement and yellow flowers on the beach.

The dual images are given a temporal dimension of an implied lyric voice before being enlarged. The sea becomes not only movement but also a powerful massiveness with its own myth and mission; the implication is unmistakably that of eternal and overwhelming power. But the flowers are also featured. Now the flower is but a solitary yellow plant broken and swept up onto the sand. The implications are in clear opposition to the sea: singularity, fragility, insignificant residue thrown up on the beach by the all-powerful sea. At this point, the human dimension of the "other" is clearly linked to the plant on the sand; the eyes of the "other" are tied to the plant and flee from the power and roar of the sea. The metaphor of sea as universe contrasting with the singularity of the single plant comes together with the beholder.

The poem now unites the lyric voice and the "other," thus proposing the singularity of human life as against life in general, for we are dust and it is to dust we will return. The final development of the metaphor starts with a rejection of three of the four pre-Socratic elements (air, fire, and water) in order to reiterate that man is "earth." Just as the rain merges with the sea in an indistinguishable mass, so our remains (dust) merge with the land, but there is a difference, for man as distinct from all other forms of life has a possibility of giving forth an expression of his uniqueness and singularity, which will be seen and will stand out albeit for a limited time as symbolized in some yellow flowers.

How have I read the text?

Ricoeurean hermeneutics aims to disclose metaphor at the fundamental intersection of the spheres of discourse characterized by language and expression. This intersection on the creation of metaphorical truth is the forced encounter of the external referentiality of the language with the internal referentiality of the text.

In Neruda's poem we must be able to incorporate such references as sea, flowers, colours, waves, and sand within a parallel structure that elaborates them in a unique expression: "blue moving the blue" and "the gold of a yellow flower held by your gaze." But there are also the intertextual references, since "we are only earth and earth we shall be" refers ultimately to Genesis 2:7 as fire, air, water, and earth refer to pre-Socratic philosophy, but there is also the sea unfolding its "myth" with its oblique reference to Paul Valéry's *Le cimetière marin*. The decisive factor in this study of the text is in the recognition of creativity as the fusion of horizons.

Literary criticism derived from Ricoeur's hermeneutics starts with the recognition that the text is analytically accessible as distinct from the psychological recesses of the author's intentions. The form brought forth by the analysis of the text is not the hidden meaning; rather, it is the requirement for reading addressed to the reader. Accordingly, the interpretation that follows analysis is a kind of obedience to this injunction that comes from the text.

The concept of hermeneutical circle is not ruled out by Ricoeur's shift in hermeneutics. Indeed, the hermeneutical circle is formulated but in new terms. It no longer proceeds from an intersubjective relation linking the subjectivity of the author with that of the reader. The hermeneutical program is a connection between two discourses, the discourse of the text and the discourse of interpretation. This connection means that what must be interpreted in a text is what it says and what it speaks about, the kind of world it opens up, discloses. The final act of appropriation is less the projection of the reader's prejudices into the text than the fusion of horizons that occurs when the world of the text and the world of the reader merge with each other.

Both Unamuno and Ricoeur hold that language cannot be reduced to a means of communication because language is first and foremost the habitat of individuals and communities of individuals. Ricoeur holds further that the metaphorical process of creative tension is a characteristic of language itself. The semantic impertinence of metaphor generates the tension that creates new meaning. His vision of reality is a dynamic one of process, and as I have presented here and in the previous chapter, this is Unamuno's philosophical foundation. Unamuno lives by Wilhelm von Humboldt's adage – man is language.

2. The Value of Literature

The principal value in reading great works of literature lies in what they can help us become. This is an age-old maxim heeded by countless generations and repeated as an article of faith from Plato's *Symposium* to the appreciations of the classics by George Santayana. But many of my generation who lived through the horrors of the Second World War and witnessed the magnitude of man's crimes against humanity have come to dismiss our tradition of humanistic learning as an inconsequential ornamentation of the leisure class. After all, it is argued, some of the most extreme violations of human rights were committed by men who read the classics, who loved music and art and were conversant with the writings of the great philosophers. I wish to offer a counterargument in support of the humanities.

The writings we consider the classics of our tradition – the works of Aristotle, Lucretius, Dante, Shakespeare, Cervantes, Milton, Goethe, Shelley, Keats, Galdós, Rilke, Proust, Joyce, and Borges, to name but a few – if they had perished before our day, as so many ancient texts have, would not have forfeited any of their truth or greatness as events, but they would have become inconsequential to us. We can neither take from nor add to their past value or inherent dignity. It is only they, these written texts, that can add to the present value and dignity of our minds – but, and this is the thesis I will defend, not because they can teach us anything about our world, not because they are to be emulated in style or design, not because we are exhorted to follow some lofty idealism through the reception of the accumulated wisdom of the past – none of these will suffice. The reading of great works of literature contributes to the making of our world insofar as they oblige us to remake our world view through their power of redescription and force us to take a stand in our response to their truth-claims. This is the general response I give to the central question of literary theory: What is literature? My argument develops a relational theory of literature and rejects the validity of all claims to definitive interpretations.

I have consistently argued that a general theory of literary criticism is a contradiction in terms, since a theory by definition is an explanation of some perceived problem or set of problems. The explanation must follow the recognition and designation of the problem. The problem we confront here is that of the purported definitive interpretation of poetry. Is there an interpretation of a text that is so certain that no reasonable person could question it? I say no. Furthermore, I think the pursuit of definitive interpretation is futile and misguided idealism. I will argue here for critical interpretation of texts that is free from the notion that critical commentary must centre on the discovery of a permanent interpretation. In particular, I believe it is imperative that critical commentary be freed from the notion that its function is to explain what is not clear about the text to ordinary readers. My theoretical position is best identified as phenomenological hermeneutics. I will proceed in three stages: first, I will make a brief statement of operating principles, drawing distinctions between my position and that of Romantic hermeneutics in the past and post-structural theory in the present; second, I will discuss the idea of the text; and, finally, I will outline the consequences of phenomenological hermeneutics for textual study.

Since 1960 the position we now identify as phenomenological hermeneutics has developed as a consequence of the writings of Hans-Georg Gadamer, especially his *Truth and Method* (1960), the later writings of Martin Heidegger, and primarily the work of Paul Ricoeur, notably *La métaphore vive* (1975), *Interpretation Theory* (1976), *Hermeneutics and the Human Sciences* (1981), and *Temps et récit* (3 vols., 1983–5).

The dialectic of philosophical hermeneutics is the core that holds together the theories of such thinkers as Gadamer, Habermas, and Ricoeur.

The dialectic explanation and understanding has three general propositions. The first is that it is impossible to know anything where there was not a presupposition to the inquiry. Pre-existing systems of inquiry are always inherently part of the way we conceive our purposes and choose the means to realize them. A second general proposition, common to philosophical hermeneutics, is an anti-idealist position, which reworks the dialectical logic of Hegel and rejects his conclusion of an Absolute. This means that philosophical hermeneutics accepts the irreducible contingency of both the thinker's own strategies and of reality itself. The truth that emerges from these theories is the truth of self-knowledge.

The third general proposition is that there is an intentional structure in both explanation and understanding. There is intentionality behind explanation in the very choice of subject and in the way the thinker addresses his object of inquiry; there is also an intentional framework in the social conditions of the thinker that affects his understanding. And these two intentional structures are dialectically related. There are no absolutes; there is no definitive truth; but there are means of reflecting on how it is that the thinker knows what he thinks he knows.

I now turn to phenomenological hermeneutics and comment on the principles of inquiry derived from Heidegger, Gadamer, and Ricoeur that constitute a theory of literature. Phenomenological hermeneutics is a reflective theory of interpretation grounded in the presuppositions of phenomenological philosophy, derived from questioning this subject–object relation. Through this questioning we first observe that the idea of objectivity presupposes a relationship that encompasses the supposedly isolated object. This encompassing relationship is prior to and more basic than any categories we may wish to construct. Heidegger's term for this fundamental relationship is being-in-the-world (*Sein und Zeit*, 78–90).

The Heideggerian term expresses the primacy of belonging, of partaking of the world, which precedes reflection. This term and others similar to it in the work of Gadamer and later phenomenological philosophers all attest to the priority of the ontological category of *Dasein*. This is the epistemological and psychological category of the subject that reflects on itself. Thus we can say with Ricoeur that "the most fundamental phenomenological presupposition of a philosophy of interpretation is that every question concerning any sort of 'being' [*étant*] is a question about the meaning of that 'being'" (*Hermeneutics*, 114).

The first principle of phenomenological hermeneutics is that every question we ask concerning the text to be interpreted is a question about the meaning of the text. The meaning of a text is to be derived from an inquiry into the make-up of a text, which is form, history, the reading experience, and the interpreter's self-reflection.

The second principle of phenomenological hermeneutics is that the traditional model of textual communication, which moves from writer to text to reader, is here supplanted by a bifurcated model that construes two separate and parallel relationships: first, in temporal priority, the writer–text relationship, and second, the text–reader relationship. The term *author* is reserved as a value-concept of the historical context.

The writer–text relationship is akin to the creative process in any human endeavour by which man's labour individuates his work as a unique statement of self. But once the work is given over to the readers, this relationship has ended; there is no retroactive control over the created work; just as in the case of natural children, they are individuals who will find their own way. The psychological intentions of the writer or parent are of no consequence except to him or her. Textual intentionality must unfold before the reader as part of the reader's experience.

For the reader to grasp the meaning of a literary text, he must be able to recognize its singularity as the composition of an author. The style of the literary work of art is not to be sought in the historicity of the author but rather in the very form of the text. This aspect must be further developed if the author's role is not to be a source of confusion and misunderstanding. Since style, be it that of an artisan making a cabinet or of an author writing, is labour that individuates, it is the sign of composition of structuration that produces an individual work, and therefore it retroactively designates its author. Thus it is that the distinctive individuating features of a producer are an essential part of stylistics in literary criticism and that the term *author* is a value-concept in literary history. The singular configuration of the literary work of art and the singular configuration of the author are strictly correlative. Unamuno showed that he understood the nature of writing and the writer when he argued that man individuates himself in producing individual works. The signature of the author is the mark of this relationship.

The essential characteristic of a literary work is that it transcends the psychological and sociological conditions of its production and thereby comes into a new relationship that cannot be circumscribed. This new relationship is an unlimited series of readings, each of which is itself situated in its own sociological, psychological, and cultural context. Thus the third principle of phenomenological hermeneutics is the recognition that the text has been cut off from its original context and has been thrust into an alien context through the act of reading.

I emphasize again that there is no longer a situation common to the writer and the reader. When we have rejected the search for the psychological intentions of another person – the author – that were supposedly concealed behind the text, and when we do not want to reduce interpretation to post-structuralist free play, what remains as our domain of inquiry? I posit that the task of interpretation is to explicate the type of being-in-the-world that is unfolded in and through the text.

Following Gadamer, we concur that the human condition is essentially a dialogue of realization for the person belonging to and interacting with a tradition in a community of commentary. The fourth principle of phenomenological hermeneutics, derived in part from *Truth and Method*, is that for the reader, the hermeneutic encounter is one of overcoming the initial alienating strangeness of the text. The metaphor of distance serves to describe this encounter and the ensuing tension. In other words, there is an initial antinomy between text and reader, an opposition between the alienating distanciation and the thrust towards appropriation by the reader. I hasten to add that this is not an either/or proposition but rather a process rooted in the problematic of the literary text. Ricoeur wrote that "in my view, the text is much more than a particular case of intersubjective communication, it is the paradigm of distanciation in communication. As such, it displays a fundamental characteristic of the very historicity of human experience; namely that it is communication in and through distance" (*Hermeneutics*, 131).

The fifth principle of hermeneutics I am proposing describes the central process of appropriating the text in the reading experience. "Appropriation" is the English translation of the German *Aneignung*, used first by Ricoeur in 1972 and later by Robert Weimann. The term means to make one's own what was initially alien. As I stated earlier, the task of phenomenological hermeneutics is to overcome the cultural distance and historical alienation of the text. Appropriation is achieved only insofar as the meaning of the text is actualized for the present reader. Appropriation, then, is the actualization of meaning in a text addressed to a reader. It is consequently a dialectical concept of dynamic process whose result is an event of taking over what was initially the thought of others. The reading experience as an event in present time, set in the midst of the historicity of the reader, is the new event that replaces the writer's event.

If we begin the task of interpretation with the understanding that the literary text has an autonomous status with regard to the author, we have three clear options for studying the text: we can explain it in terms of its internal relations, its structure; we can respond to it, read it, and comment on it; or we can attempt to relate these two – that is, the formal explanation with regard to understanding the reading experience. This latter course is that of phenomenological hermeneutics, and in order to take it we must encounter the text as form, but also as a historical, distant event, and finally as a historically present event. Consequently, our sixth principle is that the starting point is the formal organization that is subsequently tied to the traces of its historical origins, but it is clearly and openly reconstituted as a contemporary event for the reader, who is the necessary agent of meaningfulness. The reader's function becomes that of the assimilating concretizer created by the experience of reading a poem and thereby participating in the poetic world of the text.

The seventh principle of the hermeneutics I am sketching will be a clarification of what it can attain and what it cannot. Phenomenological hermeneutics differs from Romantic hermeneutics in at least one essential proposition: whereas nineteenth-century hermeneutics sought to link the content of literary texts to the psychological disposition of the author or to the social conditions of the community in which the texts were produced, phenomenological hermeneutics is ultimately directed at examining the text as a reconstituted reality that takes in historical considerations but is grounded in the phenomenon of the reader's appropriation. We must also take care to distinguish our enterprise from any literary or textual criticism of an anti-historical character, such as structuralism or post-structuralism. The seventh principle is that we must recognize that fixed meaning is impossible to establish and that conflict between interpretations is inescapable; rather than evade this fact, we seek to participate in the tradition of humanistic commentary, which Ricoeur called the hermeneutics of the textual refiguration and configuration of world.

These principles of phenomenological hermeneutics that I have outlined constitute a literary theory and set out a path for literary criticism to follow. In summary, these are as follows: 1. Every question we ask concerning the text is a question about meaning. 2. There are two separate and parallel relationships: author–text and text–reader. 3. Text transcends the conditions of production and comes into a new relationship that cannot be circumscribed. 4. Hermeneutic encounter is one of overcoming the initial alienating distance of the text for the reader. 5. Appropriation is the process of actualization of meaning in a text addressed to a reader. 6. The starting point of criticism is the study of the formal organization of the text. 7. Fixed meaning is impossible to establish since the text is inexhaustible.

I now return to the central concept of the literary text in order to comment subsequently and briefly on the consequences of this theory for literary criticism. The final dimension of the literary text is the hermeneutic level that is self-understanding on the part of the commentator. Recall that the first three dimensions are the formal or semiotic, the historical, and the phenomenological, which is the reading experience. What links phenomenological hermeneutics to hermeneutics in general is the premise that the literary text is the medium through which the reader–commentator–critic understands himself. This idea is grounded in Gadamer's insistence on the reader's subjectivity. A text that is appropriated by a reader is thereby applied to his present situation. But the initial distance of the text is not erased by appropriation; rather, an alienating situation is transformed into one of understanding without the illusions of Romanticism. Appropriation is thus an understanding of distance. Furthermore, and this is essential, recall that appropriation is mediated by the structural objectification of the text, since appropriation does not respond to the author or his intentions but rather to the explanation of the text as described through formal analysis. Once again, Ricoeur summarizes our position:

> Perhaps it is at this level that the mediation effected by the text can be best understood. In contrast to the tradition of *cogito* and to the pretension of the subject to know itself by immediate intuition, it must be said that we understand ourselves only by the long detour of the signs of humanity deposited in cultural works. What would we know of love and hate, of moral feelings and, in general, of all that we call the *self*, if these had not been brought to language and articulated by literature? Thus what seems most contrary to subjectivity and what structural analysis discloses as the texture of the text, is the very medium within which we can understand ourselves. (*Hermeneutics*, 143)

This return to the consequences of interpretation is what most clearly distinguishes Ricoeur's phenomenological hermeneutics from any of the various interpretative schools derived from Heidegger. Ricoeur's insistence on interpretation as a redescription of the world, and his dismissal of the critic's implicit claim to unveil the text as a mirror of the world, has forced literary critics to take a stand on their refiguration of the world without the shield of purported objectivity or the ideal concept of authors' intentions.

Let us be clear on this matter of consequences. Ricoeur does not propose that reading great works of literature will produce great men. But, quite directly, he *does* hold that reading literature engages us in the activity of refiguring the world and that as a consequence of this activity, the moral, philosophical, and aesthetic questions of the world of action become *our* questions, to which we must respond.

The long detour of considering the humanities as they are inherited by us in literature, history, and philosophy is necessary, according to Ricoeur, because only by engaging with our cultural heritage can we find the freedom to redescribe the world in our own experience of self in the world of action. The function of literary criticism based on phenomenological hermeneutics is to move from the consideration of the text first as form, then as history, then as experience, and finally as self-understanding.

We now move from literary theory to literary criticism. The first step in this is to indicate what the goal of criticism is to be. Put simply, the aim of a mode of literary criticism unencumbered with false premises is to elucidate the critic and his readers. This is accomplished when the critic and his readers put into play the knowing appropriation of the literary work. *Putting into play* is a key concept that Ricoeur has taken from Gadamer, and we should define it carefully.

The activity of putting a text into play is not determined exclusively by the consciousness that plays – that is, the reader. The players are participants, for the activity itself has its own way of being. Putting a text into play transforms those who participate in it – the critic and his readers. The subject of the aesthetic experience is not the critic himself but rather what takes place in the activity. We often say that we play with an idea. What we mean by this common expression is that we take up an idea and engage it: there is an essential give and take, a to-and-fro movement in this activity. We also say that an idea is played out, or that a part is played, or that something is in play between one place and another. All these expressions of ordinary language reveal that putting into play is something other than the exclusive mental activity of a subject. The *in-itself* of putting into play is such that even in a solitary situation there must be something with which one plays.

Whoever is engaged in putting into play is also himself played, for the rules of the game impose themselves on the player, prescribing the to-and-fro and delimiting the field where the activity takes place. The essential point here is that there is a strict relation between putting into play and presenting a world, and this relation is absolutely reciprocal.

The definition of literature we hold is that of a tradition of texts with a maximum capacity to redescribe the world; it follows that the game we play as readers of and commentators on literature is that of world-making. As a corollary of this proposition, the literary dimension of texts, their literariness, is precisely their propensity for putting into play the heuristic fiction of the world.

The literary critic of the past well understood that art only abolished the non-metamorphosed aspects of reality. In this sense the task of the critic has always been one of recognition rather than cognition. The problem has been that this activity has been caught in a trap between the reflective Kantian tradition and speculative Hegelian tradition of philosophy. However, the proper place of criticism is not in either camp; rather, it is at equal distance from both, accepting as much from one as from the other, but opposing each with equal vigour. Consider how in a theatrical representation the critic recognizes the character and the roles that are being played and responds to them with the immediacy of the representation on stage. Drama critics of the sensibility of the late Clifford Leech clearly recognized the paradox of their critical activity. This most imaginary of human creations, the representation of life *as if,* demands our recognition before we can perceive originality. As that which is recognized, the presented being is what is retained in its essence; it is stripped of all that is accidental and happenstance. A representation of *Hamlet* demands our recognition before we can appreciate the fullness of its immediacy. There is therefore an essential link between fiction, its capacity for figuration, and the critic's task of recognizing the essential dimension of the fiction.

The four dimensions of the literary text I have outlined in this section can be recast as stages of operation for literary criticism. Let us examine them as a sketch of a mode of criticism. The first dimension of the text is the system of signs, their rules of operation and their interrelationships. This level of inquiry is one of semiotic analysis of the linguistic and structural features that every text has. At this level we respond to the general question of *how* a text operates.

The second dimension of the text is the historical. This level of inquiry stems from the presupposition that all texts and all readers are historical and that the historical dimension is always of some consequence. The historicity of the text is in implicit tension with the historicity of the reader. As discourse, it is written language addressed to someone about something. Thus, in its split reference between internal and external references, there is the undeniable dialectic of the historical ground of the text and the distinct ground of the reader. At this level we operate on semantic inquiry as we seek to bring the dialectic of past significance and present meaning into focus. The general question we respond to at this stage is *what* the text speaks about.

The third dimension of the text is the phenomenological level of the reading experience. At this level we consider experiential aspects of the text–reader relationship as we examine the textual strategies and the reader's mode of reception. Obviously, this stage of our study of the text coincides with the reader reception theory of our colleagues from Constance. This third dimension of the text therefore yields critical commentary, which we can identify as the essence of the reading experience. It should be stated once again for clarity that phenomenological reader reception theory is not concerned with the individual experience of reading but only with the essence of such an experience. The general question we pursue at this level is *what* does the text say to me.

The fourth and final dimension of the text is the hermeneutic level of self-knowledge. Here we encounter the undercurrent of tension between the text's autonomy and the assimilating force of the reader's appropriation. At this level there is a reflective assessment of what Gadamer has called the fusion of horizons; this act of dialogic unity with the text is the very core of what is called the hermeneutical experience. The question here is *how* have I read the text.

The critical commentary on a literary text must move progressively through the four stages sketched here. Any contribution towards elucidating the critic's readers will result from the conjunction of the four stages. But let us not make the mistake of treating this approach as if it were a method for determining the definitive meaning of the text. The essential aim of this mode of literary criticism is not to establish a mirage of objective truth, but rather to elucidate the shared experience of reading the text with the essential claim of the fourth dimension of the text – that the only truth we encounter is the truth of self-knowledge. This mode of literary criticism constitutes the dialogic experience of the reader–text relationship, and the structured questions we propose serve as a basis for literary criticism, as was demonstrated with poetic texts in an earlier section. This mode of literary criticism is designed to participate in the community of commentary rather than indulge in the fantasy of objective and definitive interpretation.

The primary task of a literary critic therefore is to participate in and contribute to the tradition of commentary we have inherited from the humanists. In this light, I consider Giambattista Vico to be the founder of modern relational literary criticism. An objection that has long been made to literary theories that hold the literary text to be indeterminate and the work of art to be inexhaustible is that if the truth is unattainable, then one reading experience is as good as any other. But this objection, applied to our position, arises from a lack of understanding of the full significance of phenomenological hermeneutics, for most certainly there is a quest for truth as well as a basis for determining the validity of one interpretation relative to others.

First, let us consider the question of truth. Ricoeur offered one of the most cogent arguments on the question of truth in the interpretation of texts as early as his 1972 seminar on literary theory, taught at the University of Toronto and later published with the title "Appropriation" (*Hermeneutics*, 182–93). The question of truth is tangled up in the subject–object dichotomy. Ricoeur suggests that if we give up the concept of subjectivity and treat the reader as a knowing player in the game of redescribing the world, the impasse will dissolve rapidly, for it will soon become clear that understanding must be self-understanding, that the truth of the text is in fact the truth of ourselves – or, to put it in critical terms, the truth of the literary text is the world that it unfolds in the reader's appropriation.

When we return to our initial question of the value of reading fiction, and probe into what society has gained from storytelling and the reading of fiction, Ricoeur's response is clear and powerful. He writes in *Soi-même comme un autre* (1990):

> The pleasure we take in following the fate of the characters implies, to be sure, that we suspend all moral judgment at the same time that we suspend action itself. But in the unreal sphere of fiction we never tire of exploring new ways of evaluating actions and characters. The thought experiments we conduct in the great laboratory of the imaginary are also explorations in the realm of good and evil. (164)

If the truth is tied to the fourth dimension of the text (i.e., my self-knowledge), how can one distinguish between interpretations? This, of course, is a loaded question, loaded in the sense that the issue has been shifted from the reading experience to the critical commentary. To put it very strongly, there is no possible distinction or evaluation between one reading experience and another. But it is quite another matter where there is an implicit or explicit claim of authority and knowledge by the writer of a commentary that is based on the reading experience and is disseminated for the sake of fellow readers. We are therefore involved with the general issue of the validity of critical statements. It is clear that in critical discourse, as in any other human pursuit, a wide range of talents and abilities will be used in its execution.

The means Ricoeur suggests as a basis for evaluating psychoanalytic writings can be transferred to literary criticism. In summary form, they are the following: the critical commentary must have a coherency in keeping with its own stated principles; it must also be able to meet its aims; furthermore, the criticism must be of consequence to its readers, that is, perform a useful function for them; and, finally, criticism must be written as an intelligible narrative. There is no doubt in anyone's mind that we must make value judgments when dealing with literary criticism, and what Ricoeur has proposed is in fact a general guide for judging all interpreters' performances. Consequently, a critic has as much claim as anyone else to the truth he purports to have discovered in reading a literary text, but his performance in sharing this truth is another matter. It can be coherent, accomplished, consequential, and well written, or it can be wanting in one or all of these respects.

Ricoeur has often remarked on the fundamental social value of literature – that it facilitates the human capacity to experience the suffering of others. He has taught us that it is the imagination that responds to the ethical summons to respect the reality of the past. It is mainly poetry that serves ethics as a way of recalling our debt to the dead. The imaginary obliges both poet and reader to enter into the realm of "standing for" and thereby provides a figure of what was, if one had been there to witness it.

This state of affairs at first seems paradoxical. How can poetry do more than a well-argued essay or even good reportage with photographs? The answer lies in the nature of the act of reading poetry. The reader is drawn deep into his or her own repertoire of images, memories, thoughts and then deploys them into the configuration of the poem's references. This configuration is powerful because it is from the past but cast in the images of the reader; it belongs to both the reader and the text.

Ricoeur's sense of the textual past is far more powerful than imagining what was there in the past. He argues that the past is absent for the reader and that this absence is a powerful imperative to refigure the past as part of the present. He often refers to Proust's conclusion in *Le temps retrouvé* that the refigured past is more powerful than the testimony of the past because it merges past and present in the reader's mind.

In 1988, Ricoeur gave a lecture, later published, titled "The Human Being as the Subject Matter of Philosophy," which takes his concept of refiguration into the philosophical question of the self–other relationship. I quote from the conclusion of this remarkable essay:

> I say only that the power exerted by someone on somebody else constitutes the basic occasion for using the other as an instrument, which is the beginning of violence, murder, and still more torture, this being the extreme ... There is no self-respect without respect for the other. We should even have to say that if I esteem myself, I respect myself as someone else, as another. It is the other in myself that I respect. Conscience is the witness of this internalization of otherness in self-respect. (100)

This internalization of otherness has no greater source than literature such as Proust's work and that of so many others whom Ricoeur cites and comments on in *Temps et récit*. For Unamuno the best examples of this power are in poets like Leopardi and Antelo de Quental and, above all, in Cervantes. For me the best example of this power of refiguration in literature that gives the experience of the other for the reader is in the poetry of José Emilio Pacheco. He is our contemporary voice of the imagination. One of his most powerful poems was written in response to the devastating earthquake that hit Mexico City in 1985. One has only to read "Las ruinas de Mexico (Elegía del retorno)" in order to be there in the aftermath of the tragedy. I cite from the seventh poem, fourth stanza, published in *Miro la tierra*:

> I could not give them anything.
> What good is my solidarity?
> It does not remove debris, it does not hold up buildings
> nor does it build them anew.
> On the contrary, I ask,
> in order to leave the shadows of my gloom,
> for that impossible hand
> that no longer exists or can no longer grasp
> but still extends out
> in a space of sorrow or in the realm of nothingness. (19–20; my trans.)

3. The Sense of the Other That Defines the Self in Cinema and Poetry

This section has two parts. The first elaborates the cinematographic subject from a hermeneutic perspective. I have chosen this art form because of its significance in establishing social concepts of value and thereby answering the query of what is the sense of others that defines the self. The second part turns to the sense of others in poetry, which, although not a means of mass communication, nevertheless establishes and keeps alive a collective identity as only literature can create. Unamuno writes concerning human identity at the beginning of *Del sentimiento trágico*:

> And that which determines a man, that which makes him a certain man, one man and not another, the man he is and not the man he is not, is a principle of unity and a principle of continuity … Memory is the basis of individual personality, just as tradition is the basis of the collective personality of a people. (*SW*, IV, 11)

> But man neither lives alone nor is he an isolated individual, but is rather a member of society; there is a good deal of truth in the proverb which says that an individual, like an atom, is an abstraction … Reason, what we call reason, reflex and reflective knowledge, the distinguishing mark of man, is a social product. (*SW*, IV, 29)

If we move forward seventy-eight years to *Soi-même comme un autre*, we can recognize how the argument has developed. There are two related issues at stake: How does the study of fictional characters contribute to our consideration of selfhood. And how do we expand the inquiry concerned with individual identity into an inquiry into a collective identity of a people. Ricoeur sets up a dialectic that was implied by Unamuno – the dialectic of selfhood and otherness – and he will turn that dialectic into an insight into what makes the self a capable human being, a person with an identity, but also a person who acts in the world with and for others.

In the introduction to *Soi-même comme un autre*, Ricoeur writes: "Finally, and most especially, the dialectic of the same and the other, readjusted to the dimensions of our hermeneutic of *the self and its other* [my emphasis], will prevent an ontology of act and potentiality from becoming enclosed within a tautology. The polysemy of otherness, which I shall propose in the tenth study, will imprint upon the entire ontology of acting the seal of the diversity of sense that foils the ambition of arriving at an ultimate foundation" (20–1).

In chapter 5, "Personal Identity and Narrative Identity" (113–39), Ricoeur gives us more orientation:

> To a large extent, in fact, the identity of a person or a community is made up of these identifications with values, norms, ideals, models, and heroes, in which the person or the community recognizes itself. Recognizing oneself *in* contributes to recognizing oneself *by*. The identification with heroic figures clearly displays this otherness assumed as one's own, but this is already latent in the identification with values which make us place a "cause" above our own survival. An element of loyalty is thus incorporated into character and makes it turn toward fidelity, hence toward maintaining the self. (121)

Ricoeur, knowingly or not, has given us the most profound key to understanding Unamuno's self–other dialectic. Ricoeur writes:

> The fact that conscience is the voice of the Other in the sense of others is something that Hegel enables us to think, to the extent that conscience is tied to the reconciliation of two as yet partial figures of mind: judging consciousness and acting consciousness. In this way, the phenomenon of split consciousness crosses through the entire *Phenomenology of Spirit*, from the moment of the desire of the other, passing through the dialectic of master and slave, all the way to the double figure of the beautiful soul and the hero of action. It is important, however, that the ultimate reconciliation leaves us puzzled with respect to the identity of that other in "openly confessing itself by the vision of itself in the other." (353)

Unamuno's fiction is full of the self–other dialectic. Just three examples should suffice here. In 1917 Unamuno published *Abel Sánchez,* a tragic novel of the lifelong envy that devoured the life of the protagonist Joaquín Monegro. He spent his entire life wanting to have what his best friend, Abel Sánchez, had. Abel died of natural causes in Joaquín's arms, but Joaquín was convinced that he died because of his envy, which had descended into hatred. But the death of his other was also to be his own end, for he could not live without his other. Then in 1920, Unamuno again took up the theme of the conflict between the self and the other that moves from a master–slave relationship to its reversal. This book is *Tres novelas ejemplares y un prólogo,* and the specific text in question is "Nada menos que todo un hombre" (*OC,* II, 1008–36). Alejandro, a self-made man of great wealth, takes the most beautiful woman in the city as his wife. Alejandro's *machista* pride drives his wife, who only wants his love, into an asylum. The reversal of roles ensues when Alejandro becomes the slave of his dying Julia. In a furious outburst to save her from her failing health, he attempts a blood transfusion only to die with her. In her last words, she asks him "Who are you?" (1035). He answers, "Nothing more than a man that you have made by your love and your self" (1035). This being for oneself turns into being for my other who makes me be what I am. In 1926, while Unamuno was in political exile in Hendaye, France, he wrote a drama for the stage titled *The Other.* The drama debuted in 1932. The theme is personal identity between two identical twins. The brothers have been rivals for the love of the same woman. After the wedding, the brothers meet in the house of the newlywed, they quarrel, and one brother kills the other. The survivor now thinks he has become his dead brother. But the drama ends with an indeterminate play of opposites, and we never know who is the survivor and who is the victim. The nurse who has served them from birth, and who can tell them apart, refuses to do so and says that both have died. Where there is no identity there is no difference.

In *Soi-même comme un autre,* Ricoeur prepares us for our consideration of the cinematic character and collective identity:

> The mediating function performed by the narrative identity of the character between the poles of sameness and selfhood is attested to primarily by the imaginative variations to which the narrative submits this identity. In truth, the narrative does not merely tolerate these variations, it engenders them, seeks them out. In this sense, literature proves to consist in a vast laboratory for thought experiments in which the resources of variation encompassed by narrative identity are put to the test of narration. (148)

I have chosen two very different characters and modes of characterization, which I plan to use dialectically to demonstrate fundamental changes in concepts of representation of the filmic subject.

Casablanca, the classic romance of the reluctant American hero, directed by Michael Curtiz and starring Humphrey Bogart and Ingrid Bergman, was released in 1942. *Frida,* the filmic biography of the Mexican painter Frida Kahlo, starring Ofelia Medina, was produced in 1984, directed by Paul Leduc. In this section I comment on two modes of representation of the filmic subject; I describe these two modes as linear and non-linear characterization. Examining a three-and-a-half-minute clip from each film, I discuss the phenomenological facts of viewing in a hermeneutic exploration of two filmic characters.

Six minutes into *Casablanca*, a single-engine Fokker flies over a crowd and over the sign of Rick's "Café Americain" and lands at the airport. A delegation of German officers greets Major Stroesser of the Gestapo, who has come to Casablanca to supervise the capture and perhaps execution of the Czech nationalist leader Victor Laszlo. Stroesser is greeted by his officers and also by Captain Renard, the prefect of police in this North African outpost of Unoccupied France. As they walk from the plane to the waiting automobiles, Stroesser inquires into the fate of the person who killed two German couriers and took from them letters of transit signed by General de Gaulle guaranteeing the bearer the right to leave French territory. Renard, smiling, informs Major Stroesser that the killer is known and will be arrested that very evening at Rick's. He adds: "Everyone goes to Rick's." To which Stroesser responds: "I have heard of this café and about Mr. Rick himself." In ten seconds, Rick's significance has been introduced.

In the next scene we see a full shot of Rick's, followed by a close-up of its neon sign. The camera enters the café on the heels of a couple who have just been greeted. The camera focuses first on Sam, who is singing at the piano, then flits from table to table picking up fragments of conversation from the customers, who are a virtual cross-section of politically displaced persons along with the thieves, prostitutes, and smugglers they attract. The camera leaves the main saloon and follows the waiter known as The Professor as he enters a private area where the gambling casino is situated. As he serves a group of card players in the casino, a woman asks him if he will please ask Rick to join them for a drink. The waiter replies that Mr Rick never drinks with customers. A man at the table tells the waiter to mention that he ran the second-largest bank in Amsterdam. The waiter replies that that would not impress Rick and that the former director of the largest bank in Amsterdam is now the café's chef. Rick's character has been built up through multiple references but has yet to be seen or heard.

The camera now approaches a table in a tight shot so that we see only a man's hands and mid-torso; a waiter hands a voucher book to the unseen man, who takes it and signs "O.K. Rick." For a couple of seconds the camera lingers on his hands, the cigarette in the ashtray, the chessboard and the game he is playing solo; he has just taken a white bishop. Only then does the camera pan slowly up to his face. The build-up has been continuous from the moment Captain Renard mentioned Rick's café to Major Stroesser. The character exudes strength, self-confidence, intellectual power, and, most of all, control of his domain. The next scene in this short segment demonstrates the extent of the character's control. The doorman looks to his table for a visual sign of approval or rejection of each person who asks to enter the casino part of the café. A couple enters, followed by a well-dressed middle-aged man. When Rick gives the sign of refusal, the doorman closes the door on the latter. The man protests angrily and takes out his business card. Rick comes over from his table and confronts the man. The would-be customer demands admittance. Rick tears up the business card, hands it back to the man, and tells him his cash is good at the bar. When he asks if Rick knows who he is, Rick answers that he does and that he is lucky to have access to the bar. The diminutive Ugarte, played by Peter Lorre, who came in while Rick was confronting the angry customer, remarks with admiration that Rick dismissed the Deutsche Bank as if he had been doing it all his life. A tight-lipped Rick asks what makes him think he hasn't. Ugarte visibly shrinks.

In this way we are introduced to the protagonist. Rick's character will be further fleshed out, but the contradictions in this dominant figure have been established. The linear mode of characterization has so far been both rapid and striking. First, Rick is a key figure in the expatriate life of Casablanca. Second, his café is a privileged centre of activity. Third, as the one who controls this space, he is central to political activity in Casablanca. Fourth, he appears to be politically non-aligned and to be prospering by providing services to both Free France and the Third Reich. Fifth, he expresses marked anti-Nazi political views. This kernel of tension will expand into an existential metaphor of freedom. But before I enlarge on the linear mode of characterization in the creation of the filmic metaphor, let us look at the other film segment.

Frida is a biographical film about the extraordinary life of the Mexican painter and political activist Magdalena Carmen Frieda Kahlo Calderón de Rivera, better known as Frida Kahlo. She was born in 1907 and died just after her forty-seventh birthday in 1954. The film is unsettling because of the absence of dialogue and the extreme fragmentation and apparent random succession of scenes. Its more than one hundred separate scenes are grouped into ten segments, each segment framed by the same scene, taken from a variety of camera angles, of the dying Frida. I have chosen for commentary a three-and-a-half-minute segment starting at the ninth minute of the film.

There are five scenes in this segment. First, the camera moves slowly over a group of peasants celebrating the Day of the Dead, who are remembering the recently assassinated Emiliano Zapata. It is 1917; Frida is ten years old and a keen observer. While the group sings the lament of his death and the invocation that he lives on, the camera zooms in on photographs of him and on the votive candles that have been lit in his honour. Forty seconds after Frida appears as the observer, the scene ends abruptly and we see the aftermath of an accident. The eighteen-year-old Frida is carried into a house with a steel bar protruding from her hip. As she cries out in pain, a strong man pulls, turns, and twists the shaft until he manages to remove it. The film editing is again sharp. The next second, we approach the dying Frida in her bed, her face reflected in a bedside mirror. The scene lasts one minute and twenty-two seconds.

The next scene is in a carpenter's shop. The camera pans slowly through the shop from a fixed position, encountering obstacles until it halts on a painting that the seated Frida is observing. It is 1939; she is thirty-two years old. She is examining her painting titled *The Two Fridas* – two seated representations of herself, mirror images of each other, holding hands. One is dressed like a nineteenth-century European, the other in a Mexican Tehuana costume. The European Frida has a surgical instrument in her hand; she is cutting the artery from her exposed heart and is bleeding onto her white dress. The Mexican Frida holds an amulet in her hand with a portrait of Diego Rivera as a boy. Although her heart is also exposed, there is no cross-section representation, as is the case with the European Frida.

The camera approaches the painting from an oblique angle, then moves up close to only the European half of it, then turns to focus on the observing Frida, focusing on her face. One can see the painting reflected in her eyes. The camera moves back and captures the full painting. There is another look at Frida observing the painting, followed by a return to the painting, now focusing on the Mexican Frida; finally, the camera returns to Frida, who is still intently examining the painting. She breaks the brush she has been holding with both hands. Not a word has been spoken; the scene has lasted one-an-a-half minutes.

The last scene in this clip follows instantly. The camera moves in slowly from a distance on Frida, her father, and her sister; it is 1916, and Frida is nine years old. She is having her photograph taken by her photographer father. She is seated in a formal pose, wearing an elegant white dress. Her sister is seated off to the side and is observing. The scene ends with the camera closing in tight on Frida's face as the photograph is taken.

The discontinuity is softened only because all of the scenes concentrate on Frida. It is possible to date the fragments because all of the scenes are clearly identifiable as incidents in her life. In three-and-a-half minutes we have moved from a ten-year-old in 1917, to a young woman of eighteen in 1925, to a dying woman of forty-seven in 1954, to the thirty-two-year-old Frida in 1939, and finally to the nine-year-old child in 1916.

Can any of these fragments be expanded to achieve a sense of narrative event in the film? Non-linear characterization creates a constant incompatibility of one image with its successor; the brevity of each image is a disruptive factor as well, and because there are no verbal images, the viewer is forced to configure visual metaphors. There are two constants in this characterization: first, physical pain, and second, representation, be it through memory, mirror reflections, photography, or painting – and of course, the film itself as photography.

Let us compare the two modes of characterization, not as simple accumulations of information but rather as what they are in the experience of the viewer: processes of redescription in a semantic field of meaning construction. In ordinary terms, the two segments offer us a limited human experience with a fictional other.

In both cases the six bits of information that confront the viewer operate within a specific historical time frame. In *Casablanca* the year is 1939, France has fallen to Nazi Germany, and Unoccupied France is still an indeterminate zone, not quite as open as Switzerland, Sweden, and Portugal but not as restricted as Occupied France. In *Frida* the period is post-revolutionary Mexico, 1917 to 1954. That time is marked by events in Mexico; by the Russian Revolution, the rise of fascism in Italy and Germany, the Spanish Civil War, and the Second World War; and by the US interventions in Nicaragua and Guatemala (not in 1980 but earlier, in 1920 and 1950).

The six markers or truth-claims in the *Casablanca* segment are as follows: (1) the name "Rick's" is seen as the plane flies overhead, is mentioned by the prefect of police, and is repeated by the Gestapo major, and all of this gives Rick an anticipated significance; (2) Rick's name is repeated and is then a subject of conversation between the waiter and the customers; (3) we see Rick's signature before we see him; (4) we see his hands and his activities of smoking and playing chess; (5) we then see his face and upper body in a position of authority and control; and (6) we see him exercise power by refusing access to the German banker. These truth-claims are entirely sequential and linear and are fully coordinated in the characterization of Rick, the reluctant American hero. Rick's authority in *Casablanca* depends almost entirely on his maintaining a neutral indifference to his ideological enemies – Germany and Vichy France.

The truth-claims in *Frida* appear to be a random succession of images: (1) the face of the ten-year-old taking part in the Day of the Dead ceremony; (2) the body of the young woman in extreme pain; (3) the body of the mature woman in pain, and her mirrored reflection; (4) the artist, her work, and the camera; (5) the painting itself and its images of duality and pain; (6) the girl as the subject of a photograph – that is, the filmic photograph of the taking of a photograph. The succession is completely non-linear. The configuration is one of multiple images that make up personal identity, that of the artist and her artistic persona. If *Casablanca* offered a linear build-up of the hero, *Frida* gives us a play of images in the indeterminacy of the subject as other. And because there is no pre-established paradigm of hero in the case of Frida, the viewer must attempt to fit each new bit into some overall schema of the biographical person that was, not the fictional persona that is.

The linear characterization of Rick as hero has its roots in an established narrative process; the non-linear characterization of Frida reflects a creative metaphorical process, one in which fragments constantly change and rearrange themselves even after the film has ended. *Casablanca* is a powerful closed filmic text; *Frida* is an unstable and threatening open text. Rick is a fictional character, the exemplification of a modern hero; Frida was an actual person and is depicted through a swarm of visual images that are not narrativized. Although filmic subjects are the creations of cinematographic art, there is no doubt that part of the redescriptive process is that we are dealing with two different things – a literary narrative and a life story; thus the filmic subjects of the two films operate by means of different truth-claims of identity.

These two films provide us with the basic data for discussing the relationship between personal and literary identity. When we speak of a fictional character, what does this term imply and presuppose? Basically, we can say that the fictional character has a set of distinctive markers, physical and behavioural, that allow us to reidentify that individual as the same one we encountered earlier. This includes external markers such as physical features and, most of all, a name. The behavioural markers can be identified through various interrelated actions. Both Rick and Frida have physical markers. However, Rick has much more developed behavioural markers than Frida. At least in preliminary terms, Rick is more knowable as a character than Frida.

Let us now move to a secondary level in this hermeneutic probe of subject. This second level is the finite perspective of world-making. Here, character appears as a way of living, of existing in terms that are related to my own process of existing in the world I remake each day, in accordance with my perspectives of order. This is not simply a world of things, time, and space; it is also, primarily, a world of ideas, values, and others. On this level, character designates those lasting dispositions towards value judgments and towards others as subjects by which a person is recognized. On this level, Rick has a stance towards the world that we will continuously associate with him. Besides loving freedom and Elsa and despising bullies and Nazis, what he demonstrates in this segment is courage, toughness, authority, mental agility, and self-control. These character traits set Rick on the path to the narrativization of personal identity, as demonstrated in Woody Allen's *Play It Again, Sam*. In that film, the character's identification with Rick displays the otherness of the characterization he has assumed as his own, but this identification is already latent in the identification with the values the hero personifies.

Going further, exploring the filmic subject in *Frida,* consider that every narrative, be it novel or film, unfolds a textual world of its own. The more unique the world that has been constructed, the more will it prevent us from entering except as curious voyeurs of the exotica of the other, who is never our other but only the object of our fantasies. The subject in the narrative becomes a subject as our other to the degree that we can accept the character's fate as a human fate. But this is not a simple matter of eliciting empathy.

The life story of each of us is caught up in the life stories of others. Whole sections of my life are part of the life story of others – of my family, my friends, my companions in work and in leisure. But this personal entanglement in life stories differs markedly from personal entanglement in literary stories: the former are open-ended and in process, while the latter have been worked out in the narrative plot – or have been in the accepted wisdom of how we read a novel or view a film. A breakthrough on this matter has been phenomenological hermeneutics, which has helped us to interpret postmodern narratives and to go beyond our contemporary dialectic of the space of experience and the horizon of expectation. But I would also claim that it has given us a new reflective approach to art of other times.

The subject in *Frida* becomes an "as if" human subject for the viewer. This can be explained if we examine the process of figurative appropriation as the complex experience that it is rather than some naive notion of model substitution. The filmic text/viewer relationship in *Frida* can only be characterized as struggle. There is a struggle at every level of reception from the most basic level of knowing what is going on in the film, to the more complex ideological issues of the Marxist concept of history, to the most problematic issue of trying to respond to someone else's acute physical pain. Of course, the film is a retrospective review of a life story, but because this life story does not flow temporally, the viewer must try from the outset to make sense of the fragmented remembrances of a dying woman's life. So the first point to make is that although the filmic text is a retrospective series of remembrances, the viewing of it – in Ricoeur's terms, the viewer's *configuration* of it – is a present of actualization.

This hermeneutic examination of *Frida* indicates that because the filmic narrative is one we must construct ourselves through our responses to a series of almost one hundred visual images, it is *our* configuration that we measure against that of the life story. Our narrative and Frida's biography, far from being mutually exclusive, are in fact complementary. Stories of another's life are objectified through writing and narration, but in this film the life story returns to life through the path of our figurative appropriation.

The last issue I address is the nature of the filmic subject in the reflective make-up of the viewer. For this, I must inquire into the intimate relationship between the figure of the subject and that of the viewer who is the imagining subject. I will do so within the limitations of the two films discussed and, specifically, the two sequences I have described. For decades, we have heard protests against film portrayals of violence, pornography, and racial and other forms of discrimination. Some people find these portrayals offensive, and others contend that they induce or legitimize antisocial behaviour in others. Claims about artistic freedom become questionable once one accepts, as I do in this section, that there are strong links between art and life. My response to this debate has three parts that represent, respectively, the human body, otherness, and the repertoire of world-making.

The constancy of a self's identity is anchored in the body. Again, Rick and Frida serve as my examples. In both segments, the two characters are fully clothed. It is only in Frida's painting that her upper body is partly uncovered. Yet the body language of both characters is a formidable part of the visual imagery. Rick exudes strength and control without having to demonstrate it. With Frida we are responding to a face in physical pain without the lacerated body appearing. The closest we come to this is when the steel bar is removed from her hip. The strength of visual images of the body lies not in depiction itself but in motion or lack of it. Rick's status as a hero is strengthened by his body language as he walks over to personally throw out the Nazi, which makes Ugarte cringe even more. The only movement Frida makes in the segment's fragments is to break the brush she has been holding in her hands without our seeing it. The relative lack of movement in Frida is the determinate visual aspect that entangles us in imagining the pain and fury behind the indeterminate non-verbalized look of the woman. The constriction of movement is more powerful than movement itself.

The second aspect of the subject we are considering can be stated directly as the dialectic of self and other as the very dialectic of identity. I know who I am, above all and in all cases, because I know I am not other. The identity of being the same is bound up with the conviction of physical continuity. The self is not constituted by mere self-designation as a subject of discourse, action, or narrative. There is a more radical self-grounding that is the will to be separate, that must have otherness, as the radical guarantee of sameness for the subject.

Rick's others are all around him, and they are all subordinate. His subject is defined in contrast to his many others. The dialectic of self/other in *Casablanca* is completely concentric in that the others are all others to Rick and there is no other subject who has the capacity to define himself or herself with Rick as other. There is but one exception, and this is the other Rick who had happier days in the flashback scenes in Paris with Elsa. It is only this Rick who has the capacity to make the Rick of *Casablanca* other. The characters in the film, including Elsa and the Czech hero, Victor Laszlo, serve only to define the attributes of Rick's character as his others, specifically the woman he loves and the man he admires – two highly positive if somewhat obscured traits in the Rick of *Casablanca*.

Frida has no other than the other created by her through memory or through her painting. These other Fridas make the dialectic of identity one of profound introspection and indeterminacy. The film sequence's principal visual image has the seated Frida looking intently at her painting of her own duality. Frida the painter observes with extreme concentration the painting of a European and a Mexican representation of herself, linked through a single artery. The Mexican mirror image has the photograph of her husband, Diego Rivera, as a child; the other image has severed the artery so that both images are bleeding to death. And we are observing them both as the seated Frida observes and as the painted Fridas observe each other. Where here is the subject? The identity of the woman is the indeterminate core of the film. She looks and possibly thinks as Virginia Woolf once wrote: "It is no use trying to sum people up. One must follow hints, not exactly what is said, nor yet entirely what is done" (*Jacob's Room*, 29). Woolf's creative genius has plunged us into the dialectic of self and other. If the other is unknown except through the manner of our seeing him or her as our necessary complement, what can we do with the painted alter-images of the subject as the self's others? Do they give her her identity? Or does her identity still depend on others whose separateness is overt? Frida's others are many: her husband, Diego; her father; her sister; Trotsky; Zapata; and numerous friends and lovers, both men and women. Frida's subjects are unknown because her others do not define her with their separateness; rather, they launch her on a constant search for her inner other. We must look at her as subject and, in our manner of seeing, see our own reflection as we redescribe our world through her powerful indeterminate challenge of love, betrayal, pain, joy, suffering, and sensuality.

This inquiry has to do with the viewers' involvement with the filmic subject – Rick, the reluctant hero, and Frida, the silent, motionless, restrained woman with expressive power and a passion for life. In the film/viewer relationship, viewers' self-projections towards the filmic subject are an essential part of their dialectic present. What does the otherness of these subjects amount to when they become *our* others? Human reflection is primarily the voice of the other in us. In film, speech is comparable to gesture because what speech is charged with expressing is in the same relation as intention is to gesture.

My remarks about how the signifying apparatus works already involve a theory of significations. My corporeal awareness of the objects in my surroundings is already implicit in my body and presupposes no thematization or representation of my body. Signification arouses speech as the world arouses my body – through a mute presence that awakens my intentions without deploying them. In me as well as in the listener who finds it in hearing me, the significative intention is no more than a determinate gap to be filled with words – the excess of what I intend to say, over what is being said or already has been said. So Rick, as our other, speaks to action and to our often muted or deferred desire for action. There is a need to act and to act in support of people, ideas, beliefs, and so on, but there is also a form of paralysis of the self who finds himself incapable of initiating action as a meaningful response to life. Because Rick's subject embodies action, we need only to know if we will let him act on *our* behalf as well as on his own. The aptitude for being affected through the injunction of principle constitutes a condition of our own identity.

In Frida's case, it is her suffering that, as subject, she offers us. It is through her other's suffering that we find our own capacity to know ourselves as our other's other. In the final analysis, the more we work at the configuration of the filmic subject of Frida Kahlo, the more we will be drawn into her world of passion and pain, and this entanglement – which will never be explicitly narrativized – must ultimately be our own configuration of this life story. The pieces of the puzzle are given, the segments are all punctuated with pain and remembrance, but the narrative itself is the one we give the filmic text.

All cinematic subjects are incomplete and require the viewer's participation to complete them. So I conclude with some general observations about the impact of the cinematic subject on the viewer's process of imaginative world-making. First, the cinematic character as a special kind of narrative identity performs a mediating function for the viewer. This mediation between similarities and differences in the other is what I construct within me. Cinematic subjects are powerful imaginative variations on identity. In this section I have taken two opposite poles in the modalities of filmic characterization. At one pole we find the linear mode in a story of love set early in the Second World War. The story has definite characters: Elsa, loyal and passionate, a contradiction resolved by her surrender to Rick, who must "do the thinking for all"; Laszlo, a man with a cause, who would give his life for his political beliefs and who is prepared to risk almost certain capture and death to save Elsa. Finally, there is the protagonist, with his strong personal ethics, his apparent pragmatism, his unquestioned qualities of leadership, and his love for Elsa. The linear development of these personal and collective conflicts tests the resolve of the filmic character as reluctant hero. At the other pole is the undeveloped plot of *Frida*. The biographical context serves for the examination of the character's identity. Frida does not have a definite character, although she certainly has political beliefs as strong as and perhaps stronger than Rick's. She expresses her love of Diego but also a much more complex sexuality, which is a mode of being-in-the-world. She desires a sexual relationship with Leon Trotsky yet rebukes Diego for his many infidelities, especially with her own sister. She enjoys both heterosexual and homosexual relations in a sense of heightened sexuality. She knows physical and psychological pain and is able to express the pain of living through her art. She does not have a definite character although her presence in the film is powerful and almost overwhelming.

The contrast in these two films between narrativist and non-narrativist delineations of the subject reflects the spectrum of the imaginative construction of the other as known, as unknowable but present. To what extent are these characters part of culture? Under the rubric "Otherness of Other People," Ricoeur moves the inquiry from individuals to the community of others who form part of the self's world: "the reception of works of fiction contributes to the imaginary and symbolic constitution of the actual exchanges of words and actions. Being-affected in the fictive mode is therefore incorporated into the self's being-affected in the 'real' mode" (*Soi-même comme un autre*, 330).

A good example of how identity is shaped by the popular configurations of others is found in Gabriel García Márquez's novella *Eréndira* and the film script he wrote for it. I saw the film in the company of Ricoeur, who pointed out to me that the young protagonist was a quite ordinary young woman with no physical or artificial attributes that would lead one to think of her as a sex symbol. Yet she was completely transformed into the ultimate object of male sexual desire through the word-of-mouth campaign her grandmother had organized. Ricoeur's point was that the young woman's *reputation* was the source of the ensuing frenzy.

We gain or lose in estimation because of what others say to us. In life as in art, the result can be disappointment when the subject spoken of does not measure up to the image created by others; or, to the contrary, the subject can be enhanced in the mind of the perceiver because he *sees* what he has *heard* – as is the case with Eréndira. The rival prostitutes claim that she is only an ordinary young woman, no more or less attractive than any other. Yet the men who crowd around to have sex with her see only a goddess of love, far above any woman they know.

It is important to stress Ricoeur's concept of art in relation to the idea of humanity. In *L'homme faillible*, Ricoeur wrote: "Works of art and literature and, in general, works of the mind, insofar as they not merely mirror an environment and an epoch but search out man's possibilities, are the true objects that manifest the abstract universality of the idea of humanity through their concrete universality" (123). The commentary I have given of the filmic subject is an attempt to realize Ricoeur's concept of the power of art in cinema.

If we now turn to poetry as an expression of cultural identity, whatever the political structures that arbitrarily separate and join peoples, and if we redraw the lines and say that in reading literature we are dealing with a group identity that expresses a community's configuration of the world and that also, and most important, is shaped by what it takes in from other language groups, we encounter an entirely new alignment of authors, works, and relationships than what we presently view as national literature.

My central concern here is the making of cultural identity. My argument draws from an especially rich philosophical tradition that examines cultural identity in terms of language. My commentary is based on Ricoeur's *Soi-même comme un autre*. I argue that literature achieves meaningfulness through referentiality. But I also argue that historicist theories that reduce referentiality to the author's circumstances are reductive, and furthermore, that subjectivist approaches that ignore textual historicity are impressionistic. The referentiality that is central to my thesis is multiple and tensional. Because the literature of a people is part of the community's social context of reading and writing rather than a separate fixed body of prescribed texts, it becomes social reality.

My theory of referentiality is a hermeneutics of fictional reference in which terms gain meaning through four simultaneous operations: (1) ostensive reference to the semiotic system, (2) socio-cultural reference through language, (3) textual auto-reference, and (4) experiential reference to the reader's world view. Because the referential operations are simultaneous, interpretation of the reading experience that strives to become significant commentary must approach the reading dialectically as an open-ended source.

The extent of our understanding of a text can be measured by the fullness of our appreciation of the context in which the statement was made and its relative accessibility to us. The context, as I have indicated, can be characterized as a complex dialectic of expressive systems. It is neither fixed nor complete; it is a dynamic event, a temporally marked intersection of referential systems, and as such, it cannot be reduced to a determinate configuration. Thus it is that we can say that the reading and writing of literature is a normatively regulated communicative action with an argumentative handling of truth-claims. The argumentative handling of truth-claims is precisely what serves the community in the ongoing process of cultural identity. This communicative action takes place in the community and in a specific sociolinguistic context, but is always bringing into the community as many truth-claims from other communities as it is redescribing its own. This is why the cultural intertext must become an essential part of the interpretation of the literary aspect of cultural identity.

The interpreter always begins with confidence and with the certainty that the interpretive commentary will approximate the insight already achieved. But the more the interpreter works at explaining his or her previous understanding, the more the text will reveal previously unsuspected aspects, so that in time, what had been the initial understanding will have changed through the search for satisfactory and effective explanation. The interpreter comes to a new understanding when the explanatory process has ended; but this new understanding is just as vulnerable as the initial understanding, and the interpreter can propose it as valid only because, like Don Quijote, he dares not test the home-made helmet once again. If the interpreter were to reopen the explanatory process, the seemingly stable understanding so carefully constructed would again begin to unravel. Meaning is a dynamic encounter, a crossing and criss-crossing of referential operations. An interpretation that draws out of the dynamic event is nothing less than an arbitrary reduction of meaning to the position of understanding where the interpreter happened to be when he or she broke off.

So the question is, how can we discuss a dynamic and unpredictable event without imposing closure? My preliminary response is that the interpretation I propose is a hermeneutic examination of the reading experience rather than a historicist promotion of an abstract construct arbitrarily designated as an accurate determination of the work itself. Such reductionist interpretations are the result of one or two referential operations taken out of the reading experience and put forward as fixed and definitely accurate expositions of the work's meaning.

The commentary that follows consists of a heuristic plan that presents the conceptual framework through an explanation of the four referential operations that are simultaneous. The concluding interpretation brings together the referential systems in a dialectic process of questioning and being questioned that is the text/reader relationship.

1. Ostensive reference to the semiotic system. The sign system of a natural language is made manifest through the effective production of a communicative pattern. This is true even when there is the semantic impertinence of metaphor in the utterance that disrupts the production of sense. When this occurs, the remaining pattern keeps open the possibility of a new sense arising from the ruins of the pragmatic or literal sense. For example, let us consider the following lines from *Piedra de sol* by Octavio Paz:

> Green domain without end. Like
> a blinding flash of wings
> when they open in the middle of the sky. (237; my trans.)

The key signs are the functional words *like* and *when*. Beyond the obvious grammatical usage, we must recognize the functional role the signs perform in establishing the pattern of relationships. *Like* performs the sense-making function of resemblance and transfer. Thus, the pattern is one of A resembles B, and when attention is called to this resemblance, there is a shift in focus whereby B gains in sense through the transfer of characteristics of A. In our present example, there is a double indeterminate aspect because we cannot immediately recognize how "green domain" can be said to resemble a "blinding flash," and furthermore, we cannot grasp how wings that unfold in the sky can produce a blinding flash. *When* serves to produce temporal specification in the subordinate line. The semantic problem is that it is not clear how the temporal specification of opening wings in the middle of the sky can produce a blinding flash.

The point of our discussion under the heading of ostensive reference to the semiotic system is that there is a functional pattern that controls our response by channelling us into a process of thinking. A is like B when the temporal specification is given; therefore, green domain is like a blinding flash, but this is a blinding flash of wings when they open, unfold in the middle of the sky. The suddenness of opening up in the middle of the sky is the essential control sign for the passage.

2. Socio-cultural reference through the ideological models of the specific language. The socio-cultural inference here is to power, dominance, and sudden disruption of this hitherto unchallenged domain. The referentiality is not the direct ostensive reference but rather an indirect inference through the semantic indicators and their paradigmatic

relationships; domain without end sets in motion clear patterns of power and domination.

Equally strong is the referential power of "blinding flash" in the middle of the sky as a disruption of the unbroken dominance. Also, the reference to the bird that suddenly opens its wings has inferences of singularity amid uniformity. The most significant factor is that in terms of the socio-cultural inference, the "green domain" without end is oppositionally situated to its comparative counterpart "blinding flash of wings."

3. Textual auto-reference. The textual references are both intratextual and intertextual, and they are explicit. The intratextual references build on the cited lines. A few lines later, Paz's text reads: "Like a bird turning the forest / to stone with its song," and a few lines after that: "A sudden presence like a burst of song / like the wind singing in the fire."

The sudden appearance of the bird takes on power that could not have been anticipated in the earlier verses. It is the birdsong that can petrify the entire forest. In the third segment, the reference is once again to the sudden eruption of song, now compared to the wind singing in the forest fire. The intratextual significance of this system is that it opens with the whole and juxtaposes it with the singular only to reverse it and have the singular spread and overwhelm the whole.

Some ten lines later, the lyric voice enters the poem through the singular presence of point of view:

> I move across transparencies as though
> I were blind. A reflection erases me,
> I'm born in another, Oh forest of
> enchanted pillars, I move
> through the arches of light into
> the corridors of a diaphanous fall. (238; my trans.)

Intertextuality abounds throughout this long poem, and in the particular case of the bird imagery of the first part, there is a masterful appropriation of the first stanza of "Retorno" by the Spanish poet Juan Ramón Jiménez:

> The world's thousand towers against a golden sunset
> raise their beauty before my thoughts
> an ecstasy of stone of one thousand structures
> in a blinding flash transports me silent and blind.

In Jiménez's poem the "blinding flash" comes as a result of thought, of meditation on man's work, and transports the lyric voice blind and mute to genesis. In contrast, in Paz's poem, the blinding flash is genesis; it is the beginning that plunges man into a green, unending domain, like wings suddenly unfolding in the middle of the sky. The point of view of presence in the hitherto uninhabited world turns the forest to stone. The lyric voice enters shortly after and attempts to return (*retorno* as in Jiménez's poem) to genesis and thus regain his identity as man.

4. Experiential referentiality. The basic principle of indeterminate reference in interpretation is that the reader must strive to ground the openness of the text in some form of personal consistency that makes sense. So it would appear that closure and ethnocentricity on the part of the reader are unavoidable and a necessary part of reading. This is the position taken by deconstruction theory, and on the whole, it is valid. But there is an alternative, and that is phenomenological hermeneutics. The reader can construct the necessary consistency without imposing closure on the text by accepting that this textual meaning is one of a number of possible constructs. This can be achieved by exposing the logocentric understanding of the text to the dialectic force of explanation.

There are at least four operations of referentiality in making sense of the text, and they are, as I have stressed, simultaneous. Some operations are instinctive, grounded in the training we have received; others require explicit choices. The semiotic mode of reference merely makes possible a meaningful reading; it limits the number of possibilities on formal grounds but leaves all determination open. The socio-cultural mode of reference privileges certain possibilities of meaning but at the same time greatly enriches the text by linking its features to the cultural matrix of the language. Textual referentiality also privileges and enhances the text, but instead of linking it to the social background, it ties it into the conventions and history of other texts and their genres. The fourth mode of reference, experiential referentiality, which concretizes the text, is of course the most restrictive, since the reader must make a number of choices in the configuration of meaning, thereby partly limiting the text. Such a referential operation would indeed be a logocentric reduction of the text and would undercut its creative power by fixing meaning – but only when the interpretation is isolated from other interpretations. What I propose is a dialogic interpretation that is in process, that is open-ended, that proposes meaning and meaningfulness, not to close the text but so that the interpretation will be contested by other readers. This is the cultural intertext. Thus it is that the distance between text and reader becomes a bridge rather than a gulf, for distance that is grounded into two historicities is distance that becomes a bridge.

The interpretation that follows is limited not only because I consider just a small fragment of *Piedra de sol,* a long poem of 584 lines, but also because I privilege only one set of images. The poem opens and closes with a coda I do not treat here. My commentary is on lines 10 to 44 and on the imagery of genesis and presence. The thirty-four lines I discuss follow the coda; in four stanzas, they move progressively from reality without individual presence until, in a blinding flash, wings unfold in the middle of the sky and there is singularity. The second stanza introduces a temporality that prophesies the joy and suffering of consciousness. The third stanza introduces the human gaze, the viewpoint that makes the world and that can also petrify it in memory. The body of the other is present in the gaze. The fourth stanza adds the first person of the lyric voice, who can know himself only through the female other. The lyric voice gains the world through the body of the female other. This reflection is ephemeral. He has not yet discovered the meaning of reality, which is neither *I* nor *you,* but *we.*

What is the role of poetry in the action of being in the world? Ricoeur provides us with the orientation. When we read or hear a poem, what is our subjective response to the images and metaphors? In *L'homme fallible,* Ricoeur writes about perception and feeling: "Feeling is understood, by contrast, as the manifestation of a relation to the world that constantly restores our complicity with it, our inheritance and belonging in it, something more profound than all polarity and duality" (*Fallible Man,* 85). The reader gains an understanding of the poem by projecting values on the very appearance of the world. What appears to us as a quality is a manifestation of the moment, the phase, the state of the orientation. By means of this manifestation, the tendency tells us where it is. In the fragment of the poem I discuss here, there emerges a lyrical configuration of beginnings, beginnings of world, of consciousness, of self, and of identity. These beginnings have emerged in our experience through a creative process that knows no national boundaries.

Various interpretations have been offered for these lines. A widely accepted one is that this is a genesis paradigm. But I propose that this is a unique genesis, one in which there is no God and no Satan to tempt mortals into transgression. Nor is there a pantheon of gods plotting and scheming to outdo one another, using mortals as their pawns.

In this genesis there is the world, inhabited by man and woman and transformed by them into their habitat. A genesis paradigm that does not place the human being in a permanently subservient role and that does not recognize transgression of the divine will has profound social implications. Recorded history would have been vastly different if such a beginning had been part of Western culture as it was of India's. If there is no paradise lost, there is no damnation and, as Rabindranath Tagore's father, the great Hindu philosopher Debendranath Tagore taught, in human affairs a person's mind and heart alone must rule.

I began this discussion with the hermeneutic proposition that the argumentative handling of truth-claims serves the community in the ongoing process of cultural identity. My concept of cultural identity is that of a dynamic identity, an identity that has a centre, but a *moving* centre. Dynamic cultural identity constitutes a changing horizon in the sense that it is, above all, a living set of ideas about the self and the self's community. Without a doubt, the dynamic cultural identity of the United States, for example, draws from both logical identity and Platonic identity, but its parameters are constantly changing, as a detached observer can easily recognize. It follows that the very life force in a dynamic concept of cultural identity comes from ideas that are proposed, contested, accepted, or negated regarding the self's relation to the community. Conflicts among literary interpretations address particular issues that are significant to specific communities, but because the fundamental stakes are common to all communities, cultural intertextuality traverses the world with so much ease that Marshall McLuhan's global village becomes an appropriate historical indicator of our times.

Phenomenological hermeneutics examines the literary text in the context of the linguistic community where it originated. This examination entails continuous cultural interchange. The movement of texts and ideas among linguistic communities is so wide-ranging and so complex that the very idea of linguistic isolation today, even for the tribes of the deep Amazon Basin, is patently absurd. We can measure the extent of our refigurative understanding of a text by the fullness of our appreciation of the context in which that text was made and the community in which it is received.

Meaningful human action takes place within a linguistic community that shares the same values and prejudices and interpretations of common events. Only within this aggregation of collective memory do cultural identities emerge – identities that can be in conflict with others that occupy the same space, as we know well from Israeli-occupied Palestine and the break-up of Yugoslavia. Radical bifurcations in cultural identity can have tragic consequences, for example, the Spanish Civil War (1936–9). Deepening fissures in a cultural identity can give rise to political parties that coalesce around the resulting differences. But even in the case of the violent self-destruction of a cultural community, we must recognize that such polarities and conflicts are part of the same identity. With regard to Spain, the war against Napoleonic France at the beginning of the nineteenth century, and the Carlist conflicts that punctuated that century, help us understand how, under specific circumstances, a people is capable of tearing itself apart. The cultural intertext I have used here offers us a means for moving in and out of the dynamic centre of gravity that a cultural identity constitutes.

The cultural intertext would be of marginal significance were it not for the powerful role it plays in the development of popular culture, primarily in the making of images of hierarchy and images of governance. These images, be they national symbols or social stereotypes, always have great potential to displace truth, justice, and social equality. What these remarks bring to my argument is the problematic of social reality. The same culture has two faces within its own domain and it also projects a duality outside. This reflects a drive for survival and continuation as well as an insatiable need for self-expression. It is all too clear for historians that a culture can be both beautiful and monstrous. What interests me here is how this duality is exported to other cultures.

The cultural intertext necessarily changes when it is "exported" because it moves into different discursive communities. The vast differences that separate, say, India, Spain, and Mexico must be pondered if we seriously intend to understand the transmission and power of the cultural intertext. One way for us to cope with the multiple contexts in which the cultural intertext moves is to examine not the author's intended target but rather the possibility for the reader to make sense of the intrusion from another culture. Even the simplest configuration of the social dimensions for the cultural intertext has an affective component. Cultural contexts other than that of the author can be neither predicted nor controlled, and this fact leads directly to a situation in which unanticipated variables are capable of generating chaos. What *is* largely predictable are the culturally derived targets in the originating point of the intertext sequence. The culturally intended reading of the text depends overwhelmingly on cultural indicators shared by the author and the reader. For example, a specific text may have been meant as ironic or playful, but when such a text is exported into a culture that lacks the necessary cultural indicators for the ironic reversal, the cultural intertext mutates.

Cultural intertextuality as an integral part of the making of the world we live in covers the entire range of discursive practices and cannot be approached as simple usage of loan words or images. The model proposed here reflects a non-linear approach to cultural reality, one that recognizes the full extent of the present crises in theories of representation. Culture is thus seen as a construct of collective identity and value exchange. The fundamental failure of past models was that they amounted to attempts to move towards universal subjectivity. Our hermeneutics situates the community in specific material reality, has a commitment to the historically specific, and, consequently, narrates the history of cultural intertextuality.

When does a group become a community? Hannah Arendt gives basic orientation: "It is when shared values lead to the collective action of acting in concert toward the ends of the common good, that the group has moved toward a greater unity which can continue as long as the shared traditions and values are kept alive" (*Crises*, 143). It is undoubtedly true that literature and, especially, cinema play a fundamental role in keeping shared values alive or calling them into question, as the case may be.

4. Explanation and Understanding of the Visual Metaphor

The goal of interpretation is to produce understanding so that specific meanings can be shared with other readers. But whose understanding is at stake, and what has supposedly been understood? We might answer: Some aspects of texts that have been taken by the critic-interpreter to have meaning. But we must not fall into the common trap of postulating that everything has meaning, for there are many things that do *not* have meaning, and this is so not because they are hermetic or unintelligible, but because the application of meaning to them is not warranted. It is a logical error to hold that anything that can be described can be interpreted and evaluated, for not everything has a meaning to it. I can describe a geometrical shape such as a square or a cube, I may even engage in a discussion of how well a specific version of a square meets my description, but all of this is meaningless unless the object described has a function. Interpretation is on a separate ontological level than either description or evaluation.

According to Ricoeur, interpretation is a conscious operation whether formally or informally constituted and denotes the basic operations of *explanation* and *understanding*. The objects of our attention can be taken up by explanation, but not all explanations will be satisfactory. To explain is to remove the strangeness from the object being considered, to make it more familiar. The call to explain is not usually a request to redescribe unknown objects, but rather to clarify how these objects fit into the critic-interpreter's context. When these objects fit into our context, they have meaning.

I begin this inquiry into the nature of interpretation with a closer examination of the normal activity we designate as explanation. When I say something that is unclear to my intended recipient and I am asked to explain what I have said, I respond by elaborating on what I take to be the context of my remarks and the situation I intend to bring about in this context through my statements. In doing so, I am attempting to remove the strangeness that caused the lack of understanding. When historical events or natural phenomena are explained, the speaker attempts to place them in the context of the known or to fit them into a broader scientific or philosophical framework. Individual objects do not usually call for explanation; the task of explanation comes into play only when there is a problem in fitting those objects into an established context. Thus, the context the explanation addresses is a requisite condition for meaning. That is why painters and other artists are so often unable to explain their works: the intelligible context in question belongs primarily to the recipient and not to the producer. If the explanation of a work of art is related to its historical context, there is the problem of distinct contexts, for the historical context of a work is the context of the producer and not usually the recipient. If a personal context is used, then once again, there is a problem of differing contexts, for the context called upon is that of the critic-interpreter and not that of the recipients of the work of art. There is also the possibility that the explanation for the work of art will be given on the basis of the technical tradition used in its production. Here the explanation attempts to show how the work has been put together, and thus the context is the system of relationships between the work itself and other related works. This mode of explanation has a practical advantage and a degree of validity, but because it essentially evades the question of what is in the work itself that makes it a work of art and not just another man-made composition, a gain in meaning is not faced.

If explanation is social in its basic origin and purpose, understanding is individual in its basic orientation. But it is because of the confrontation between explanation and understanding that interpretation can be a shared meaning. The encounter of explanation and understanding is the dynamic source of the act of criticism. Interpretation is here characterized as a highly specialized commentary written for readers interested in the work of art.

Interpretation expresses the general process of explanation and understanding. Explanation ends when meaning has been conveyed and understanding appears to be complete. The problem is that understanding is never complete. Thus, to interpret a work of art is to appropriate here and now its intentionality. To explain is to bring out the structure of the work of art – that is, to comment on its internal organization in the context of the tradition of art.

In practice, critic-interpreters vary in the direction they give interpretation. That direction ranges from extensive explanation with only summary conclusions to a brief explanation followed by a thoroughly argued sense of understanding. But in all cases the movement between explanation and understanding is the force that produces the interpretation.

In an interview published in French in 1995 (*Critic and Conviction*, 171ff), Ricoeur was asked why he so rarely wrote about his love of art and music. His response opens another window onto our understanding of his hermeneutics. He reminds us that when we experience a work of art, we are in the presence of the artist's intention to signify much more than a topical reference. The multiple meanings derived from the viewer's aesthetic experience are united only in the work itself. The explosion of meanings is limitless, since it materializes in each encounter with each person experiencing the work of art. In other words, our interpretation of a work of art is but a temporary and limited attempt to capture the rush of significance. The aesthetic experience itself is more interesting than any interpretation and can only be described as the explosive encounter of the person viewing it and the work itself. In this experience, polysemia rules. The work of art is in movement as long as we are in the encounter.

In a later question, the interviewers asked Ricoeur who his favourite artists were. His list was long and varied, with a marked preference for twentieth-century abstract painters, but including some sculptors: Pierre Soulages, Alfred Manessier, Jean Bazaine, Piet Mondrain, Wassily Kandinsky, Paul Klee, Joan Miró, Jackson Pollock, Francis Bacon, Marc Chagall, Jacques Lipchitz, Jean Arp, Anton Pevsner, Constantin Brancusi, Henry Moore, Yves Tanguy, and Antoni Tàpies.

Ricoeur was asked why he so strongly preferred twentieth-century non-figurative art. He answered that for years he had rejected classical painting until he went to a 1994 grand exhibition of works by Nicolas

Poussin (1594–1665), an artist greatly admired by Picasso. It was as if he was seeing this French master for the first time. An eye trained in non-figurative art can focus on the extraordinary play of colour and line and the perfect balance between these elements. His objection to classical art had to do with its predisposition to narrativize, as if the scene being depicted was a mere illustration. A good example of Ricoeur's non-figurative perspective on Poussin involves *The Assumption of the Virgin* (1626), now in the National Gallery in Washington, D.C. In that painting, three cherubs fill the Virgin's tomb with flowers, which take the place of the risen body. The Virgin is accompanied in her ascent by numerous small children, who, unlike the cherubs, do not have wings. The Virgin looks to heaven in ecstasy while two of the small children pull back the clouds as if they were draperies, revealing the beatific vision only to her eyes. The painting displays a mastery in capturing movement. The twisting, turning, swerving children lead our eye up towards the divine vision, which is just out of sight. All of this swerving and twisting is controlled in turn by two Greek columns, which vertically frame the central scene together with the horizontal lines of the open tomb in the painting's foreground. The use of lines to frame the scene, and the multiple curves that lead us up to the hidden vision and the floating body of the Virgin, are an expression of movement frozen in time within a balanced frame of line and colour. It is in this context that Ricoeur recalls Picasso's admiration.

But Ricoeur's most telling statement in this part of the interview comes when he names Pierre Soulages (1919–), Alfred Manessier (1911–93), and Jean Bazaine (1904–2001) as particularly important artists. These three painters were of the same generation, contemporaries of Ricoeur; all were French abstract painters in the loosely defined postwar "School of Paris." Although they worked with sharp independence from one another, they had faced common experiences: the Second World War, the German Occupation (1939–45), and the intellectual leadership of Emmanuel Mounier (1905–50), who was very close to Ricoeur.

Mounier had argued since 1934 that artists must be free from any form of indoctrination, be it fascism, communism, or even Catholicism. In the dark days of the German Occupation, he argued with great conviction that individual liberty is essential to artistic creation if people are to survive in spirit as well as in body. In *Personalism* he wrote that

> the excess of labour in our lives still hides from us the fact that the poetic life constitutes a central aspect of personality, and ought to be reckoned as

> essential as our daily bread. Transcendent as it is, sublime in the proper sense of the word, art cannot be reduced either to the greed for sensation of the intoxication of life, nor is it, when embodied in its works, reducible to the pure contemplation of the idea, nor to the constructive power of the mind. It is the sensitive expression, throughout the whole range of our existence, of life's intimately unexpected character. (77–8)

Ricoeur met Mounier in 1932 when he was studying philosophy at the University of Rennes. Then after the war he began to attend the conferences organized by Mounier at Châtenay-Malabry. The primary role that Mounier assigned to art as a means to enrich life is strongly visible in Ricoeur's concept of art.

The postwar painters Ricoeur singled out have attested to the intellectual and political debt they owe to Mounier. Their work, which Ricoeur knew so well, helps us discern a pattern in Ricoeur's appreciation of their painting. Jean Bazaine, the oldest of the three, once wrote that

> this temptation to draw forth from oneself what for the world is shapeless and unsettling, the very signs, the scars of one's most secret inner movements, has been the painter's *raison d'être* since painters have existed. But it cannot mean that forms (and combinations of forms) from nature are to be rejected, for the forms on the canvas, as nonfigurative as they may be, even when they pass through us and leave us, have to come from somewhere. *Art of our Century* (in Ferrier and Le Pichon, 481)

A good example of Bazaine's work, much admired by Ricoeur, is *Il Palombaro* (1949), now in the Ludwig Museum. The artist has used the elements derived from Cubism, but the painting is one of rhythms in line and colour, and just beneath the surface is a play of natural forms. It was this primordial revelation of movement that Ricoeur praised.

In 1941, Parisian artist Alfred Manessier joined Jean Bazaine and others in occupied Paris to form the group "Twenty Young Painters in the French Tradition" to advocate individual liberty as essential to art. His paintings, such as *Nuit de Gethsémani* (1952), tap natural forms as a distant source; they are compositions of elaborate relations of line, curve, and colour. Ricoeur was attracted by the indeterminate open polysemia of Manessier and Bazaine, which defies narrativization.

Perhaps the most intriguing of the three artists for Ricoeur was Pierre Soulages, whose artistic career had marked parallels with that of Ricoeur himself. Almost seven years younger than Ricoeur, Soulages emerged from the war's cruelties refusing to paint anecdotal or documentary canvases. His paintings are stark, are mostly monochromatic, as we can see in *Composition* (1949), now hanging in Centre Pompidou in Paris. Soulages explains his work and, in the course of these remarks, provides us with powerful clues for linking his work to that of Ricoeur:

> If the involuntary figurative anecdote is not to be found in my painting, no doubt it is because of the importance given in it to rhythm, to that throbbing of forms in space, to that cutting up of space by time. Time seems to me to be one of the preoccupations expressed in my painting; time seems to me to be at the center of my approach to painting, time and its relationship with space. (in Ferrier and Le Pichon, 687)

The artist's intentions, like the viewer's explanations, reduce the painting to only one aspect of its almost limitless expressions. Both the explanation of the artist and that of the critic do not even begin to penetrate the enigma the painting represents. A painting constantly takes from other representations, and in so doing it produces the multiple and limited meanings we ascribe to it. Soulages states his credo clearly: "I have always thought that the more limited the means, the stronger the expression: That may explain the choice of a small palette" (687). This is without question a phenomenological approach to painting: "Because painting is an adventure into the world, it signifies the world. Because it is a synthesis, it signifies it in its totality" (687). Soulages believed that if in figurative painting an artist introduces reciprocal relationships with the world, in the case of non-figurative painting the artist "introduces other relationships: For viewer and painter alike, the world is no longer looked upon but lived, it has become part of the experience they have of it" (687). He sees his own art as markedly differing from figurative painting: "There is no human faith more exalting than that which draws a great deal of humble attention to what is born rather than attempting to codify the past only to invent a future just like it" (687). He concludes in the spirit of Ricoeur: "It seems to me that what happens in a painting which, from an object in the making, suddenly comes alive, defies description" (687).

In the hermeneutics of painting we have a phenomenon akin to photosynthesis in plants: the presence of light converts carbon dioxide into oxygen; in the same way, when we look at a work of art, the viewer's perception of and reaction to the artist's figuration is a process of configuration whereby the viewer converts the artist's imagery into the viewer's own repertoire of meaningful images. Art interpretation comments on this process of appropriation.

To return to the question the interviewers first asked: Why had Ricoeur not written about art and painting in particular? His answer was simple: he *had* done so, but not in a French publication. In 1973, he had travelled to Forth Worth, Texas, where he gave a series of lectures that were later published in English as *Interpretation Theory* (1976). I cite some of the relevant passages:

> Far from yielding less than the original, pictorial activity may be characterized in terms of an "iconic augmentation," where the strategy of painting, for example, is to reconstruct reality on the basis of a limited optic alphabet. This strategy of contraction and miniaturization yields more by handling less. In this way, the main effect of painting is to resist the entropic tendency of ordinary vision – the shadow image of Plato – and to increase the meaning of the universe by capturing it in the network of its abbreviated signs. (40–1)

> Because the painter could master a new alphabetic material – because he was a chemist, distillator, varnisher and glazer – he was able to write a new text of reality. Painting for the Dutch masters was neither the reproduction nor the production of the universe, but its metamorphosis. (41)

> Impressionism and abstract art, as well, proceed more and more boldly to the abolition of natural forms for the sake of a merely constructed range of elementary signs whose combinatory forms will rival ordinary vision. With abstract art, painting is close to science in that it challenges perceptual forms by relating them to non-perceptual structures. The graphic capture of the universe, here too, is served by a radical denial of the immediate. Painting seems only to "produce," no longer to "reproduce." But it catches up with reality at the level of its elements, as does the God of the *Timaeus*. Constructivism is only the boundary case of a process of augmentation where the apparent denial of reality is the condition for the glorification of the non-figurative essence of things. Iconicity, then, means the revelation of a real more real than ordinary reality. (42)

Ricoeur's marked preference for abstract painting has deep philosophical roots and is part of his ontology, which is fully expressed in

Temps et récit (III, 88) and *Soi-même comme un autre*. The configuration of the work of art and the binding together of elements of its expression are not possible if the artist and the viewer do not share a prefiguration of the world. It is in refiguration that the viewer's partial comprehension of the configurational act can be conveyed to others, with the basic understanding that this is not the aesthetic experience itself, but only a by-product that adds to the range of possibilities for the work of art, which is inexhaustible. The artist sets out not to copy the world but to create it; this is so with all great artists from the earliest to the abstract painters Ricoeur so admires. The act of creation must overcome the limitations of the canvas; it must not just capture but transcend a moment in time. Ricoeur explains this challenge in *Temps et récit:* "An even more intractable aporia ... has to do with the ultimate unrepresentability of time, which makes even phenomenology continually turn to metaphors and to the language of myth, in order to talk about the upsurge of the present or the flowing of the unitary flux of time" (III, 243). But the painter must translate his iconic forms into a myth, and to do so, he must make the objects represented merely heuristic devices, in order to reach back into the prefigurative of experience. Or, as in the case of abstract painters like Soulages, the artist must do away with the figurative altogether, in order to create new figurative dimensions for himself and the viewer. As early as 1952, in "The Wish and Endeavor for Unity," Ricoeur had set out the basic thought for these ideas on art, which he would later recognize as applying to Soulages's work:

> For this primordial stratum of all experience is the always pre-existing reality; it is always-already-before and I come too late to express it. The world is the word I have on the tip of my tongue which I will never express; it is there, but scarcely have I begun to say it when it is already the world of the scientist, the world of the artist and the world of such and such an artist: of Van Gogh, of Cézanne, of Matisse, of Picasso.
>
> The unity of the "world" is too prior to be possessed, too lived to be known. It vanishes as soon as it is recognized. This is perhaps why a phenomenology of perception, which would try to furnish us with the philosophy of our being-in-the-world, is a wager akin to the quest for paradise. The unity of the world against which all "attitudes" stand out is merely the *horizon* of all these attitudes. (*History and Truth*, 194)

Ricoeur is fascinated by the creative process of the painter as he makes his world, which he suggests is the artist's configuration as it is derived from the prefigurative he shares with his viewers. He turns to the historian Louis O. Mink and his seminal article "History and Fiction as Modes of Comprehension" to develop what we refer to as the configurational act and to expand beyond writing to the iconic creation of the painter. From *Temps et récit*:

> What system of a priori concepts organizes an experience that otherwise would remain chaotic. Plato aims at this categoreal comprehension, as do most systematic philosophers. The configurational mode [proposed by Louis O. Mink] puts its elements into a single, concrete complex of relations ... Comprehension in the broad sense is defined as the act "of grasping together in a single mental act things which are not experienced together, or even capable of being so experienced, because they are separated by time, space or logical kind." In short, "comprehension is an individual act of seeing-things-together, and only that." (I, 159)

A Soulages painting in its particular configuration sees things together and not as discrete units. It thus becomes an inexhaustible source for creation in the configurative act of the viewer. The viewer's configuration of the iconic metaphor becomes for Ricoeur a profound experience equal to a religious vision. Again I quote from *Interpretation Theory*:

> My experience [viewing a painting] cannot directly become your experience. An event belonging to one stream of consciousness cannot be transferred as such into another stream of consciousness. Yet, nevertheless, something [of what I experienced] passes from me to you. Something is transferred from one sphere of life to another. This something is not the experience as experienced, but its meaning. Here is the miracle. The experience as experienced, as lived, remains private, but its sense, its meaning, becomes public. (16)

These iconic metaphors cannot be described because they are not translatable; rather, they create their own meanings in the viewer's response. The viewer experiences them as a kind of chain reaction: each nascent meaning calls forth another metaphor, and another; each stays alive long enough to conserve its power to evoke a whole. Yet each has the ability to engender a conceptual diversity, an unlimited number of potential interpretations at a conceptual level in the viewer's experience.

This iconic polysemy of abstract art would seem to rule out any meaningful role for the commentator, be he the artist himself or a critic. It would seem that there *is* no refiguration, that the aesthetic experience a work of art offers is sharply restricted to the individual viewer confronting the painting. Ricoeur's response is one of the most important developments in twentieth-century criticism of art and literature. I cite from "Structure, Word, Event," first published in *Esprit* (1967), then in translation in *Philosophy Today* (1968), and finally collected in *The Conflict of Interpretations* (1974):

> The phenomenon of polysemy is incomprehensible if we do not introduce a dialectic between sign and use, between structure and event ... It is the most interesting [case] because we thereby marvelously come upon what I have called the exchanges between the structures and the event. In fact this process presents itself as a convergence of two distinct factors, a factor of expansion and, at the same time, of surcharge. (93)

Throughout this book I have gone to great lengths to point out direct or indirect concordances between Unamuno and Ricoeur. With regard to painting, Ricoeur is the philosopher and Unamuno the poet. Unamuno did not contribute to art criticism, but he did give us a long poem that articulated his experience as the viewer of a painting – Diego Velázquez's starkly powerful *Christ on the Cross* – contrasting it with the other painting of the Crucifixion attributed to Velázquez (now in Museo Nacional del Prado). The viewer has turned poet, whose role is more than commentator. Unamuno as poet recognizes his place in the almost limitless expansion of art in the refiguration of life. Ricoeur's comments on the richness of reflection are Unamunian although they were made without his being familiar with Unamuno's poetic reflections. Ricoeur writes: "Reflection is blind intuition if it is not mediated by what Dilthey called the expressions in which life objectifies itself. Or, to use the language of Jean Nabert, reflection is nothing other than the appropriation of our act of existing by means of a critique applied to the works and the acts that are the signs of this act of existing" (*The Conflict*, 17).

Finally, this miracle of art, this aesthetic experience of the viewer and subsequent expansion of that experience, is impossible without freedom for the artist, the viewer, and the viewer as commentator – in other words the figuration, configuration, and refiguration of the work of art. Ricoeur's philosophy of art begins with the viewer's dialectic of engagement, but as we have also pointed out, the horizon of the community is always in the background. Nowhere does he state this more clearly than in *Freud and Philosophy*:

> The constitution of the self is not completed in an economics and a politics, but continues on into the region of culture. Here too the psychology of personality grasps only the shadow, that is to say, the aim, present in each man, of being respected, approved, and recognized as a person. My existence for myself is dependent on this constitution of self in the opinion of others; "my self" is shaped by the opinion and acceptance of others. But this constitution of subjects, this mutual constitution through opinion, is guided by new figures which may be said to be "objective" in a new sense. These objects are no longer things, as are the objects in the sphere of having; they do not always have corresponding institutions, as do the objects in the sphere of power. These new figures of man are to be found in the works and monuments of law, art and literature. The exploration of man's possibilities extends into this new kind of objectivity, the objectivity of cultural objects properly so-called. Even when Van Gogh paints a chair, he at the same time portrays the absent man; he projects a figure of a man, namely the man who "has" this represented world. Thus, the various modes of cultural expression give these "images" the density of "thingness"; they make these images exist between men and among men, by embodying them in "works." It is through the medium of these works and monuments that a human dignity and self-regard are formed. (509–10)

Unamuno on Painting

In the vast sweep of Unamuno's works, one text stands out as a masterpiece in the interpretation of painting: the poem *Cristo de Velázquez* (1920). Unamuno wrote this long poem of 2,540 verses over a ten-year period as a meditation on Velázquez's *Cristo Crucificado* (1632), which Philip IV donated to the Benedictine convent of St Placido. Since 1829 it has been in the Museo del Prado. There is a somewhat similar painting from 1614 by the court painter Francisco Pacheco. The contrast between Pacheco's painting and Velázquez's is striking. The Velázquez painting is minimalist; there is only the body of Christ on the cross, and the background is completely black. The figure of Christ is illuminated, especially the torso. There is a glow around Christ's head. It is a huge painting, 2.48 by 1.69 metres. Unamuno saw in this painting a dialectic of an almost overwhelming image of death accepted. His poem describes the body of Christ in detail, with a wealth of symbolism from centuries of texts on the divinity of Christ and the difficult acceptance of his death.

The painting's most striking aspect is the dialectic between what it shows and what it does not. There is no blood, no lacerated body, nor is there any sign of the physical agony of the Crucifixion. The serenity the painting emanates is in direct contrast to the bloody representations of Christ on the cross so popular in Spain and in Spanish America. The serenity of Unamuno's interpretation represents Christ's calm acceptance of death. There is a powerful dialectic between the rage against death so often expressed by Unamuno and the soft, calm acceptance of death as necessary. One is reminded of K's inexplicable acceptance of death in Franz Kafka's *The Trial*. But what is an enigma in Kafka's work is here a sacrifice offered by Christ, who has willingly gone to his death as the Paschal Lamb to redeem mankind from finality. The ensuing dialectic between absent rage and calm acceptance, between finality and the promise of the Resurrection, between rational rejection of the Resurrection and faith, comes forth not as an either/or but as living unto death, which means living this life in such a way that death will be a tragedy because of the loss to our others.

Unamuno's sources of his meditation on Velázquez's painting are largely Protestant liberal thinkers of the nineteenth century, especially Carl Harnack (*Lehrbach der Dogmengeschichte*, 2nd edition, 1894) and Albrecht Ritschl (*Die christliche Lehre vonder Rechtfertigung und Versöhnung*, 1874). Nelson R. Orringer's full study of these sources is *Unamuno y los protestantes liberales* (1985). The most complete study of Unamuno's poem is J. Guillermo Renart's *El Cristo de Velázquez de Unamuno* (1982).

Notwithstanding the obvious differences between Ricoeur's approach to painting and Unamuno's poetic response to Velázquez's painting, they share this ground: each philosopher's dialectic gives priority to the viewer's configuration and rejects narrative determinations that are alien to the experience of the artwork. Ricoeur approached nonfigurative art as a primordial invitation for the viewer to create his or her own vision; Unamuno's dialectic between the image and the absent but implicit image of the tortured body of Christ forces the viewer to either grapple with the distance between the visible serenity and the implicit rage or look away. In both philosophers, however, the visual image achieves its fulfilment in the viewers' interpretation.

Let us ask again to what extent painting is a factor in the cultural expression of a community. Does painting have the power of refiguration that we recognize in literature? Has the graphic declaration of freedom by Soulages and his colleagues resonated in the cultural identity of France, or is its significance confined to a select minority of art critics? The complexity of the cultural network has many minor and major discursive elements. Our task in hermeneutics is to include as many as we can in our discussion of refiguration.

5. Ricoeur's Hermeneutics

In 2005 the work of Paul Ricoeur came to an end. We have now had time to reread and rethink his philosophy. This section is in fact a postscript. It is the result of rereading my previous work on Ricoeur and rethinking his *La métaphore vive* (1975) and *Temps et récit* (1983–5). This overview has taken a year to complete and is contemporaneous with the completion of this book in 2014. At the centre of this rereading is the question of the place of literary works in the quest to understand time and create new meaning. Ricoeur wrote: "What fails is not thinking, in any acceptation of this term, but the impulse, or to put it better, the hubris that impels our thinking to posit itself as the master of meaning. Thinking encounters this failure not only on the occasion of the enigma of evil but also when time, escaping our will to mastery, surges forth on the side of what, in one way or another, is the true master of meaning" (*Temps et récit*, III, 261).

Over somewhat more than forty years, Ricoeur achieved what no other philosopher had accomplished before. He developed a philosophy of interpretation of human action, beginning with the subject as defined by his or her action in the social group, followed by the discursive manifestation of this cohabitation, and culminating in an examination of the subject's sharing of the world through the common practice of world-making as the social prefiguration of narrativity.

Ricoeur is such a formidable thinker because of his extraordinary knowledge and use of the classics of Western philosophy. He considers Augustine's *Confessions* and Aristotle's *Physics* to be the dual sources of our tradition. They are very different – one is Greek, the other biblical – but they come together as our philosophical heritage. Ricoeur puts it this way: "Western thought has two archaic inspirations: the Greek and the Hebraic. It is in the background of Augustine's phenomenology that we hear the voice of the second one, just as we heard the voice of the first one in the background of Aristotle's *Physics*. The inscrutability of time, but also the diversity of figures of what is beyond time, give rise to thought for a second time" (*Temps et récit,* III, 264).

The story of Ricoeur's development of a comprehensive philosophy of language begins in 1948, the year he was appointed Chair of Philosophy at the University of Strasbourg. He began a rereading of the philosophical tradition, a project that clearly prefigured two characteristics underpinning all his subsequent work: a clear attachment to rationalism, and a concentration on the affective and volitional dimensions of human life. This trajectory at once set him apart from the directions taken in the Parisian milieu of Barthes, Derrida, and Foucault, but it was also the basis for his rational "rapprochement" with post-structuralism decades later.

Le volontaire et l'involontaire (1950) follows Edmund Husserl's method but also gives indications of Ricoeur's independence from Husserl's strict analytic approach. Ricoeur concerned himself with the body and with the situatedness of a consciousness. He recognized the need for a detour through the empirical social sciences demanded by the very situatedness of the human body, but his aim unequivocally remained self-understanding. In 1955 he published *Histoire et vérité*. This was his first, but not his last, attempt to develop an ethics of social action. The two-volume *Finitude et culpabilité* (1960) consisted of *L'homme faillible* and *La symbolique du mal*. In the latter book Ricoeur made a bold move away from Husserl's phenomenology and turned his full attention to the philosophy of language and to hermeneutics. This new direction resulted in *De l'interprétation: Essai sur Freud* (1965). Ricoeur's emerging hermeneutic theory was featured in the introduction to this work and subsequently developed through a series of essays that were published in book form as *Le conflit des interprétations* (1969). He argued that understanding is achieved only through the dialectic of opposing perspectives, which transcends the fossilized position each perspective has inherited. The dialectic is an open-ended contest that is never resolved but nevertheless elucidates the positions of both participants.

In May 1971, Ricoeur embarked on the new hermeneutics when he delivered the lecture "From Existentialism to the Philosophy of Language." This was later published as the appendix to the English translation of *La métaphore vive*. He gave the following explanation: "The kind of hermeneutics which I now favour starts from the recognition of the objective meaning of the text as distinct from the subjective intention of the author. This objective meaning is not something hidden behind the text. *Rather it is a requirement addressed to the reader*. The interpretation accordingly is a kind of obedience to this injunction starting from the text" (emphasis mine). This new hermeneutics was directed to what the encounter between text and reader opened up, what the engagement disclosed. He was still at the beginning of this radical shift within hermeneutics, and a number of major challenges lay ahead for him, including exchanges with his post-structuralist contemporaries, Foucault and Derrida.

In his next three books – *La métaphore vive* (1975), *Interpretation Theory* (1976), and *Temps et récit* (1983–5) – Ricoeur developed the hermeneutic post-structuralist response to Derrida and Foucault. In *La métaphore vive* he moves us away from the rhetoric of metaphor, which treats metaphor as a trope of resemblance to the semantic viewpoint, which is differentiated from the rhetorical one because the framework of word is replaced by that of the sentence; thus metaphor is now more than a trope, it is an impertinent predication. And this philosophical trajectory culminates in a third level: the hermeneutic point of view. The move now is from the level of the sentence to that of the text, poem, novel, or essay. The viewpoint changes correspondingly from that of rhetoric, wherein the problem to be considered is the form of metaphor as a figure of speech; to that of semantics, where the issue is metaphoric sense; and finally to that of hermeneutic, where the concern is the reference of metaphor and its power to redescribe reality. This last position was in complete opposition to the intellectual fashion of the day, which held poetic discourse to be essentially non-referential and centred on itself.

Ricoeur's achievement in *La métaphore vive* was to introduce the concept of split-reference, which is the foundation of a post-deconstruction hermeneutics. Ricoeur is speaking of two worlds, one of which is fictional because it is projected by the work. It is the world of the work. But as readers who concretize the work, we also belong to the world of praxis in which we live, and the two are completely entwined. On the one hand, the world of the fictional work can only be constituted insofar as the reader has a world of praxis from which to draw the necessary assumptions that fill out the fictional discourse. On the other, the reader as reader displays her or his action so that the actual world is the world of praxis. Reading a poetic text is the decisive intersection between the world of the work and the world of actual praxis, because it is through the engagement that there is a transfer from the fictional world to the real world. Works of literature are closed systems only when they are not read. A work that is read is caught up in the tension between the two worlds. The reader engaged in the act of reading follows a trajectory of meaning as the dynamic course of the text is once more brought to life; the reader not only rekindles it but extends it beyond the text into the world of praxis. The structuralist distinction between the inside and outside of the text has been created by a methodological decision that is quite removed from the act of reading itself. But the eradication of the inside/outside dichotomy is also arbitrary because of its insistence that there is no stable meaning of the poetic text and therefore no possible shared meaning.

Ricoeur unequivocally states that it is the task of his hermeneutics to reopen this closure and to reinsert the world of the text into the world of praxis, fully recognizing that not everything is a text and that all texts belong to a culture. By reopening the arbitrary closure imposed on literature, he goes far beyond the interpretation of the poetic text; he takes on the task of formulating a hermeneutics of willed action. As early as 1971, he began to sketch out the problem of interpretation of willed action in his lecture "The Model of the Text: Meaningful Action Considered as a Text" (1971), but it was not until the publication of the three volumes of *Temps et récit* that his works' comprehensive design became apparent. In an interview with Charles Reagan in 1982, by which time the first volume had already been completed, he made this significant observation on his hermeneutics: "that not everything is a text in the sense that texts themselves are the product of a culture and have an origin, a truth, and also implications and effects in life and human action" (105).

The reinsertion of texts into the world of praxis is itself part of the process of reality that hermeneutics recognizes. Ricoeur's ontological model is that of a spiral that accounts for both change and continuity in temporal identity. In ontological terms the text begins not with an author but with the reader. It is the reader who responds to the demands of the text and, in so doing, makes the textual world. This is the point of entry into the cycle of creation and re-creation. The configuration of the text is similar to our configuration of the action we perceive or the stories we are told, which are also texts. The dynamic course of the text does not, however, end with its rendering, for the reader prolongs the dynamic encounter beyond the text itself and into the world of praxis by talking and writing about the configuration of the text. In other words, the idea of the inside and the outside of the text is rejected. The configuration of the text is a form of mediation between the individual and the community of readers to which the reader belongs. The act of reading (or hearing the oral text) has the powerful potential of creative interpolarity. By reading we interpolate the world of the text, which may begin as an unlearned experience of imaginative response but can proceed to the learned experience of reflection and into the ongoing praxis of living.

The highest achievement of an author's text is, therefore, to become a mediator between the reader and his world, between the reader and members of the community, and between the reader and himself or herself. It is this mediating stage in the process of communication that generates the refiguration of reflective response. Refiguration is the realization of the mediating potential that the text has released. We refigure the text when we talk or write about the configuration experience. We write and speak for others and to others and thus invite dialogue about the configuration of the text. It would be naive to say that the dialogue is about the text, as this would beg the question of whose text is under consideration. The engagement in communicative exchange about these matters is generally what we consider literary criticism to be, and it is the tradition of such exchanges that we invoke in the name of literary criticism, for the critic or commentator can equally call into the debate Theodor Adorno or Matthew Arnold as well respond to Richard Rorty or Stanley Cavell.

Both in the tradition itself and in the quotidian substratum of a community's sense of itself, there is, of course, a cumulative effect to these exchanges and debates. Such collective identity bespeaks values and ideologies that are often in conflict. This collective matrix of the community's linguistic make-up is the prefigurative that has made it possible for a reader to read a text and to respond to its implicit and explicit referentiality. Ontologically speaking, Ricoeur concludes that fictional characters have life stories with pasts no less real than those of historical figures. The cycle of world-making is constant: the cultural community lives in discourse and produces texts that embody that discourse; the reader is able to reinsert the text into praxis because he or she shares the prefigurative with the author's text; finally, readers reflect on the configurative experience of making the text, and this reflection is what can be shared with others and thereby replenish the matrix of the prefigurative. There is a constant loss and gain in the process, but there are also ideas and textual sources that go on generating new responses.

It is from these pages that one can draw out the fuller implications of Ricoeur's hermeneutics to date. Ricoeur identifies three major features of the hermeneutics of the self. (1) The reflective process of hermeneutics must move in its interpretive purpose through a series of analytical examinations into the purported problems of interpretation. This important first feature reasserts Ricoeur's fundamental premise of rational inquiry. (2) The hermeneutics of self engages in the dialectic of selfhood and sameness. This feature clearly distances the hermeneutics of self from the philosophies of the *cogito:* "To say self is not to say I. The I is posited – or is deposed. The self is implied reflexively in the operations, the analysis of which precedes the return toward this self" (*Soi-même comme un autre,* 18). (3) The final dialectic is that of selfhood and otherness. The significance here is that the otherness Ricoeur delineates is not the otherness of comparison but rather the otherness that is constitutive of selfhood as such. Thus Ricoeur argues that the selfhood of oneself implies otherness to such an intimate degree that one cannot be thought of without the other (*Soi-même comme un autre,* 20). To these three features Ricoeur puts four questions that will be the working stations of the hermeneutics: (a) Who is speaking? (b) Who is acting? (c) Who is talking about himself or herself? (d) Who is the moral subject of imputation?

The implications of the hermeneutics of the self extend into a number of fields: political science, sociology, law, and the ethics of all of these. Ricoeur writes: "It is this search for equality in the midst of inequality, whether the latter results from a particular cultural and political condition, as in friendship between unequals, or whether it is constitutive of the initial positions of the self and the other in the dynamics of solicitude, as this defrays the place of solicitude along the trajectory of ethics" (*Soi-même comme un autre,* 192).

Ricoeur's hermeneutic argument moves to the exchange between esteem for oneself and solicitude for others, which "authorizes us to say that I cannot myself have self-esteem unless I esteem others *as* myself. 'As myself' means that you too are capable of starting something in the world, of acting for a reason, of hierarchizing your priorities, of evaluating the ends of your actions, and having done this, of holding yourself in esteem as I hold myself in esteem" (*Soi-meme comme un autre,* 193).

Ricoeur's last book, *Parcours de la reconnaissance* (2004), published fifteen months before his death in May 2005, consists of three expanded lectures first given in Vienna and Fribourg. Despite failing health, he was determined to finish what he considered to be his tribute to friendship. He closes the book with a quotation from Montaigne's *Essais:* "In the friendship I speak of, our souls mingle and blend with each other so completely that they efface the seam that joined them and cannot find it again. If you press me to tell why I loved him, I feel that it cannot be expressed, except by answering: because it was he, because it was I" (263). It was my privilege to be his friend and to be able to spend some time with him in the days before his death.

If Ricoeur's hermeneutics has a conflictive quality, one must also acknowledge his unwavering commitment to reciprocity, which rises above the instinctive "eye for an eye, tooth for a tooth." This transcendence of conflict is achieved through the exercise of reason, which invariably prevails in Ricoeur's philosophy.

In Ricoeur's numerous readings of texts, his hermeneutics is always open, suggesting the possibility of other readings and of readings counter to his own. In this practice we have clear evidence of the conflictive nature of interpretation, of his recognition of a counterargument, and, just as important, of his respect for the other's right to contradict and of an implicit invitation to dialogue, not in order to reject the counter-reading, but to learn from it. Ricoeur's strict discipline in writing and his modest denial of his own importance are part of a basic premise that the application of reason is the only way to engage the other so that one may enhance the possibility of dialogue and, thereby, of a shared gain in understanding.

In his analysis of narrative in both history and fiction, Ricoeur concludes that all human conceptualization of time is derived from narrative. But there are limits to narrativity that reach an impasse for the creation of new meaning. The narrative is the language of plot, the description of the purported world, and the characterization of the agents of action, in an ordered progression, but the creation of new meaning is not *in* time and is not subject to narrative order. It is here that Ricoeur complements narrative with metaphor. Only through the metaphor of lyric poetry can there be an attempt to bring to language the flux of consciousness. I cite Ricoeur again: "These metaphors in no way constitute a figurative language that we might translate into a literal language. They constitute the only language available to the work of returning toward the origin" (*Temps et récit*, III, 267).

To sum up, in *La métaphor vive* Ricoeur introduced the power to redescribe reality through metaphor, and in *Temps et récit* he developed the full process of figuration, refiguration, and prefiguration in the interpretation of narrative. The metaphor's redescription of reality and the hermeneutics of narrative figuration together give the sense of being-in-the-world.

Redescription of the world and the refiguration of the narrative constitute the exigence to think more and speak differently. The power of reflection or refiguration of memory, and the capacity to create new meaning through metaphor, are the philosophical foundation we need in order to comprehend the power of language.

At this juncture, to be clear on these matters, let us revisit Ricoeur's metaphorical redescription and the refiguration of life stories. He explains metaphorical redescription in *La métaphore vive* as the unique human capacity to overcome contradiction and imagine new meaning. T.S. Eliot has given us a classic example in *Burnt Norton*. I cite from the Faber and Faber edition of 1944:

> Or say that the end precedes the beginning,
> And the end and the beginning were always there
> Before the beginning and after the end.
> And all is always now. Words strain,
> Crack and sometimes break under the burden,
> Under the tension, slip, slide, perish,
> Decay with imprecision, will not stay in place,
> Will not stay still. (12)

The transformation of words into material objects of decay allows us to glimpse the process,

> Between un-being and being.
> Sudden in a shaft of sunlight
> Even while the dust moves
> There rises the hidden laughter
> Of children in the foliage
> Quick now, here, now, always –
> Ridiculous the waste sad time
> Stretching before and after. (13)

The metaphor forces us to step back and redescribe the reality of living. Now turning to the refiguration of the multiple figurations of narrative, the most cogent example is in Proust's *Le temps retrouvé*. The long trajectory of eight volumes of *À la recherche du temps perdu* yields numerous moments of reflection on the past. The reflection of refiguration brings the past into the present. In the revisiting of narrative, memories turn into refiguration as the narrator actualized the past.

The narrative in this last volume of eight in Proust's work is remarkable because the reader shares in the multiple figurations of lived experience, which become meditation and reflection on the meaning of life and the creative process of writing. I cite from Frederick Blossom's English translation of *The Past Recaptured*:

> One prerequisite to my book, such as I had conceived it just now in the library, was that I plumb to the very bottom impressions which I should first have to re-create with the aid of my memory (387) … The fear of ceasing to be myself had formerly caused me horror and especially with each new love that came to me – for Gilberte, for Albertine – because I could not endure the idea that one day he who had loved them would exist no longer, which would be a sort of death (389) … This dimension of time which I had once vaguely felt in the church at Combray I would try to make continually perceptible in a transcription of human life necessarily very different from that conveyed to us by our deceptive senses. There are, it is true – this was proven to me, as has been seen, by sundry episodes in this narrative – many other errors of our senses which distort for us the true aspect of this world (397) … There came over me a feeling of profound fatigue at the realization that all this long stretch of time not only had been uninterruptedly, lived, thought, secreted by me, that it was my life, my very self, but also that I must, every minute of my life, keep it closely by me, that it upheld me, that I was perched on its dizzying summit, that I could not move without carrying it about with me. (401)

This is an extraordinary narrative, one in which the configuration that narrator and reader have together devised of places, persons, and events so clearly turns into the reflection of refiguration. If configuration is the initial and essential grasping of the narrative depiction by which the reader gains a modicum of meaning, then refiguration is the reflective process that gives us depth of understanding. This movement from configuration to refiguration is the basic source of human self-awareness. The only element that must be added is the creative explosion of new meaning that metaphor gives in the redescription of reality. Such is Ricoeur's legacy to all who in reading find themselves.

Conclusion

Unamuno and Ricoeur on Making Sense: The Dialectic of Order and Disorder

Unamuno's concept of culture has been central to the thesis of this book. In *Del sentimiento trágico* he wrote this concise definition of culture: "Culture is composed of ideas and solely of ideas ... everything made was made by the word, and the Word was in the beginning" (*SW*, IV, 334, 339).

Taking Unamuno's words further, for a working definition of culture, we can say it is a changing network of discursivity. It follows that the hermeneutics of culture concerns itself with interpreting discursive practices in the history of the community in question. The problem with most cultural studies to date has been the notion that specific facets must be isolated from the whole and abstracted in order to be examined. This amounts to an autopsy of sundry cultural practices. The dynamic interchange and reality of culture has been almost entirely eclipsed by this neo-positivistic examination of cultural practices.

By taking into account Ricoeur's hermeneutics of literary refiguration as a significant factor in the cultural process, we will have completed the argument of this book. Ricoeur writes in *Soi-même comme un autre:* "The actions refigured by narrative fictions are complex ones, rich in anticipations of an ethical nature. Telling a story, we observed, is deploying an imaginary space for thought experiments in which moral judgment operates in a hypothetical mode" (170).

The concept of order as a factor in human action functions as a paradigm for control over contingent circumstance. Years ago, in conversation with Jorge Luis Borges, he and I discussed the idea of order. I asked him about his sense of order and randomness. His answers have remained a fundamental part of my thinking. We were sitting in a near-empty classroom at the University of Toronto where he was scheduled to speak. He turned to a wastebasket located near the door; it was half full with debris. He asked if there was any order in the wastebasket. I said that if there was, it was not apparent to me – it appeared to be the normal random collection of midday garbage. He said that my response in itself could be construed as expressing a sense of order in what I considered to be normal midday garbage. But then he took the basket and turned it over on a table. The empty milk and juice containers, the empty lunch bags, folded newspapers, and so on, spilled out. He said: "Look at it now on the table. Have I not created a special order by putting it on the table?" Order, therefore, is an imaginative configuration that deals in systems and totalized things. Without the things, garbage in this case, or a system like language, there can be no order except as an idea, a mental need that gives it sense. Furthermore, he stated, there can be no order unless there was, and is, the possibility of disorder. The two are dialectically linked. He added, "Now, then, if we were to put up a mirror to our table display of garbage we would have begun the process of duplication that is art." A few months later, I read an essay by Paul Weiss in *The Concept of Order*, edited by Paul G. Kuntz. Weiss wrote:

> Disorder is an excess of order; it occurs when there are too many orders imposed upon a set of entities … Order is selective and restrictive; it provides a channel through which to move from one entity to another; it helps to organize things in such a way that they can be understood. Disorder instead provides too many channels through which to move from one entity to another, too many alternative ways in which to understand. (16–17)

Weiss then proceeded in the next paragraph to make an observation about the sense of order and disorder similar to the one Borges had made:

> A case of disorder would be a leap, a miscellany, a heterogeneity of entities that are not similar in colour, origin, shape, place, meaning, or value. These entities logicians call members of a class; mathematicians say that they make up an aggregate or a set. Though distinct, they are sufficiently joined to be together in one group. But the ways in which they can be related are too many. It is a disorder, contrasting with the usual arrangement of the positive integers 1, 2, 3, 4, 5 … which offers only one way to move from one number to another. (17)

Of course, Weiss was not concerned either with the spatial order created by Borges or with mirror duplication, both of which, as I have suggested, are part of the imaginative order of configuration. So when we speak of order we are also speaking of disorder, and order is always a configuration of something actual or virtual. Although no one particular order is required, there must be some way of grasping the whole. Weiss continues that order "is a means by which we can move clearly and easily from one entity to another. If we get rid of all particular orders we are left with a set of aggregated elements which can be interrelated in an endless number of ways'" (17).

The spatial order of the debris on the table has affinities to a plastic work of art: it is a configuration of space. The mirror duplication brings into the discussion the whole spectrum of representation and the inversion of the double. The idea of order is imposed by the knowing imagination of those who look upon it as spatial configuration. Why, we should ask, need this be so? Why do we impose order on objects? This imposed order does not invent relationships but rather takes up one aspect of things and ignores others. Again Weiss comments that the order one tries to impose is an order that is present in the original conglomeration of orders. The imposed order is selected out of the indefinitely many that are present. Sense demands order – where there is sense, there must be order. As Wittgenstein states: "The confusions which occupy us arise when language is like an engine idling, not when it is doing work" (*Philosophical Investigations* [132], 51) – or, in our terms, making sense.

But let us inquire how it is that we impose order onto a poetic text in our quest for sense, metaphorical sense. In 1967, Octavio Paz wrote about writing poetry in the following poem-letter to the Spanish poet León Felipe:

Poetic writing is

learning to read

the empty spaces of writing

in writing

not traces of what we were

paths

toward what we are. (*Ladera este*, 91; my trans.)

Line one, "Poetic writing is," can be read as a metapoetic fold; it states an already always circle and marks the absence of an origin. The signifiers are the signified in this endless repetition. Line two, "learning to read," at first appears to be a referential statement that makes sense outside the poem because it alludes to a tradition that privileges writers and readers as the custodians of the book. But this security is deceptive and short-lived, for the line deconstructs itself; it is not that writing is learned by reading, but that poetic writing is learned by reading what is *not* written, the empty spaces, the void, the absence that lies behind the presence of the script:

learning to read

the empty spaces of writing

in writing.

The blanks of writing are found in writing itself as the absence that makes the presence possible.

"Poetic writing is" comes to us both as a line in a poem and as an elaboration of differences. What *is* said can be said only because of what was *not* said, and what was *not* said is contained in what *was* said. In other words, once again we are faced with the concept of the fold in which there is no beginning and no end, only repetition.

Line five, "not traces of what we were," also appears to be referential and thus invites closure. Apparently the prevailing ambiguity from empty spaces or blankness that is in writing is dissipated by virtue of an analogy between absence and a forgotten past; the traces of those who lived but did not write are all that is left by the countless dead. But once again, in lines six and seven, the text deconstructs itself. The negation of the trace of the past is the path of the present, and therein appears the third fold; in this case it is a time fold. Our trace of the past and our rejection of it is the present of living, an already always movement forward. Deconstructive readings, of course, exploit the multiple dualities positioned on opposite sides of the copula as a pure sign of predication. Poetic writing is identified with reading the absences of poetic writing. Therefore identification does not distinguish, differentiate, or establish uniqueness through the copulative action; it does the opposite – it merges the two acts into one that sinks into absence. Thus the identifying power of the copula is turned in on itself, deconstructing the ostensive aim of the enunciation of giving singularity to the subject.

The second and third lines also self-destruct, for what is to be read is not the stated, but the non-stated. The absent is the object of this reading, not that which is present. Thus, the reading of absence destroys the response to the written presence. Of course, there can be no absence without presence, but the absence that is to be read denies the very presence that makes it possible. In short, reading becomes creative negativity. The last opposition turns on the reader and juxtaposes the traces of what we were to the being that we are. There is a chiasmus of *caminos*/paths. However, since what we are depends entirely on the traces of what we were, the being of what we are does not yet fully exist, but can only be sought after. Reality becomes a constant flow out of nothingness into becoming.

At this point it would be useful for us to compare random occurrence with the force of purpose in human affairs. We would fall into a complete muddle if we were to revert to logocentric thinking that opposes chance with design or purpose. The act of dumping a wastebasket is certainly a purposeful action, yet the contents of that basket are the result of random occurrences. My point, however, is that one is necessary to the other. Certainly, the words in a poem are carefully and purposely selected by the poet, but the response to these words cannot in any way be controlled by the poet. Each reader responds given her or his repertoire. Wittgenstein puts it in these words in *Zettel:* "A poet's words can pierce us. And that is of course causally connected with the use that they have in our life. And it is also connected with the way in which, conformably to this use, we let our thoughts roam up and down in the familiar surroundings of the words" ([155], 28).

This commentary succinctly sums up the relation of purpose to chance. Let us see how the two, chance and design, come together perfectly by examining another poem by Octavio Paz, "Apremio/Compulsion" from *Salamandra*:

It runs and lingers in my head
Slow and hurtling ahead in my blood
The hour passes without passing
And in me sculpts itself and vanishes

I am bread for its hunger
I am the heart it leaves behind
The hour passes without passing
And this that I write disintegrates it

Love that passes and affixes sorrow
in me battles in me reposes
the hour passes without passing
body of quicksilver and ashes

gauges my chest and does not touch me
perpetual weightless stone
the hour passes without passing
and it is an inflamed wound

The day is short, the hour immense
hour without myself and its sorrow
the hour passes without passing
and in me flees and is chained.

Salamandra, 68 (my trans.)

The five stanzas of the poem are based on the oxymoron; a series of oxymorons creates an order out of the disorder of internal contradiction. The hour passes without passing, it runs yet waits, it sculpts yet vanishes. The self is in battle and repose, the body is quicksilver and ashes; nothing can be more contradictory than the empirical designation that it gouges the chest without touching it and that it is a perpetual weightless stone, but the contradiction is also internalized as the self flees and remains chained. The hour that causes this contradiction further turns the self into its bread and its heart and the writing of the poem itself disintegrates time.

This series of contradictions, oxymoronic figures, cannot have predictable responses since their very force is tensional explosion, as Poulet would say. These elements in Weiss's terms lead to disorder because they have too many possibilities, not because they do not have any. In other words, polysemic indeterminancy is a phenomenon of disorder within the ordered sequence of the poem. But we should go further and probe how the oxymoronic verse causes disorder and how we can respond to it in critical terms.

I wish to acknowledge the collaboration of Professor Étienne Guyon, former Directeur de l'École normale supérieure in Paris, in developing the scientific analogy with hermeneutics.

Edward Lorenz developed the scientific concept of strange attractors in 1963 to explain the instability in the behaviour of the earth's atmosphere. Lorenz's model uses a qualitative rather than a quantitative approach. His first observation was that the system constantly expends energy and does not gain in momentum; if it were not for new and external forces of energy, it would come to a dead end. These points of major dissipation of energy are attractors. There is a convergence of energy that cancels itself out. But these points of convergence are not stable (i.e., always the same in their use of energy), nor are they periodic (they are temporally unstable since they can come and go in the most unpredictable ways). These points are called strange attractors because they are points of convergence but are also radically unstable. Stephen H. Kellert describes this phenomenon:

> This apparent contradiction is reconciled by one of the main geometric features of strange attractors: a combination of stretching and folding. The action of a chaotic system will take nearby points and stretch them apart in a certain direction, thus creating the local divergence responsible for unpredictability. But the system also acts to "fold" together points that are at some distance causing a convergence of trajectories in a different direction. (14)

The five stanzas and twenty lines of the poem provide us with a formal sequence that is markedly similar to other poems by Octavio Paz that utilize contradiction and oxymoron. To map out the sense-making possibilities of this configuration of strange attractors and stable attractors, we require a conceptual space that encompasses all of the poem's referential attractors. Each of these attractors will be a point in the conceptual space that can be related to any number of the paradigmatic sets that each other attractor contains. The reconstruction of the attractors I have presented creates a configuration of possible relationships or, in terms of physics, a simulated phase space. This map of possibilities takes each as a topological point with a set of coordinates to the other attractors, each with a multitude of paradigmatic attributes. The linkage between attractors is mapped out, but which of the many attributes will be connected is random, depending on the reading. The problem of meaning is in fact the problem of representation – the problem of representing the heterogeneous diversity of types of knowledge in the different contexts of understanding. We understand and interpret texts to the extent that we are able to contextualize them. On this most important point, semiotics, hermeneutics, and experimental physics are very close. The common concern is to connect understanding to contextual preunderstanding through the work of inquiry.

There is a deep link between the imaginative configuration of phenomena in science and literature, and this link is the educated imagination responding to contingency, chance, and indeterminacy. The biologist Robert May writes:

> One thing is certain. Biological systems, from communities and populations to physiological processes, are governed by nonlinear mechanisms. This means that we must expect to see chaos as often as we see cycles or steadiness. The message that I urged more than ten years ago is even more true today: not only in [biological] research, but also in the everyday world of politics and economics, we would all be better off if more people realized that simple nonlinear systems do not necessarily possess simple dynamical properties. (95)

The creative force of the imagination, the force of vision that characterizes the work of both the poet and the scientist, is such that they tap their experience in order to create a "what if" world in the laboratory and an "as if" world in the poem. But they make these worlds in order to transgress them, for their aim is to share in the reality we make in the art of living.

The inscription of language onto diverse systems ranges from relatively simple systems such as an EXIT sign, which has a minimum of rules and a limited range of meaning, to complex systems, which are extensively rule-governed and have an almost limitless range of meaning. Poetry is a complex system within which some signs appear with much greater frenquency than others because of their specific symbolic properties. Others have been frequent in one historical period but not another, and still others make but rare appearances in poetical systems. Some signs in specific combinations make their way from one poetic system to another, forming specific and new textual configurations while retaining the trace of their previous place in the other poetic system. The concretizing agent who recognizes the transference from one poetic system to another is in every case the reader.

"Complex adaptive systems" is the term used in science today to designate the non-linear dynamics of living systems, whether they are competing trees in a forest, colonies of bacteria, communities of animals, or human societies. Natural languages are most certainly complex adaptive systems, and within natural languages the mode of expression we call poetry can serve as a paradigm for research on how language works. The human need to make sense of what is said puts into play a host of symbolic connotations elicited from the reader's repertoire, along with generic and intertextual usages reflected in the configuration, as well as the social connotations of the historical context of both text and reader. These variables interact with one another and are constantly changing the configuration of reading in fully unpredictable ways. These shifting relationships present an open-ended range of possibilities of poetic meaning since all the variables also change over time.

If we look at a poem as a complex adaptive system, we find that the poetic system goes through a phase transition from order to randomness as the interaction between the text and the reader gradually increases and intensifies. A system can develop extravagant complexity at the boundary between order and randomness or sense and non-sense. The poetic text as a complex adaptive system moves towards that boundary through the natural process of readerly expectation. The key to analysing these systems is the interaction between text and reader. The more the interaction increases, the more quickly the system moves from sense to non-sense and then to the critical point of either complete breakdown or the emergence of a new metaphorical sense that has literally risen from the ruins of the initial sense.

To sum up this description of poetry as a complex adaptive system of signs, I make four points: (1) poetic systems are composed of discrete units we call signs, (2) these are continuously adapting during a reading, (3) they may adapt in an entirely novel manner in subsequent readings, and (4) although the signs are simple in their lexical rendering, in a text they gather information about their new contextual environment by eliciting relevant previous imaginative configurations out of the random play of the reader's making of meaning.

Since a poetic system of signs is a rule-governed complex system, the various formal properties of a particular formulation can be examined in detail. The major distinguishing feature of a poetic system is that unlike in simple systems, where assigned meaning is obvious and self-evident, in poetic systems meaning cannot be assigned until the inscription becomes a text, that is, until the system is activated through the reader's interaction. When writing becomes a text it is given specific parameters; most of all, there is transference from potential semantic possibilities to a specific reader's meaning. The use of the term "becomes a text" explicitly indicates that writing becomes reading and that meaning is forthcoming as the action of the text/reader relationship unfolds. Poetic meaning is neither the property of the writing nor the creation of the reader, but rather the interaction between writing, now constituted as text, and the reader, to whom we will henceforth refer as the concretizing agent. This agent does not decode the inscription using the global system of a natural language. Only the novice translator does this. The concretizing agent must bring about the transference from virtual meaning to actual meaning, but this is necessarily incomplete and will always be incomplete except for those moments when the concretizing agent completes it in ways that are often unexpected.

The object of the reader's play with words is to make meanings. In creating meanings out of certain clusters of signs we call images and metaphors, the reader compresses the referential information into models of schemata, which are used to anticipate and react to changes in the evolving meaning. Over time the reader modifies those schemata to reflect new information, elicited in the ongoing response to the poetic signs. Of course, not all poetic systems are the same. Some systems have fewer polysemic signs. These systems lack the momentum in the reading experience to develop explosively into new contexts of meaning; highly charged polysemic systems, by contrast, expand so rapidly that they shoot off into radically divergent contexts. They bifurcate again and again, generating a non-linear and unreproducible response between different parts of the same system. We can therefore only generalize in a limited way. When a sign operates as a polysemic sign it takes on the functions of a mobile bifurcating sign.

Thus the inscribed system is a fixed, rule-governed system with specific formal characteristics, but on reading, it becomes a non-linear process as the signs become a text through interaction with the reader's epistemological system. In this way we have shifted focus from the semiotics of the written sign system to the semantics of the non-linear process that is reading. The reading of the poetic text can be described as a complex adaptive system with a limitless number of mobile agents, for each sign can become a catalytic agent of bifurcation in a response system. The latent polysemia comes to the fore as the sign is catalysed into meaning; these are meanings that could not have been anticipated.

Here I am going far beyond the celebration of creativity, by claiming that there are non-linear approaches to knowledge. The attainment of this form of knowledge depends heavily on an educated imagination making the initial configuration and, subsequently, on the rational articulation of refiguration that can explain the net gain in meaning. The gain in meaning is the result of the reader's response to the semantic impertinence of metaphor. This tensional process obliges the reader to make sense of the patterns of bifurcations that are the making of an "as if" world as well as to develop an acceptable explanation for phenomena that do not respond to established rules.

Ricoeur's philosophy of interpretation is unique in twentieth-century philosophical work on language. Ricoeur views language as mediation rather than a code or object, and he addresses philosophers as well as his colleagues from the human sciences with equal clarity and conviction. He defines hermeneutics as the consideration of the ensemble of religious, literary, and juridical texts offered to interpretration of communities of listeners and readers. This position constitutes the philosophical foundation of my concept of literary culture as the source material of the author, who redescribes it in his or her individual expression in the literary text.

Cultural interpretation has developed numerous methods and theories throughout the long history of textual exegesis. Ricoeur's hermeneutics is one of the few modes of interpretation that has a philosophical basis that is not teleological. His hermeneutics is rooted in a fully articulated ontology. His interpretation begins with the encounter with the subject and the search for an understanding of meaning. This encounter is what he calls the configuration of the text or of the subject under examination. This is the interpreter's drive towards grasping the fullest meaning of the subject in question. This is the everyday experience not only of reading a text but also of understanding the world we live in. Because we are not alone either in the world or in the reading of texts, there will be differences, some minor and others major disagreements with other interpretations. Such conflict of interpretations is common to all open societies.

Ricoeur views the conflict of interpretations as a positive force leading to revision and reconsideration and, in some instances, rethinking the interpretation. This phase is what he calls the refiguration of meaning in our interpretations. In the normal process of discursive engagement the conflict of interpretations leads to the cultural distillation of elements that pass into the cultural archive of the community of interpreters. This archive is the wellspring of discursive debate, which in turn becomes the legacy of all who have access to it. Every time we draw ideas from the archive we are immersed in the depository of prefiguration of our culture. In this way we produce ideas, images, and narratives that will be appropriated and reinvented in a new context of configuration. What we do in the interpretation of texts, we also do in our engagement with the world. Our interpretation of the world we live in has been developed through the continuous configuration of experience; this experience in turn has been the subject of refiguration in the conflict of interpretations. Consequently, it has been deposited in the archive, from which we may or may not draw, depending on our own circumstances of living. Ricoeur's sources in creating his hermeneutics have been Martin Heidegger and Hans-Georg Gadamer.

Unamuno's cultural hermeneutics develops directly out of the conflict of interpretations that confronted him throughout his adulthood. The existential base of this hermeneutics is his struggle to live with and from the irreconcilable differences in life. Unamuno's sources are also German, primarily nineteenth-century Protestant theologians. He began with Albrecht Ritschl, *Die christliche van der Rechfertigung und Ver Versöhnung* (1894), but also Wilhelm Herrmann, *Die Wahrheit der Christlichen Religion* (1888), as well as Georg Wobbermin, *Thelogie und Metaphysik* (1901), and the most daring of Ritschl's followers, Ernest Troeltsch, *Systematische Christliche Religion* (1909). All of these sources have been fully documented in *An Unamuno Source Book* (María Elena and Mario Valdés, 1973) and in Nelson R. Orringer's commentary, *Unamuno y los protestantes liberales* (1985). Unamuno saw his own writing, especially *Del sentimiento trágico de la vida*, as destined to join in the conflict of interpretations with his predecessors in the struggle that is reality. What Unamuno did not explicitly express as a hermeneutics is, without question, a hermeneutics in his literature as I have discussed in this book.

References

Citations from texts in French and Spanish are from the published translations in most cases. When there are no published translations or the translation is wanting, the translation is mine. The dates given for all cited texts in Spanish or French are those of the original publication.

Works by Paul Ricoeur

The Conflict of Interpretations: Essays in Hermeneutics. Trans. Kathleen McLaughin, Sweeney, et al. Evanston: Northwestern UP, 1974.

Le conflit des interprétations. Essais d'herméneutique. Paris: Seuil, 1969.

The Contribution of French Historiography to the Theory of History. Oxford: Clarendon P, 1980.

The Course of Recognition. Trans. David Pellauer. Cambridge, MA: Harvard UP, 2006.

La critique et la conviction. Entretien avec François Azouvi et Marc de Launay. Paris: Calmann-Lévy, 1995.

Critique and Conviction. Trans. Kathleen Blamey. New York: Columbia UP, 1998.

A l'école de la phénoménologie. Paris: J. Vrim, 1986.

Fallible Man. Revised and trans. Charles Kelbley. New York: Fordham UP, 1986.

Freedom and Nature: The Voluntary and the Involuntary. Trans. and Introduction by Erazim V. Kohák. Evanston: Northwestern UP, 2007.

Freud and Philosophy: An Essay on Interpretation. Trans. D. Savage. New Haven: Yale UP, 1970.

"Gabriel Marcel and Phenomenology." In *The Philosophy of Gabriel Marcel*. Ed. Paul Arthur Schilpp and Lewis Edwin Hahn. La Salle: Open Court, 1984. 471–98.

Hermeneutics and the Human Sciences: Essays on Language, Action, and Interpretation. Ed. John B. Thompson. Cambridge: Cambridge UP, 1981.

Histoire et vérité. Paris: Seuil, 1955.
"History and Hermeneutics." *The Journal of Philosophy* 19, no. 73 (1976): 683–95.
History and Truth. Trans. Charles Kelbley. Evanston: Northwestern UP, 1965.
L'homme faillible. Paris: Aubier–Editions Montaigne, 1960.
"The Human Being as the Subject Matter of Philosophy." In *The Narrative Path: The Later Works of Paul Ricoeur*. Ed. T.P. Kemp and D.M. Rasmussen. Cambridge, MA: The MIT P, 1989. 89–101.
Husserl: An Analysis of His Phenomenology. Trans. Edward G. Ballard and Lester E. Embree. Evanston: Northwestern UP, 1967.
"Intellectual Autobiography." In *The Philosophy of Paul Ricoeur*. Trans. Kathleen Blamey. Chicago: Open Court, 1995. 3–53.
De l'interprétation. Essai sur Freud. Paris: Seuil, 1965.
Interpretation Theory: Discourse and the Surplus of Meaning. Fort Worth: Texas Christian UP, 1976.
Le juste I. Paris: Editions Esprit, 1995.
The Just. Trans. David Pellauer. Chicago: U of Chicago P, 2000.
Le juste II. Paris: Seuil, 2001.
Lectures on Ideology and Utopia. Ed. George H. Taylor. New York: Columbia UP, 1986.
"Life in Quest of Narrative." In *On Paul Ricoeur: Narrative and Interpretation*. Ed. David Wood. London: Routledge, 1991. 20–33.
"Love and Justice." In *Paul Ricoeur: The Hermeneutics of Action*. Ed. Richard Kearney. London: Sage, 1996. 23–39.
La mémoire, l'histoire, l'oubli. Paris: Seuil, 2000.
Memory, History, Forgetting. Trans. Kathleen Blamey and David Pellauer. Chicago: U of Chicago P, 2004.
La métaphore vive. Paris: Seuil, 1975.
"The Model of the Text: Meaningful Action Considered as a Text." *New Literary History* 5, no. 1 (1973): 91–117.
Oneself as Another. Trans. Kathleen Blamey. Chicago: U of Chicago P, 1992.
Parcours de la reconnaissance. Paris: Éditions Stock, 2004.
Philosophie de la volonté. Le volontaire et l'involontaire. Paris: Auber, 1950.
Reflections on the Just. Trans. David Pellauer. Chicago: U of Chicago P, 2007.
Réflexion faite. Autobiographie intellectuelle. Paris: Esprit, 1995.
A Ricoeur Reader: Reflection and Imagination. Ed. Mario J. Valdés. Toronto: U of Toronto P, 1991.
The Rule of Metaphor. Trans. Robert Czerny. Toronto: U of Toronto P, 1978.
Soi-même comme un autre. Paris: Seuil, 1990.
La symbolique du mal. Paris: Aubier, 1960.
The Symbolism of Evil. Trans. Emerson Buchanan. Boston: Beacon Press, 1969.

Temps et récit. Tomes I–III. Paris: Seuil, 1983, 1984, 1985.
Du texte á l'action. Essais d'herméneutique. Paris: Seuil, 1986.
From Text to Action: Essays in Hermeneutics. Trans. Kathleen Blamey and John B. Thompson. Evanston: Northwestern UP, 1991.
Time and Narrative. 3 vols. Trans. Kathleen McLaughlin and David Pellauer. Chicago: U of Chicago P, 1984–8.
"What Is Dialectic?" In *Freedom and Morality*. Ed. John Bricke. Lawrence: U of Kansas P, 1976. 173–89.

Works by Miguel de Unamuno

Abel Sánchez and Other Stories. Trans. Anthony Kerrigan. Washington, DC: Regnery, 1996.
La agonía del cristianismo. Madrid: Compañía Ibero Americana, 1931.
The Agony of Christianity. Trans. Kurt F. Reinhardt. New York: Frederick Ungar, 1960.
Cancionero. Obra completas, vol. 6. Madrid: Escelicer, 1969. 949–1424.
"Civilización y cultura" [1896]. In *Obras completas*, vol. 1. Madrid: Escelicer, 1968. 992–7.
"Cómo se escribe y para qué sirve la historia," "Notas íntimas y reflexiones políticas del joven Unamuno." *Cuadernos de la cátedra Miguel de Unamuno*. Salamanca: Universidad de Salamanca, 2006. 42, 189–210.
"Cómo se hace una novela" [1927]. In *Obras completas*, vol. 8. Madrid: Escelicer, 1968. 709–69.
"De la correspondencia de un luchador" [1909]. In *Obras completas*, vol. 3. Madrid: Escelicer, 1968. 269–72.
Diario íntimo [1902]. In *Obras completas*, vol. 8. Madrid: Escelicer, 1966. 777–880.
El espejo de la muerte [1913]. In *Obras completes*, vol. 1. Madrid: Escelicer, 1968. 1127–36.
"Faith" [1900]. In *The Agony of Christianity and Other Essays*. Trans. Anthony Kerrigan. Princeton: Princeton UP, 1974. 148–55.
"La fe" [1900]. In *Obras completas*, vol. 1. Madrid: Escelicer, 1968. 962–70.
"La gloria de Don Ramiro" [1909]. In *Obras completas*, vol. 1. Madrid: Escelicer, 1968. 269–74.
"Heráclito, Demócrito, y Jeremías." In *Obras completas*, vol. 4. Madrid: Escelicer, 1968. 1422–5.
"How to Make a Novel." In *Novela/Nivola*. Trans. Anthony Kerrigan. Princeton: Princeton UP, 1976. 381–484.
"La locura del doctor Montarco" [1904]. In *Obras completas*, vol. 1. Madrid: Escelicer, 1968. 1127–36.

"The Madness of Doctor Montarco." In *Abel Sánchez and Other Stories*. Trans. Anthony Kerrigan. Washington, DC: Regnery, 1996. 179–206.
"Mi religión" [1907]. In *Obras completas,* vol. 3. Madrid: Escelicer, 1968. 259–63.
"My Religion." In *The Agony of Christianity*. Trans. Anthony Kerrigan. Princeton: Princeton UP, 1974. 209–17.
"Nicodemo el fariseo" [1899]. In *Obras completas,* vol. 7. Madrid: Escelicer, 1968. 365–85.
Niebla. Ed. Mario J. Valdés. Madrid: Cátedra, 1985.
"Nieve" [1922]. In *Obras completas,* vol. 1. Madrid: Escelicer, 1968. 506–8.
"Notas sobre el determinismo en la novela" [1898]. In *Obras completas,* vol. 9. Madrid: Escelicer, 1968. 769–73.
Obras completas. 9 vols. Madrid: Escelicer, 1966–71.
Our Lord don Quijote: The Life of Don Quixote and Sancho Panza with Related Essays. Trans. Anthony Kerrigan. Princeton: Princeton UP, 1967.
"Paisajes del alma" [1918]. In *Obras completes,* vol 1. Madrid: Escelicer, 1968. 503–5.
De patriotismo espiritual. Artículos de La Nación de Buenos Aires (1901–1914). Ed. Victor Ouimette. Salamanca: Ediciones Universidad, 1997.
Paz en la guerra [1897]. In *Obras completas,* vol. 2. Madrid: Escelicer, 1968. 89–301.
Plenitud de plenitudes y todo plenitud! [1904]. In *Obras completas,* vol. 1. Madrid: Escelicer, 1966. 1171–82.
"Por el son a la visión" [1943]. In *Obras completas,* vol 4. Madrid: Escelicer, 1968. 496–9.
Recuerdos de niñez y mocedad [1908]. In *Obras completas,* vol. 8. Madrid: Escelicer, 1968. 97–169.
San Manuel Bueno, mártir [1933]. Ed. Mario J. Valdés. Madrid: Cátedra, 1979.
"El secreto de la vida" [1906]. In *Obras completas,* vol. 3. Madrid: Escelicer, 1968. 876–85.
Selected Works of Miguel de Unamuno. Trans. Anthony Kerrigan. 6 vols. Princeton: Princeton UP, 1972.
Del sentimiento trágico de la vida [1912]. In *Obras completas,* vol. 7. Madrid: Escelicer, 1968. 109–302.
En torno al casticismo [1895]. In *Obras completas,* vol. 1. Madrid: Escelicer, 1968. 775–869.
The Tragic Sense of Life. In *Selected Works,* vol. 4. Trans. Anthony Kerrigan. Princeton: Princeton UP, 1972.
Tres novelas ejemplares y un prólogo [1920]. In *Obras completas,* vol. 2. Madrid: Escelicer, 1967. 971–1036.
La vida de don Quijote y Sancho [1904]. In *Obras complates,* vol. 3. Madrid: Escelicer, 1968. 51–256.

Other Works

Abel, Olivier. "Paul Ricoeur's Hermeneutics: From Critique to Politics." In *Between Suspicion and Sympathy: Paul Ricoeur's Unstable Equilibrium*. Ed. Andrzej Wiercinski. Toronto: The Hermeneutic P, 2003. 11–21.

Apollinaire, Guillaume. *Idéogrammes Lyriques*. Paris: Gallimard, 1966.

Aranguren, José Luis. "Sobre el talento religioso de don Miguel de Unamuno." *Arbor* 11, no. 36 (1948): 485–503.

Arendt, Hannah. *Crises of the Republic*. New York: Harcourt Brace Jovanovich, 1972.

– *The Human Condition*. Chicago: U of Chicago P, 1958.

– *Lectures on Kant's Political Philosophy*. Chicago: U of Chicago P, 1982.

Aristotle. *The Complete Works of Aristotle*. Revised Oxford translation. 2 vols. Ed. Jonathan Barnes. Princeton: Princeton UP, 1984.

Barrett, William. "Afterword: Unamuno and the Contest with Death." In Miguel de Unamuno, *The Tragic Sense of Life in Men and Nations*. Trans. Anthony Kerrigan. Princeton: Princeton UP, 1972. 361–74.

Beardsley, Monroe C. "Order and Disorder in Art." In *The Concept of Order*. Ed. Paul G. Kuntz. Seattle: U of Washington P, 1968. 191–218.

Benítez, Hernán. *El drama religioso de Unamuno*. Buenos Aires: U de Buenos Aires, 1949.

Bergson, Henri. *Creative Evolution*. Trans. Arthur Mitchell. New York: H. Holt, 1911.

Blake, William. "Songs of Innocence and of Experience." In *Blake: The Complete Writings of William Blake*. Ed. Geoffrey Keynes. London: Oxford UP, 1966. 210–22.

Blanco Aguinaga, Carlos. *El Unamuno contemplativo*. Mexico City: Colegio de México, 1959.

– "Unamuno's yoismo and Its Relation to Traditional Spanish Individualism." In *Unamuno Centenial Studies*. Ed. Ramón Martínez López. Austin: U of Texas P, 1966. 18–52.

Blundell, Boyd. "Creative Fidelity: Gabriel Marcel's Influence on Ricoeur." In *Between Suspicion and Sympathy*. Ed. A. Wiercinski. Toronto: The Hermeneutic P, 2003. 89–102.

Borges, Jorge Luis. *This Craft of Verse*. Ed. Calin-Andrei Mihailescu. Cambridge: Harvard UP, 2000.

Braudel, Fernand. *El Mediterráneo y el mundo mediterráneo en la época de Felipe II*. Trans. Wences-Roces. Mexico City: Fondo de Cultura Económica, 1976.

Carr, David. *Time, Narrative, and History: An Essay in the Philosophy of History*. Bloomington: Indiana UP, 1986.

Cerezo Galán, Pedro. *Las Máscaras de lo trágico: filosofía y tragedia en Miguel de Unamuno*. Madrid: Trotta, 1996.

Chevalier, Jacques. "Entretiens avec Bergson." *La Table ronde* 137 (May 1959): 9–28.

Clavería Arza, Carlos. *Temas de Unamuno*. Madrid: Gredos, 1953.

Collado, Jesús Antonio. *Kierkegaard y Unamuno: la existencia religiosa*. Madrid: Gredos, 1962.

Cruz Hernández, Miguel. "La misión socrática de don Miguel de Unamuno." *Cuadernos de la Catédra* 3 (1952): 41–53.

Deleuze, Gilles. *The Logic of Sense*. Trans. Mark Lester with Charles Stivale. Ed. Constantin V. Boundas. New York: Columbia UP, 1990.

Derrida, Jacques. "White Mythology: Metaphor in the Text of Philosophy." In *Margins of Philosophy*. Trans. with additional notes by Alan Bass. Chicago: U of Chicago P, 1982. 207–171.

Dupriez, Bernard Halsall. *A Dictionary of Literary Devices*. Trans. Albert W. Halsell. Toronto: U of Toronto P, 1991.

Eliot, T.S. "Burnt Norton." *Four Quartets*. London: Faber & Faber, 1944. 7–13.

Esclasans, Agustín. *Miguel de Unamuno*. Buenos Aires: Juventud, 1947.

Fernández, Pelayo Hipólito. *Miguel de Unamuno y William James: un paralelo pragmático*. Salamanca: Cervantes, 1961.

Ferrater Mora, José. "On Miguel de Unamuno's Idea of Reality." *Philosophy and Phenomenological Research* 21, no. 4 (June 1961): 514–20.

– *Unamuno: Bosquejo de una filosofía*. Buenos Aires: Sudamericana, 1957.

Ferrier, Jean-Louis, and Yann Le Pichon. *Art of Our Century*. Trans. Walter D. Glanze. New York: Prentice Hall, 1989.

Foucault, Michel. *Les mots et les choses: une archéologie des sciences humaines*. Paris: Gallimard, 1966.

– *The Order of Things: An Archeology of the Human Sciences*. New York: Random House, 1970.

Frank, Anne. *The Diary of a Young Girl: The Definitive Edition*. New York: Bantam, 1997.

Frye, Northrop. *Anatomy of Criticism: Four Essays*. Princeton: Princeton UP, 1957.

Gadamer, Hans-Georg. *Hegel's Dialectic: Five Hermeneutical Studies*. Trans. Christopher Smith. New Haven: Yale UP, 1976.

– *Truth and Method*. Trans. Garrett Barden and John Cumming. New York: Seabury P, 1975.

García Blanco, Manuel. "La cultura alemana en la obra de Miguel de Unamuno." *Romanistisches Jahrbuch*, no. 8 (1957): 326–35. Hamburg.

García Márquez, Gabriel. *Cien años de soledad*. Buenos Aires: Sudamericana, 1967.

– *One Hundred Years of Solitude*. Trans. Gregory Rabassa. New York: Harper & Row, 1970.

Gleick, James. *Chaos: Making of a New Science*. New York: Basic Books, 1987.

González, Antonio, O.P. "Unamuno: Fe y descreimiento." *La Torre* 11, no. 42 (April–June 1963): 107–43. Puerto Rico.

– "¿Unamuno en la hoguera?" *Asomante* 12 (1961): 29–42. Puerto Rico.

González Caminero, Nemesio, S.J. *Unamuno: Trayectoria de su ideología y de sus crisis religiosas*. Comillas: U Pontífica, 1948.

Guy, Alain. "Miguel de Unamuno, Pélerin de l'absolu." *Cuadernos de la Cátedra Miguel de Unamuno* 1 (1948): 75–102.

Harnack, Adolf von. *Lehrbuch der Dogmengeschichte*. Freiburg: JCB Mohr, 1888–90.

Hawking, Stephen. "Stephen Hawking Will Now Take Your Questions." *Time*, 15 November 2010, 4.

Hegel, G.W.F. *Hegel's Philosophy of Mind*, from the 1830 ed. by W. Wallace and A.V. Miller, with revisions and commentary by M.J. Inwood. Oxford: Clarendon P, 2007.

– *The Phenomenology of Mind*. Trans. J.B. Baillie. New York: Harper & Row, 1967.

Heidegger, Martin. *Basic Writings from Being and Time (1927) to The Task of Thinking*. Ed. David Farrell Krell. Trans. Frank A. Capuzzi and J. Glenn Gray. New York: Harper & Row, 1976.

– *Being and Time*. Trans. John Macquarrie and Edward Robinson. [Translation of the 17th ed. of *Sein und Zeit*, 1927]. New York: Harper & Row, 1962.

– *Early Greek Thinking*. Trans. David Farrell Krell and Frank A. Capuzzi. San Francisco: Harper & Row, 1984.

– "The Origin of the Work of Art." In *Basic Writings*. Ed. David Farrell Krell. Trans. Frank A. Capuzzi and J. Glenn Gray. New York: Harper & Row, 1977. 149–87.

– "The Question Concerning Technology." In *Basic Writings*. Ed. David Farrell Krell. Trans. William Lovitt. New York: Harper & Row, 1977. 287–317.

– *The Question of Being*. Trans. William Kluback and Jean T. Wilde. New York: Twayne, 1958.

– *El ser y el tiempo*. Trans. José Gaos. Mexico City: Fondo de Cultura Económica, 1951.

Holmes, Oliver Wendell. *The Autocrat of the Breakfast Table*. London: J.M. Dent & Sons, 1906.

Hook, Sidney. *Pragmatism and the Tragic Sense of Life*. New York: Basic Books, 1974.

Horgan, John. "The Death of Proof." *Scientific American*, October 1993, 93.

Hunter, J.F.M. *Essays after Wittgenstein*. Toronto: U of Toronto P, 1973.

Ilie, Paul. *Unamuno: An Existential View of Self and Society*. Madison: U of Wisconsin P, 1967.

Iser, Wolfgang. *The Act of Reading: A Theory of Asthetic Response*. Baltimore: Johns Hopkins UP, 1978.

Jervolino, Domenico. "Gadamer and Ricoeur on the Hermeneutics of Praxis." In *Paul Ricoeur: The Hermeneutics of Action*. Ed. Richard Kearney. London: Sage, 1996. 63–79.

Jiménez, Juan Ramón. *Antología poética*. Ed. Francisco Javier Blasco. Madrid: Cátedra, 2010.

Kearney, Richard. "Between Oneself and Another: Paul Ricoeur's Diacritical Hermeneutics." In *Between Suspicion and Sympathy*. Ed. A. Wiercinski. Toronto: The Hermeneutic P, 2003. 149–60.

– *Dialogues with Contemporary Continental Thinkers: The Phenomenological Heritage*. Manchester: Manchester UP, 1984. 17–46.

Kellert, Stephen H. *In the Wake of Chaos: Unpredictable Order in Dynamical Systems*. Chicago: U of Chicago P, 1993.

Kerrigan, Anthony. "Translator's Foreword." In Miguel de Unamuno, *The Tragic Sense of Life in Men and Nations*. Princeton: Princeton UP, 1972. vii–xxviii.

Kierkegaard, Søren. *Concluding Unscientific Postscript to the Philosophical Fragments*. Trans. David F. Swenson. Ed. Howard J. Hong and Edna H. Hong. Princeton: Princeton UP, 1992.

Klemm, David E. *The Hermeneutical Theory of Paul Ricoeur: A Constructive Analysis*. Lewisburg: Bucknell UP, 1983.

LaFuente, Avelina Cecilia. *Antropología filosófica de Miguel de Unamuno*. Sevilla: Publicaciones de la U de Sevilla, 1983.

La Rubia Prado, Francisco. *Alegorías de la voluntad: pensamiento orgánico, retórica y deconstrucción en la obra de Miguel de Unamuno*. Madrid: Libertarias, 1996.

Laing, R.D. *The Divided Self*. London: Tavistock, 1960.

Le Guern, Michel. *Sémantique de la métaphore et de la métonymie*. Paris: Larousse, 1973.

Lowe, Walter J. "Introduction." In Paul Ricoeur, *Fallible Man*. Trans. Charles Kelbley. New York: Fordham UP, 1986. vii–xxxii.

Manya, Joan. *La teología de Unamuno*. Barcelona: Vergara, 1960.

Marcel, Gabriel. *Pour une sagesse tragique et son au-delà*. Paris: Plon, 1968.

– *Tragic Wisdom and Beyond*. Including Conversations between Paul Ricoeur and Gabriel Marcel. Trans. S. Jolin and Peter McCormick. Evanston: Northwestern UP, 1973.

Marías, Julián. "Love in Marcel and Ortega." In *The Philosophy of Gabriel Marcel*. Ed. P.A. Schilpp and L.E. Hahn. La Salle: Open Court, 1984. 553–72.

– *Miguel de Unamuno*. Madrid: Espasa-Calpe, 1943.

May, Robert. "The Chaotic Rhythms of Life." In *Exploring Chaos: A New Guide to the New Science of Disorder*. Ed. Nina Hall. New York: W.W. Norton, 1993. 82–95.

Menchú, Rigoberta. *I, Rigoberta Menchu: An Indian Woman in Guatemala*. Trans. Ann Wright. Ed. Elizabeth Burgos Debray. London: Verso, 1984.

Merleau-Ponty, Maurice. *Sense and Nonsense*. Trans. H.L. Dreyfus and Patricia A. Dreyfus. Evanston: Northwestern UP, 1964.

Meyer, François. *L'ontologie de Miguel de Unamuno*. Paris: Presses Universitaires de France, 1955.

Molina Cruz, Mario. "¿Dónde estarán nuestros dioses?" In *Volcán de Pétalos. Ya' byalhje xtak yejé*. Mexico City: Estudios Culturales y Publicaciones, 1996. 69.

– "La maldición de la noche triste." In *Volcán de pétalos. Ya' byalhje xtak yejé*. Mexico City: Estudios Culturales y publicaciones, 1996. 89.

– "Testimonio." In *Volcán de pétalos. Ya' byalhje xtak yejé*. Mexico City: Estudios Culturales y publicaciones, 1996. 17.

Mounier, Emmanuel. *Personalism*. Notre Dame: U of Notre Dame P, 1989.

Neruda, Pablo. "Oda de unas flores amarillas." In *Libro tercero de las odas*. Santiago, 1957. 47.

Nietzsche, Friedrich. *Thus Spoke Zarathustra: A Book for All and None*. Trans. Walter Kaufmann. New York: Viking P, 1966.

– *The Will to Power*. Trans. Walter Kaufmann. New York: Random House, 1967.

Nozick, Martin. *Miguel de Unamuno*. New York: Twayne, 1971.

Olson, Paul R. *The Great Chiasmus: Word and Flesh in the Novels of Unamuno*. West Lafayette: Purdue UP, 2003.

Orringer, Nelson R. *Unamuno y los protestantes liberales*. Madrid: Gredos, [1912]1985.

Ouimette, Victor. *Reason Aflame: Unamuno and the Heroic Will*. New Haven: Yale UP, 1974.

Pacheco, José Emilio. *Miro la tierra*. Mexico City: Era, 1986.

Paz, Octavio. *Arbol adentro*. Barcelona: Seix Barral, 1987.

– "Carta a León Felipe." In *Ladera este*. Mexico City: Editorial Joaquín Mortiz, 1969. 89–94.

– *Libertad bajo palabra*. Obra poética. Mexico City: Fondo de cultura económica, 1960.

– *Salamandra*. Mexico City: Joaquín Mortiz, 1969.

Pellauer, David. "Paul Ricoeur and Literary Hermeneutics." In *Between Suspicion and Sympathy*. Ed. A. Wiercinski. Toronto: The Humanities P, 2003. 370–8.

– *Ricoeur: A Guide to the Perplexed*. London: Continuum, 2007.

Pérez, Janet. "Rhetorical Integration in Unamuno's *Niebla*." *Revista Canadiense de Estudios Hispánicos* 8 (1983): 49–73.

Plato. "Cratilo," "Teetetes." In *Platón. Diálogos*. Trans. Francisco Larroyo. Mexico City: Porrúa, 1996. 249–349.

Proust, Marcel. *A la recherche du temps perdu*. Paris: Gallimard, 1954.

– *The Past Recaptured*. Trans. Federick A. Blossom. New York: Random House, 1932.

Rabaté, Colette, and Jean Claude Rabaté. *Miguel de Unamuno. Biografía*. Madrid: Taurus, 2009.

Rawls, John. *Justice as Fairness: A Restatement*. Cambridge, MA: Harvard UP, 2001.

Reagan, Charles E. *Paul Ricoeur: His Life and His Work*. Chicago: U of Chicago P, 1996.

Reinhardt, Kurt. F. "Introduction." In *The Agony of Christianity*. Trans. Kurt F. Reinhardt. New York: Frederick Ungar, 1960. vii–xxxviii.

Renart, Juan Guillermo. *El Cristo de Velázquez de Unamuno: Estructura, Estilo, Sentido*. Toronto: Anejos de la Revista Canadiense de Estudios Hispánicos, 1982.

Rendtorff, Jacob Dahl. "Paul Ricoeur's Poetic Ontology." In *Between Suspicion and Sympathy*. Ed. A. Wiercinski. Toronto: The Hermeneutic P, 2003. 379–97.

Ritschl, Albrecht. *Die christliche Lehre von der Rechtfertigung und Versohnung*. Bonn: Marcus, 1870–4.

Salcedo, Emilio. *Vida de Don Miguel: Unamuno en su tiempo, en su Espana, en su Salamanca*. Salamanca: Anaya, 1964.

Sánchez Barbudo, Antonio. *Estudios sobre Unamuno y Machado*. Madrid: Guadarrama, 1959.

Sánchez Cuesta, Manuel. "Miguel de Unamuno: Epistolario y hermenéutica." *Revista de Filosofía* 6, no. 10 (1005): 467–71. Madrid.

Saussure, Ferdinand de. *Course in General Linguistics*. Trans. Wade Baskin. Ed. Charles Bally and Albert Sechehaye. New York: Philosophical Library, 1959.

Sedwick, Frank. "Unamuno the Essayist and His Detractors." *Modern Language Forum* 62, no. 2 (July 1957): 101–12.

– "Unamuno, the Third Self and *Lucha*." *Studies in Philology* 54, no. 3 (1957): 464–79.

Serrano Poncela, Segundo. *El pensamiento de Unamuno*. Mexico City: Fondo de Cultura Económica, 1953.

Sinclair, Allison. *Uncovering the Mind: Unamuno, the Unknown, and the Vicissitudes of Self*. Manchester: Manchester UP, 2001.

Sparshott, Francis. *The Theory of the Arts*. Princeton: Princeton UP, 1982.

Steiner, George. *Martin Heidegger*. Chicago: U of Chicago P, 1989.

Tagore, Rabindranath. *The Gardener*. London: Macmillan, 1913.

Thomas, Dylan. "And Death Shall Have No Dominion." In *The Poems of Dylan Thomas*. Ed. David Jones. New York: New Directions, 1971. 49–50.

Updike, John. *S*. New York: A.A. Knopf, 1988.

Valdés, Mario J. *Death in the Literature of Unamuno*. Champaign: U of Illinois P, 1964.

– "Paul Ricoeur and Literary Theory." In *The Philosophy of Paul Ricoeur*. Ed. Lewis Edwin Hahn. La Salle: Open Court, 1995. 259–84.

– *Phenomenological Hermeneutics and the Study of Literature*. Toronto: U of Toronto P, 1987.

– *Shadows in the Cave: A Phenomenological Approach to Literary Criticism Based on Hispanic Texts*. Toronto: U of Toronto P, 1982.

Valdés, Mario J., and María Elena de Valdés. *An Unamuno Source Book*. Toronto: U of Toronto P, 1973.

Valery, Paul. *Le Cimetiere marin*. Paris: Emile Paul, 1920.

Ward, James. *Psychological Principles*. Cambridge: Cambridge UP, 1920.

Weil, Eric. *Logique de la Philosophie*. Paris: Vrin, 1950.

Weiss, Paul. "Some Paradoxes Relating to Order." In *The Concept of Order*. Ed. Paul Kuntz. Seattle: U of Washington P, 1968. 16–18.

Welsen, Peter. "Personal Identity as Narrative Identity." *Between Suspicion and Sympathy*. Ed. A. Wiercinski. Toronto: The Hermeneutics P, 2003. 192–202.

White, Hayden. *Metahistory: The Historical Imagination in Nineteenth-Century Europe*. Baltimore: Johns Hopkins UP, 1973.

Wiercinski, Andrzej, ed. *Between Suspicion and Sympathy*. Toronto: The Hermeneutic P, 2003.

Wittgenstein, Ludwig. *Philosophical Investigations*. Trans. G.E.M. Anscombe. New York: MacMillan, 1958.

– *Zettel*. Trans. G.E.M. Anscombe. Ed. G.E.M. Anscombe and G.H. von Wright. Berkeley: U of California P, 1970.

Wood, David, ed. *On Paul Ricoeur: Narrative and Interpretation*. London: Routledge, 1991.

Woolf, Virginia. *Jacob's Room*. London: Hogarth P, 1976.

– *Mrs. Dolloway*. London: Hogarth P, 1924.

Zubizarreta, Armando F. *Tras las huellas de Unamuno*. Madrid: Tauros, 1960.

Index

www.ingramcontent.com/pod-product-compliance
Lightning Source LLC
LaVergne TN
LVHW090159080826
844660LV00013B/868/J

* 9 7 8 1 4 4 2 6 4 9 4 6 0 *